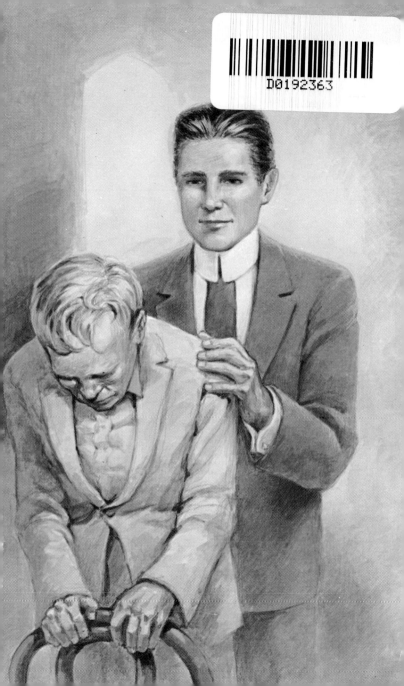

William Borden

An Overseas Missionary Fellowship Book

Mrs. Howard Taylor

MOODY PRESS
CHICAGO

COMMISSIONED

"As the Father hath sent me, even so send I you."—JOHN 20:21

Out from the realm of the glory-light
Into the faraway land of night,
Out from the bliss of worshipful song
Into the pain of hatred and wrong,
Out from the holy rapture above
Into the grief of rejected love,
Out from the life at the Father's side
Into the death of the crucified,
Out of high honour and into shame
The Master willingly, gladly came:
    And now, since He may not suffer anew,
    As the Father sent him so sendeth He you.

HENRY W. FROST, D.D.

Moody Press Edition, 1980

ISBN: 0-8024-0885-0

Printed in the United States of America

INTRODUCTION

When the death of William Whiting Borden was cabled from Egypt, it seemed as though a wave of sorrow went round the world. There was scarcely a newspaper in the United States that did not publish some account of a life which had combined elements so unusual, and letters from many lands attested the influence of its high ideals and unselfish service. It is probably true, as was stated in the *Princeton Seminary Bulletin,* that no young man of his age had ever given more to the service of God and humanity; for Borden not only gave his wealth, but himself, in a way so joyous and natural that it was manifestly a privilege rather than a sacrifice.

From Chicago, the city of his birth, came the following testimony:

"A church friend of mine, working in the office of the Western Union Telegraph Company, was much tried by the scoffings of an unbeliever concerning everything to do with religion. Whatever might be said on the other side was met with argument and denial. My friend, though an intelligent man and an earnest Christian, has little time for general reading and did not know of your son until an account of his consecrated life appeared in the daily paper. Upon reading it he at once felt that it might mean something to this unbeliever, so he laid the paper on his desk and awaited results. The scoffer read the article through, then coming to my friend said:

" 'I cannot understand it! There is no accounting for such a life.'

"He was completely silenced by the revelation of the power of God in the life your son lived. This is a small incident, Madam, but my friend has been deeply impressed and, with me, rejoices to know that Mr. Borden's biography is to be published."

A Richmond journal, reaching a hundred thousand young people in the South, admitted that Borden's theory of converting his many possessions of talent, vigorous strength and wealth into eternal values might not accord with the popular receipt for making the most of life.

"But," the editorial continued, "even though he was cut off in his early prime, before actually reaching his distant sphere of labour, it is doubtful whether any life of modern times has flung out to the world a more inspiring example. His investment has borne rich returns already and will continue to yield its peculiar fruit. There are thousands of talented and favoured young men who will, in the light of Borden's conception of investment values, come to a new view of Christian service. Material possessions and natural endowments will be appraised not by a standard of self-indulgence or worldly ambition but by their adaptability for building the Kingdom of God. Here was a fearless spirit, not fettered by worldly wisdom in the disposition of his powers and possessions, who looked out and up, beyond all these, and grasped the really great thing of value for which to spend them."

"It was not the million dollars that came to this young American," commented another editor, "which made his life a victory and his death a world-wide call to young men and women to learn the secret of that victory. It was in things that every man can share that William Borden found the way to the life which is Christ and the death which is gain. And China and the Moslem world shall yet share that gain, as his burning torch is used to kindle in other lives the fires of a like passion for Jesus Christ."

CONTENTS

INTRODUCTION

PART I—EARLY YEARS

PART II—YALE UNIVERSITY

PART III—PRINCETON SEMINARY

PART IV—AFTERWARDS

5

To

THE MOTHER
WHO LOVED AND GAVE

On the far reef the breakers
　Recoil in shattered foam,
Yet still the sea behind them
　Urges its forces home;
Its chant of triumph surges
　Through all the thunderous din—
The wave may break in failure,
　But the tide is sure to win.

O mighty sea, thy message
　In changing spray is cast:
Within God's plans of progress
　It matters not at last
How wide the shores of evil,
　How strong the reefs of sin—
The wave may be defeated,
　But the tide is sure to win.

—Selected

PART I

EARLY YEARS

"Oh, what a glorious yoke are youth and Grace, Christ and a young man!"

SAMUEL RUTHERFORD

"It is the God-governed and not the self-governed life which counts for most, which is the best worth while."

—Selected

CHAPTER 1

BOYHOOD

Born, November 1, 1887

Out of the heart are the issues of life.—Proverbs 4:23

THERE MUST BE BEGINNINGS. To those who knew Borden only in student days it may seem out of keeping with such virility and strength to present him as a child. Yet childhood comes first and is full of the germs and seeds of later developments. While he was a sophomore at Yale, for example, an unexpected discovery connected him in an interesting way with the curly-headed little fellow of ten years previously.

His elder brother had recently married, and in preparing the Chicago home for the occupation of the young couple some papers came to light that recalled a long-past experience. One Sunday afternoon when William was only six, Mrs. Borden had gathered the children around her as usual for a Scripture lesson. Several cousins of their own ages were with them, the eldest being about eleven. Apropos of something in the lesson, Mrs. Borden suggested that they should each take a slip of paper and write down what they would most like to be when they grew up.

This was done in a serious spirit. No one saw what the others had written, and all the slips were put away in a sealed envelope and forgotten. When found ten years later and returned to those who had written them, the ideals of those early days proved to have been realized to a remarkable degree. One boy had wanted to be a gentleman like his father. One of the girls wished to travel abroad, another "to help God and the soldiers of my country"—all through the world war the latter was to render exceptional service. And William had written:

I what to be an oneast man when I grow up, and true and loving and kind and faithful man.

To his last day, by the grace of God, the man could have looked into the eyes of the child without shame.

Borden's love of a good roughhouse was early foreshadowed by his devotion to active and even dangerous games. He was "a regular little monkey," his mother recalled, "for running round and having a good time." His cousin, John Whiting, was his chief ally in escapades of all sorts. Together they attended successive schools in Chicago,[1] and with another companion spent their holidays in congenial ways. It was nothing unusual for the three to start out on Saturday at five A.M., ending up at supper time, John Whiting tells us, "dead tired out."

We found that by the use of ropes we could travel along the roofs of the houses in Bellevue Place, almost the entire length of the block. For a time this afforded us considerable amusement. Another diversion was to go down to the river and put in the day knocking around among the boats tied to the various docks. We used to go all over the boats, climbing the rigging, etc. The noon meal we would get wherever we could, generally from the kitchen of one of the three houses.

Late one Saturday afternoon we decided that we wanted to play in the gymnasium of the school William and Kelso attended. That the building was locked up for the week-end made no difference. We found the cover of a coalhole loose and dropped in through that. We fooled around the gym until tired, then took a leisurely shower and dressed, not realising how late

[1] William attended the University School and the Latin and Manual Training Schools in Chicago, before going to the Hill School, Pottstown, Pennsylvania.

it was. We got out by a window which we had to leave unfastened. I was visiting William at the time and when we reached home, about seven-thirty P.M., we were met by Mr. and Mrs. Borden, worried and almost alarmed over our nonappearance. When the cause of our tardiness was discovered, we were promptly sent to bed with bread and milk for supper. It was meant for punishment, but nothing could have suited us better. We were tired and hungry, and while it was only bread and milk, the supply was unlimited.

A marked characteristic of Borden in later life was his unflinching loyalty to the doing of hard things. Fishing, hunting, sailing, all had their attractions for the boy, as may be seen from his early letters, but he seems to have loved hard jobs best of all. When he and his cousin, for example, discovered a wreck after a terrible storm and the Lake Shore Drive was flooded and covered with débris, it was second nature to turn in at once and help. A ship loaded with lumber had gone to pieces and the great timbers were lying at all angles along the shore. Seeing from the windows the work that had to be done, the little fellows of seven or eight were soon out in the storm, gathering up the lumber and putting it in orderly piles. A gang of Italian laborers appeared before long, but William and John Whiting kept on working, and at the end of the day lined up with the others and received their pay.

A chief enjoyment when about ten years old was to go down on Saturday to their uncle's foundry, some distance from Chicago, and spend their holiday working around with the men. Of this they never seemed to tire. The house of an uncle in Indiana also offered attractions along the line of work, and that of all sorts. It was a farm to which as a child William had often been sent to escape the severe winds of the Chicago spring. Of these visits his aunt wrote:

He was never idle, always inclined to make work his play and to find in work well done ample compensation for his efforts. I remember that on his visit in the spring of 1898 William wanted to make cider. His uncle told him that after years of neglect the cider-press was unfit for use and could never be made sufficiently clean again. But William cleaned the cider-press. I can see the little fellow now, making many trips up the hill for hot water, carrying his buckets two at a time. After several hours of scraping and scrubbing, the press was spotless and cider-making began.

On a visit in the spring of 1900, when he was twelve, William was up at sunrise and in the barn before the men arrived, beginning their day's work for them. This was the time he took such interest in the McKinley sawmill, making strawberry-boxes, going to work and stopping with the mill whistle. At the end of his visit Mr. McKinley handed him a sum of money, saying he had earned it, but William declined payment on the ground that it had been a privilege to learn.

On his last stay with us, May, 1912, he was the same dear, affectionate, lovable boy as of old. He arrived at six A.M. and we had an early breakfast, after which we went out on the porch and William saw the teamster, an old man of seventy-five who had been in the employ of the family for about forty years, driving toward the corn-cut. William hailed him joyously, jumped off the porch, ran down the hill and was soon beside him on the wagon. Gently he put his arm round the old man's shoulder, and when they reached the corn-crib he took the shovel and filled the wagon with corn, driving off with him and emptying the load at its destination. He then went over to the McKinley sawmill, greeting many acquaintances and helping them in their work as in earlier years.

I always think of William as I used to see him when a boy, coming home after a day's work in his blue sweater—rosy cheeks, eyes full of love and hair covered with shavings—calling to me as he started to run up the hill, hoping he had not detained supper. Was there ever another boy of his means, so humble, with a heart so full of love and with such pure thoughts!

One of the deepest things in Borden's life was devotion to his mother, and that too was very manifest in the child. From the time when he used to play quietly in her room "not to disturb her writing," and leaving his toys would steal up behind her chair to raise the wavy hair at the back of her neck and kiss her without a word, on to the days of bereavement, after his father's death, when he made time in the midst of college claims and studies to write to her every day, he was more like a lover than a son. This attitude comes out in his very first letter, written when just five years old:

Nov. 23, 1892

DEAR MAMA—I send my love to you. I wish you would come to my house. Sorry that you don't come home.

Well I am.

And a little later, on her birthday:

DEAR MAMA—I did not have enything to give you. I am very sorry that I did not enything for you. So I gave you a bunch of flowers and this letter.

Goodbye, from   WILLIAM BORDEN

He was quite a correspondent, even in those days, and the observation and attention to detail apparent in his early letters gave promise of the man whom nothing escaped.

89 BELLEVUE PLACE

DEAR GRANDMAMA—How are you feeling. I think the baby is awful cuning. It has a little cold in her head. She is 19 in. long, and weighs 6 lbs. One day the butcher came in and found the maids all so happy because it was a little baby, so he told Mrs. Hatch and Mrs. Hatch told Mrs. Stone and Mrs. Stone told Mrs. Shelden.

Goodby from   WILLIAM BORDEN

LAKE GENEVA, WIS.

DEAR GRANDMOTHER—Papa bought a new sailboat for us. We have sailed down to Golf Club and back twice. The first day we fished I caught 11 fish, Papa 11, John 3. The baby has been in the bathtub for the first time. Miss Duns has gone.

Every night the baby comes downstairs, and Mama reads John Halafax aloud to us. Papa bought a new covered carriage for Mama and the baby. We are going ciscoe-fishing to-day.— Yours truly,

W. BORDEN

89 BELLEVUE PLACE,
January, 1898

DEAR PAPA—I hope you and your father are feeling well and enjoying your visit to New York. . . . Saturday Jan. 15th it snowed all day nearly. Friday 14th we had thirteen children hear and played all sorts of games. After everybody was gone and everybody asleep except Marie, Mama and myself, we smelt gas and went searching all over the house trying to find it. We did not find it but opened some windows, by that time it was twelve o'clock. It was snowing when I went to bed, and on Saturday as I told you before. In the morning we went out by the build-out and coasted down those day-hills onto a pond of ice. There was skating but it was not good so we didn't go. About ten o'clock we came back and hitched on wagons. One time I got laughing so I couldn't hold onto my rope and let go, and then I couldn't run fast enough to catch up with it again. In the afternoon a lot of boys were out hitching, and we all hitched our sleds together and made a long train that reached from our house to the Maniers nearly. I was at the front and it pulled my arms nearly off. Kelso was at the end and it switched him all over into the curbstone and everywhere. We had supper at 7 o'clock. . . . Your loving son,

WILLIAM WHITING BORDEN

The baby is just as sweet as can be, hair is all curled.

BORDEN, INDIANA

DEAR MAMA—We have arrived here safe and sound, the train was 20 minutes late. After breakfast John and Papa went hunting, I did not go with them, papa shot one bird, he was a nice fat quail and that is all they got.

After lunch John and I went out and shot at a target with a rifle and revolver and papa went off hunting but did not get anything. He is asleep now and it is just 20 minutes of 5 and is getting dark. This is written on Wednesday.—Your loving son,   W. W. BORDEN

BORDEN, INDIANA

DEAR MAMA—Monday I was down at Mr. McKinley's saw mill, they sawed long boads off and made short ones for krates and me and another man stacked them up. In the afternoon I went with Jim McKinley up on the knobs for hay, the roads were very mudy and we had to let the horses rest. When we got back they had the big rip-saw going. . . . Monday morning Mr. Burns and I fed the pigs and then began to boil some potatoes for them. We built such a big fire that they boiled over and put part of the fire out. Tuesday morning Fraulein and Mary went out walking and I went down to the saw mill and stayed all morning. They have been getting a drag-saw ready, and will have it going before we get back in the afternoon. We were sawing a big red oak and nearly in the middle we found two big bullets. The saw had sawed them in two. It took an hour to get through sawing that one big log.

Hope all are well.—Your loving

WILLIAM

Written Tuesday.

ELKHORN LODGE,
ESTES PARK, COLORADO

DEAR GRAMA—I hope you are feeling well. The 3rd day that we were up here Papa, Mary and I went fishing over to the Big Thomson which is about half a mile south of our house, but we didn't catch anything. . . . A little while after that we went fishing again, and John caught 10 but the rest of us didn't catch anything.

About two weeks ago, this being Tuesday the 18th, John, Mary, Ella James and I went out after some of James's horses. We went out about 2 o'clock and we hunted the country high and low all over Beaver Flat and didn't get home until 8 o'clock, and Papa was just starting out in the buggy after us.

Now I'm going to tell you where we went and what we did. Well first we forded the Fall River and rode way up into Horshoe Park, but we didn't find the horses there, so we came back and crossed the river in a place where it was pretty deep and then we had to go through a lot of bushes which nearly swept us off our saddles. Then we crossed the ridge right near Deer Mountain. We found to get across into Beaver Flat that we had to go across a rail fence, so John took off some of the rails but one and then the horses jumped or stepped over the one. Well we went on and came to another rail fence and managed it in the same way. Then we came to a Barb Wire Fence! Well we finally managed to pull up one of the posts and laid it down and made the horses go over, all but mine who's name was Buckskin and he positively refused to go over, and in trying to make him go over he backed off and pulled him onto the Barb Wire and tore his pants and cut his finger.

Well, seeing my horse wouldn't go over, I had to go back and get out as best I could. . . . I then rode up into Beaver Flat about 3 miles, and was just about half way back when I met John, Ella and Mary. We went back where I'd been, only we went farther, but could not find the horses, so we went home.

On Saturday the 22nd there was going to be a Base Ball game, so we all went in the hayracks. We stopped at the Post Office and got some balls, and most everybody bought candy and gum and treated everybody to it. We got to the field which was up the Thomson a little way. They started to make the diamond. It began to rain and everybody that could got under the wagon, it stopped after a while and they practised. I will give you a copy of the score card. . . . We won as you see, and coming back yelled,

> "Ripetak, sipetak, siss bum ba!
> Elkhorn, Elkhorn, ra! ra! ra!
> Who are *we*? who are *we*?
> We are the gang from James', see!"

Here I say goodby, your loving grandson,

WILLIAM W. BORDEN

It was a happy, wholesome life, and in their father the children had an understanding friend. Every night he worked with them over their lessons, and they knew that he was no less interested in their games and sports. He was a man of few words, but the intimacies of homelife revealed the strength and nobility of his character. The following unstudied lines—written by one of his daughters upon hearing of her father's death—give an impression of his influence over his children.

Oh Lord, I thank Thee that Thou gavest me
This strength to cling to all my childhood years,
This noble man, my father, mine to be—
Though not as now—mine through eternity.
See, Lord! I am almost smiling through these tears,
For Thou hast made me rich of all mankind
By giving me to be his daughter-friend;
For his was calm nobility of mind
That, selfless, saw the truth and gave clear-lined
Full justice unto all things, to the end!

A sense of justice born of a pure heart
That loved a few dear ones, how sacredly!
Silent and grave, long hours he spent apart
In thought, until a word of love would start
A deep sweet look behind his eyes, and he
Would sit with us and talk from his great store,
Of beauty, poetry, and of great men.
And as the days and years opened the door
Of his dear heart to me I loved him more,
As I had more of love to give, and then—

Then, Lord, You took him from me and I wept.
It seemed so piteous, for I loved him so,
Until I fell upon my knees and crept
A little child to Thee, and wearied slept,
While quiet drifted down like cooling snow
Upon my throbbing heart. A voice then said,
"Dear child, give Me yourself and all your fears,
He now is living, loving you, not dead;
For him, for you, for this, My blood was shed."
And I awoke—strange—smiling through my tears.

Some of his strongest traits Borden inherited through his

father, who came of old Puritan stock. For the love of conquest which had taken the Bordens of Bourdonnaye to England with the Norman Duke (1066) was followed centuries later by the love of freedom which made them exiles for conscience' sake. To exchange the rich pastures and woodlands of Kent for the barren shore and tangled forests of New England was no easy step, but Richard and John Borden, who seem to have been brothers, were driven to it by the distress of the times. The burning of heretics had ceased in their day, but ostracism and persecution were still the common lot of "dissenters."

And so it came about that the first child born of European parents in Rhode Island (1638) was Matthew, third son of Richard Borden. Much interesting information is available concerning the family, for at an early period they joined the Society of Friends, whose practice it is to keep careful records concerning its members. "Glad should every Borden be that his ancestors were Quakers," writes their historian in California, and as one turns her illuminating pages,[1] noting the contribution of generation after generation to the development of this great country, one cannot but echo the sentiment.

The tendency of the family was always to move westward, and in the sixth generation a certain John Borden settled in Indiana, who was the great-grandfather of the William Borden of this record.

On his mother's side Borden came of a long line of soldiers, magistrates and preachers, reaching back to the early annals of English history. The best blood of the old country was in their veins, but the terrible years of Archbishop Laud's administration (1628-1640) had driven them too from the land they loved. Colonel William Whiting, who brought the name to America, belonged to the Suffolk branch of the family, and came with his wife Susannah from Yarmouth on the East Coast. With about a hundred others, they founded the city of

[1] *Historical and Genealogical Record of the Borden Family,* by Hattie Borden Weld, Los Angeles, Cal.

Hartford, Connecticut, and became members of the first church established there, under "the animated and able ministry" of the Rev. Thomas Hooker.[2]

Three generations later, Charles Whiting married the beautiful Elizabeth Bradford, a descendant of Governor William Bradford of Plymouth Colony and of John Alden, who won as his bride "the Puritan maiden Priscilla."[3] The sons of this Charles Whiting, himself a soldier, lived in the stormy days of the Revolutionary War and bore a brave part in its vicissitudes. A tribute is paid to one of them, William Bradford Whiting, in the family records, where he is spoken of as "a gentleman and a Christian, an upright, honourable man, possessing great dignity of manner and such integrity of character that his very presence was a rebuke to the wicked." In middle life he moved his home from Connecticut to Canaan, a beautiful part of the State of New York, which thus became the residence of Mrs. Borden's more immediate ancestors.

Bradford Whiting's descendants moved with the times, and the old homestead at Canaan was forsaken for regions further west. Detroit was little more than a village when Mrs. Borden's grandfather settled there; and her father, John Talman Whiting, played an outstanding part in the development of the State. Mrs. Borden (Mary de Garmo) was one of seven children, and passed on many of his lovable qualities to her son, William Whiting.

But there was something more important that she passed on

[2] The old records show that Colonel William Whiting was "one of the civil and religious fathers of Connecticut"; Magistrate of the colony, and Treasurer until his death. In his will he left the sum of five pounds toward mending the highways betwixt his dwelling and the meeting-house, and no less than twenty-five pounds to his "dear and loving Pastor toward the publication of his work on the 17th of John, and any else he doth intend."

[3] Governor Bradford, "the very prop and glory of Plymouth Colony," and John Alden were thus among Mrs. Borden's ancestors who came over on the *Mayflower*, and so were Priscilla Mullins and her parents, and a certain Thomas Rogers from whom, on the maternal side, Elizabeth Bradford was descended.

to this child, for when William was about seven years old Mrs. Borden entered upon a new experience spiritually which was deeply to affect his life. A devoted mother before, she now became an earnest, rejoicing Christian. To her, Christ was real, and fellowship with Him satisfying in no ordinary degree. Instead of losing everything when she turned to Him from the gaieties and allurements of the world, she found that she had gained not only peace with God but a new zest in living, a new joy in home and loved ones. New friends were brought into the family circle; new interests and ideals filled her life. In the Moody Church to which she transferred her membership, she found opportunities for service and the clear Bible teaching she coveted for the children. The result was very evident in the life of her younger son, who owed the strength and grasp of his spiritual convictions largely to that church home.

It was there he took his first step in open confession of Christ. Seated by his mother one Sunday morning, he heard Dr. R. A. Torrey, then pastor of the Moody Church, give the invitation to the communion service about to be held.

"Is it not time that you were thinking about this yourself, William?" his mother whispered.

"I have been," was the unexpected reply.

When the elements were handed from pew to pew, to Mrs. Borden's surprise, William quietly took the bread and wine as did those about him. Rather taken aback at this interpretation of her question, Mrs. Borden mentioned the matter to Dr. Torrey, who smiled and said:

"Let him come and see me about it to-morrow."

Young though he was, his answers to Dr. Torrey's questions made it evident that he was ready for the step he had taken, and the interview led to his joining the church in the regular way.

Another important decision was made when Dr. Torrey gave an opportunity for all who wished to dedicate their lives to the service of God to indicate this purpose by rising for prayer.

He made his meaning very plain, that it was a step of life-consecration. William quietly rose—a little fellow in a blue sailor-suit. He had to stand a long, long time while the service went on, but there was no wavering, and it was a consecration from which he never drew back.

Dependence upon prayer and love for the Word of God were becoming even then the warp and woof of his life. "Getting off to school" was a rush for him as for other boys. He hated to be late, and with books strapped on his back and cap and lunch-box in hand might be in "a tearing hurry." But, somehow, there was always time for the little word of prayer with Mother without which the day would not have been right. They would just drop on their knees together and pray that William might know in his experience the power of the blood of Jesus Christ. That was their daily prayer in those early years, and later it was that the will of God might be done in his life.

As to his love of the Bible, Mrs. Borden can never forget the picture she saw one evening on going to his room when the children had returned from a delightful party. Instead of finding William undressing, there he was, just as he had come home, in his velvet suit with knee-breeches, pumps and a stiff collar, seated on the edge of the bed, eagerly and serenely reading his Bible, from which he looked up at her with beaming eyes.

Later, on a journey round the world, his companion remarked that however long the day of sightseeing might be, the boy never failed to close it with Bible reading and prayer. All through college and seminary it was the same. Strenuous as life was for him in their Princeton home—with all his work in theology, religious and social claims, business responsibilities, and examinations looming ever in the background—when his mother went to his study the last thing at night, it would be to find him deep in the Book he loved, from which he would look up with the same glad light in his eyes.

CHAPTER 2

THE HILL SCHOOL
1902-1904. AGE 14-16

What! know ye not that your body is the temple of the Holy Ghost which is in you, which ye have of God, and ye are not your own? For ye are bought with a price: therefore glorify God in your body, and in your spirit, which are God's.—I CORINTHIANS 6:19, 20

Birthday verse given to William by his mother, when he was about eight years old, which became the keynote of his life.

THE GLORY of The Hill School when William entered it as a lad of fourteen was not its assembly hall and library, its gymnasium or athletic fields. Much of the splendid equipment of today had not yet come into existence. But the school had reached high-water mark in the last decade of the life of its great head master. What he was among his boys, four hundred of whom overflowed classrooms and dining hall, may be judged from the inscription on the simple marble that marks his resting place in the ivy-covered cloister of the chapel:

John Meigs
STRONG, IMPETUOUS, TENDER,
SERVANT OF CHRIST
MASTER OF BOYS
MAKER OF MEN
HIS COURAGE WAS THE FOUNDATION OF THE SCHOOL
HIS PASSION FOR TRUTH ITS LIGHT

"Obstacles are the glory of life" was one of his sayings, and no slackness or shirking was tolerated at "The Hill." "Prompt, alert, indefatigable himself, he demanded the same of all about him," and masters as well as boys awoke under his influence to a new, stimulating realization of what they could accomplish. There was a buoyancy, a spirit of energetic enthusiasm that was contagious, as a head master wrote who had once been on the faculty of The Hill.

> Everybody was systematically yet happily busy. There seemed to be never an idle minute. And the background of the picture was equally satisfying—a combination of perfectly-kept equipment and quiet appointments, bespeaking good breeding, artistic taste and culture. Through it all appeared a seriousness of purpose, not obtrusive yet hardly concealed by the various devices for interesting the boys in the realities of life. . . . Whether in the genial, comfortable air of the dining-room, amid the varied activity of the athletic field, or in the more rarefied atmosphere of the school-room-chapel, there was the same heartiness and stimulus, physical, intellectual and spiritual, and the centre of it all, the animating spirit of this city on the hill was "professor." . . . Its ideals were his ideals and its system was the device of his genius for making those ideals practical and applying them to the everyday problems of life.[1]

There was, under the influence of Dr. Meigs, a splendid insistence upon the sanctity of the body, "its reverent, radiant uses." With all his power he sought to make his boys understand that the strength of noblest manhood is built on purity, and that impurity is weakness and shame. "Self-reverence, self-knowledge, self-control," he believed with Tennyson, "lead life to sovereign power." But he was far from trusting in moral training alone to develop the all-round manhood he had in view. A penciled memorandum gives some of his deeper thoughts in this connection.

> The school must educate, develop, guide and instruct that spiritual faculty which, by whatever name we call it, is su-

[1] From *The Master of the Hill*, by Walter Russell Bowie, from which further quotations are made in this chapter.

preme. There is no other restraining power [than religion].
Sympathy, the innate horror of doing wrong to a fellow creature; self-respect, the innate horror of doing wrong to ourselves, are real powers in all finer natures. But a restraining
power is needed. . . . The problem of school morality will be
solved by a religious motive or none.

Coming from a great educator this statement is notable, and
the way in which he and his colleagues acted upon it gave
a character all its own to The Hill School. The religion which
John Meigs led the boys to understand and seek after was no
artificial piousness; "it was a deep and manly and straightfor-
ward choice of Christ as pattern and Master and Lord." In this
connection he noted:

As with the aspiring athlete and the eager learner, so must
it be with the young Christian. He must be taught to study
the great Book of rules for daily living; to seek his great Captain in difficulty, and to ask for guidance in prayer; to heed the
coach who has gained wisdom and victory in his longer game
of life; and to share counsels, joy and confidences in brotherly
meetings for prayer. He must realize that the test of his religious life is what he *is* and what he *does* when he is *not* on his
knees in prayer, *not* reading his Bible, *not* listening to great
preachers and *not* participating in religious meetings.

About the Sunday services of the school there was the same
naturalness and appeal to the boy "where he lives." Distinguished preachers came for the regular "Chapel," but the
characteristic thing was the Vesper Hour, when hymns were
sung and the man who knew and understood them best would
sometimes speak and always pray. One of his boys wrote:

The real picture of the Professor, which always comes clear
and distinct from memories of the old school-days, is as he sat
at his desk in the schoolroom of a Sunday evening at the song
service, and the hymn I always associate with him is "Ein Feste
Burg". . . . That is what he looked and what he was—a firm,

strong, kindly, helpful citadel. There seemed to be something in the Professor's face as he came down the aisle at the close of those song services on Sunday nights that I never quite caught at any other time, a something words will not tell.

And there were other things Hill boys could never forget, among them the Professor's utter sincerity and truthfulness and his hatred of everything mean and underhand. They remember that he never stole upon them unawares, but that "always his heavy footfall—every ounce of his great frame telling at each step—resounded through the corridors as he approached; and in the memory of that sound they find their most vivid impression of what is meant by the hatred of sham, subterfuge and unfairness."

"Truth-speaking and truth-loving" he considered "the very bedrock of character," and with these he classed obedience, which in his thought stood for "willing conformity to the right standards of the school, which all must accept who accept its life"; obedience not so much to rules as to "the high majesty of accepted duty." On this point he could have "no refusal and no evasion." To the father of a boy about to be expelled he wrote:

> His vital and fatal lack is that of obedience. He has so in-
> dulged himself that self-pleasing is the law of his life, and
> deference to a higher law seems repugnant. Your . . . experi-
> ence will reinforce my position touching the vital necessity of
> submission to law as the primal condition of moral as well as
> physical life and well-being.

Dr. Meigs was keenly alive also to the importance of organized games and athletics, on account of the moral training they afford and their contribution to purity of life. He was fortunate in having secured the services of Michael F. Sweeney, the holder when he came to The Hill, and for years afterwards, of the world's record for the high jump. A member of the faculty tells us that

He became not only the physical director of the gymnasium and track-work but also the coach and controlling spirit of all the organized games in the school. Between him and the head master there was a sympathy and understanding which grew into the most loving identity of purpose, and into all his relationships with the boys . . . Mr. Sweeney brought not only his technical skill but the power of a Christian idealism which left its deep impress on the spirit of many a lad who would hardly have been reached through any other channel.

Borden had come to the great school well grounded in the principles for which it stood. Sincerity and truthfulness were part of his character; one could never think of him in connection with any sham. There was so little self-consciousness about him, or morbid craving for appreciation, that one who knew him most intimately could say:

In all the years I was in close touch with him, I never saw him do one thing for effect.

A school friend, while he spoke of William as "a sturdy fighter," recalled also his "reserve and dignity and steady, quiet strength." Outwardly he was undemonstrative, but his home letters reveal the same warm-hearted, earnest, impetuous boy as of yore.

Sept. 27, 1902

DEAR MOTHER—To-day is the first time since I left Boston that we have seen the blue sky or sunshine. It has been raining steady since the evening I arrived until yesterday evening. I like the school very much, all the old fellows are nice to the new fellows, asking us to come and see them in their rooms, etc.

My room is in the east wing, second floor, number 4. My roommate is a very nice fellow, a little older than I am, and two or three inches taller. . . . A great many of the old fellows here knew John [his elder brother], most of them are sixth formers. All the old teachers are very nice to me and they seem very jolly, especially Mr. Rolfe, Mr. Hallock and Mr. Weed whom I suppose you met. . . .

I like Professor and Mrs. John very much from what I have seen of them so far. Many parents came down with the fellows the first day, and even some sisters. Our room is very nice; it has two large windows looking out on the quadrangle. Under the sill of each is a small window-seat which could be made quite nice if they had cushions and pillows on them. . . .

I am taking football for exercise and I am now trying for the second team, but I don't think there is much chance of my making it.

Last night they had the first meeting of the Y.M.C.A. Throop Wilder is President and John Holabird is Vice-President. The meeting was great! Throop spoke first, and then a good many of the old fellows got up and spoke. Dwight Meigs led in prayer, and then other fellows gave short prayers.

This year there are more new fellows than ever, and Professor had to turn away some because he couldn't accommodate them. I sit at Mr. Weed's end of the fifth-form table, which is right at the end of Mrs. John's table.[2]

Give my love to Granny and everybody and tell them I expect to write soon.—Your loving son,   WILLIAM

Oct. 4, 1902

DEAR SIS—I received your letter yesterday and thank you for it very much. As my roommate gets about three letters every mail, I like to get one once in a while.

Talk about work—I have six studies, Chemistry, English History, French, Greek, English and Bible History. The Eng. Comp. is fierce. We have to make a literal translation of parts

2 There were two Mrs. Meigs, beloved of The Hill School—one the mother of the Professor, who for many years had been the mainspring of its life, and the other "Mrs. John" who came to it as his bride in the fall of 1882. Of the value of her contribution to the school it would be difficult to speak adequately. "That which, joined to the influence of John Meigs himself," wrote his biographer, "more than any other thing set the tone and created the spirit of The Hill was the touch of Mrs. Meigs upon the boys. In the lovely 'sky-parlour,' up in the tower of the old stone building of the head master's house, with its wide windows looking out over the tranquil trees, many a boy in his talks with her has caught the gleam of new meanings for his life, going down to the school again with the power of finer purpose in his soul."

of Virgil and Caesar, and in class change this into idiomatic English. Then again we have to write on the character of people in the Sir Roger de Coverley papers, in the style of Steele.

We have had two Y.M.C.A. meetings, at one of which Boyd Edwards, who was at Northfield, spoke. I have joined it, also my "wife."[3] Throop Wilder is fine, he is Pres. of Y.M.C.A. and of the Athletic Association.

I am out trying for the second team, it is pretty hard work. There are a great many Chicago fellows here. . . .

Hoping you will write soon again.—I am, Your loving brother,   BILL

I haven't been homesick a bit.

Oct. 26, 1902

DEAR FATHER—Mother says you are working over the plans of our Camden house day and night. I haven't noticed any pictures of summer houses in the magazines. Harry Widener is the son of the man who owns that house you liked so much. You remember we were looking at it in a magazine at Camden last summer. . . .

We have had three football games so far. The first two were with the Haverford Grammar School and Princeton Freshmen, the score in each game was 0 to 0. The third game was a perfect cinch for us, the score being 41 to 0 in favour of Hill. Only one goal was missed. Monday [tomorrow] the annual interclass track will be held, I am going into the shot-put. It is a handicap meet, so I will have a little show but not much.

I wish you would get me a shot gun and give it me for my birthday, so that I could have it down here and shoot a little, so that I could go hunting at Christmas vacation. I will put an account of my expenses up to the present time in here.

With lots of love.—Your son,   WILLIAM

Football supplies	$3.20	Contribution	$1.00
Posters	1.05	Clothes pressed	1.00

[3] His roommate, Eugene Delarno.

Eatables	.20	Stamps	.10
Screw Driver	.14	Hill banner	.50
Book-rack	.20	Thumb Tacks	.09
Picture wire	.20	Carfare	.10
Class paper	1.90	Soda	.15
Clothes	1.00	Pillow	1.50
Epp's (i.e. tuck)	.30	Reading-room fee	1.00
Paper	.02	Epp's	1.35
Stamps	.10	Contribution	.65
Epp's	.45		
Contribution	1.00		$25.68
Window cushions	9.98		

Oct. 26, 1902

DEAR MOTHER—Last Saturday we only danced for a little while and all sat around on the floor and sang songs. I liked it much more than dancing and hope we will do it again. . . . I suppose you are waiting until Nov. 1 [his birthday] to send down anything, but when you do I wish you would send plenty of fruit and cake; and we can have jam, so I wish you would throw in a few glasses of different kinds of jelly, which help the sandwiches we have daily at 11:45.

Mr. Speer[4] was here to-day and preached, he was fine. He seems to have changed a great deal, his voice is terribly deep bass.

I will have to stop now as the Prep bell for bed has rung.

With lots of love,   WILLIAM

Jan. 18, 1903

DEAR MOTHER—We have had good weather lately, and to-day is simply fine. The sky is clear and cloudless. The air is cool and bracing. I intend to take a long walk this afternoon with some fellows.

About my examinations. I passed Algebra easy enough, and got a 100 in it I think. But I did not pass Geometry. However, Mr. Shephard let me go into the class, and I will try again to pass it Monday and he will help me, sort of tutoring and I hope to pass it to-morrow. I took an exam. in Lorna Doone and the result was rather surprising. I got 95 in it. There wasn't a single mistake in spelling or punctuation in the whole thing,

[4] Dr. Robert E. Speer.

and he had not made a single mark of correction anywhere. It was quite long, taking me nearly two hours of steady writing.

I have a terribly hard time in studying now, in fact I scarcely do anything but study. Study at night, every spare minute from the time I get up until school begins. Then at the recesses. After lunch I have about an hour and a half spare time. Then I have to prepare my lessons for the afternoon session, and then begin the same program again after supper.

Feb. 2, 1903

DEAR MOTHER—You say you like my hard work, well I don't think you would if you knew how terrible it is. I work every little spare minute that I have, almost, and when Saturday comes you're just about played out and don't get a decent rest before it begins again the next week. And then if you get a "third list" after working so terribly hard it makes you feel sort of discouraged. Our English is the worst stuff imaginable. It is Carlyle's Essay on Burns. Why it is something awful! You can't make head or tail out of it, and it takes about two hours' hard study to know anything about it at all.

We look forward to getting through with this term and scratch off a day on the calendar every day. There are now about eight weeks left of toil and drudgery. The weather here is awful too, one day it's summer and the next winter, first rain and then snow, etc.

I am losing weight quite fast now under Mr. Sweeney's work. I have lost 4 lbs. and lose about 3 lbs. a week. I will soon be a skeleton, won't I! But I guess it won't matter much. . . . Yours with lots of love,   WILLIAM

Mar. 1, 1903

DEAR MOTHER—I was very glad to get your letter as I had not had one for almost a week.

This evening we had a fine recital by Leland T. Powers of Boston. He gave Monsieur Beaucaire and was simply great. He is wonderful the way in which he can change his voice and expression from that of a woman to that of a man in an instant. You wouldn't think it possible he could change his appearance so much as he does by simply mussing up his hair, or some other little thing like that. After giving M. Beaucaire he gave a short and very funny thing about some old country parson and other country people. This simply kept us roaring all the time.

Mr. Speer was here today and preached both this morning and afternoon. Many of the fellows here criticize him, and one of the teachers. But I don't think they know what they are talking about, and it makes me sore to hear them.

I am getting to like Mr. Rolfe more and more all the time. He is simply great. Always happy and cheery, never harsh or gruff except when he has to stop fellows from rough-housing, and even then he is nice and makes a joke out of it or does something else. . . .

Just think only three weeks more of study. If I escape exams. I might be able to leave here Tuesday afternoon or evening, March 24th. My, but won't I be glad when I get out of here! I tell you it will be a relief to get away from the toil and grind of this place for a little while at least.

You must tell me about Johnny and everything you can about J——, Teddy, and anything that is going on at home.

With lots of love to everyone,—Your loving son,

WILLIAM

Mar. 8, 1903

DEAR MOTHER—I was awfully glad to hear from you twice this week.

About my coming home and my vacation, I am not in for any exams. so far, and I think I am safe for this last week. Now if I can possibly manage by toil and labour and grinding to keep out for two weeks more, then I will be safe. Just think Mother, exams begin the 24th of this month, and I hope to be able to leave that night, getting to Chicago the next evening! Only sixteen more days and I may be out of this awful working place, and the winter term will be over. You can never appreciate how terrible this winter term is. As for the length of my vacation, it will be just three weeks I think.

That he realized his hope is evident from the following letter:

MY DEAR MR. BORDEN—I am very happy to congratulate you on William's excellent record for the past term and to inform you that he is one of twenty members of the school who have been excused from all of their examinations.—Faithfully yours,

JOHN MEIGS

March 31st, 1903

The summer term brought new and varied experiences. To his mother he wrote:

April 17, 1903

The trees here have quite large leaves and fruit trees are in full bloom. Everything is fine and I think this term will pass pretty quick.

I want you to write me as often as possible and give me all the news about everything you possibly can. Sometimes I feel like punching the fellow's head who sits in the mail window and says, "Nothing for Borden," three times a day for sometimes three and four days in succession! Tell me about the doings of John, Mary and Baby, etc.

April 20, 1903

DEAR MOTHER—The weather continues simply fine here; beautiful warm sunshiny days, everything blooming as if it were midsummer.

We have lots of fun now, playing outdoor games, baseball, track, etc. The Gun Club shooting is good fun and I have improved greatly since last term. If I keep on improving I might have some chance of making the Gun Team and I will certainly work hard for it.

My studies will be pretty hard this term I think. But I can manage to get along all right, so you needn't worry. This last week I got two seconds and five firsts in subjects.

I came very near forgetting to tell you about the sermon on Sunday. Campbell Morgan was here and preached a fine sermon in the morning, which was said to be the best ever given here. It certainly was fine. It was on Mark 1:11 and 6:3. "Thou art my beloved son in whom I am well pleased," and, "Is not this the carpenter": man's view and God's view. Mr. Morgan demonstrated that it must have been the eighteen years of Christ's life of which we know nothing, save that He was a carpenter, in which He had pleased God. Then he went on to meditate on how much good an apprentice of His would have gotten. He said he did not think Christ would have talked of heaven or hell, but would have simply given him an example to follow, by His every-day life in which there was no blemish.

Some of the fellows thought it was a little long, but I did not and wanted more. It was wonderful, the way he held everyone spellbound by his talk. For five or ten minutes no one would stir while he talked, then as if to relieve the strain he would change his tone. Then the people would shift their positions slightly and settle down again and so on. It certainly was fine and I hope he comes again.

June 14, 1903

DEAR MOTHER—I got your letter from Camden and was glad to hear from you.

Now Commencement is all over and we have begun work again, at least what's left of us. For there are only fifth and sixth formers here now. . . . On Tuesday morning the swimming contests were held. Our team was scratch in the relay-race, and we got second place.

In the afternoon, it being clear, the inter-class track meet was held. It was very close and exciting throughout. The sixth form won with 43 points, we were second with 40. . . . The next morning the drill was held on the field. It was not very hot and hence the drill did not seem very bad. Our company did not drill very well and so we did not get the prize. Right after the drill, the closing exercises were held in the gym. Prizes were given out and also gold medals. . . . Eugene got three prizes of books for excellence in Latin, Greek and Bible History. I got one in Geom. I am seventeenth in the school, twelfth on second honour list and seventh in our form.

Lunch right after that was simply great. Only one table was left in, to serve stuff from, and everybody stood up. There was salmon, chicken croquettes, two or three kinds of salad, sandwiches, bouillion and everything. About half a dozen different desserts. I took a liberal portion of everything and came very near regretting it.

November 22, 1903

DEAR MOTHER—It seems a perfect age since I had any communication with the outside world. We have been to Lawrenceville, and our team got beaten by a score of six to five. It seems awfully queer—the feeling that football is over. It seems unnatural, as if something had come to an end. But I will tell you about our trip to Lawrenceville.

I was taken with the team as a sub. We left here Friday afternoon and got to Trenton about 8:00. We went to the Trenton House for the night. It is an awfully old affair, must have been there in Washington's time. The hall-ways were a regular labyrinth, and we walked a terrible way before finding our rooms. In the morning after breakfast Mr. Sweeney gave us a talk in one of the fellows' rooms. I never knew what he was like before. He was wonderful. He talked to us for about an hour on all points in football, and especially "fighting." I'm sure he thrilled every fellow, he did me I know.

After lunch we went out to Lawrenceville. The game was at 2 o'clock. Their team outweighed ours nearly twenty pounds to the man, but that didn't keep our fellows from fighting just as hard. Lawrenceville teams usually have weight, while ours have Hill spirit. In the first half no scoring was done, and the ball was in their territory most of the time. In the second half we scored a touchdown. Our man was so tired that he missed the goal, which really lost us the game. Then with only a few minutes left to play, the teams lined up again. Their weight told now and they pushed us down to about our ten yard line. We held them and punted out. They came on again, were held again, and then came on and crossed the line. They kicked the goal, making the score 6 to 5. It was mighty hard for our fellows to lose like that, and they all felt mighty badly over it. They played simply fine and nobody has any kick coming.

I hope to be home in less than three weeks from now. Not very long, is it? I'll be mighty glad to get home and see you.

I'm going to work these next two weeks, and then maybe I won't have any third week here.—Your loving son,

WILLIAM

After the Christmas vacation:

January 31, 1904

DEAR MOTHER—We have been having pretty good weather here and lots of snow. Yesterday we hired a bobsled and went coasting out here on a hill and had pretty good fun. The sled was an enormous one and held nine or ten.

A Dr. —— was here to-day to preach, he was very sad. In the morning he read a thing he called the first chapter of the Ephesians, but it wasn't out of the Bible and was as different as you could imagine. Then his sermon wasn't any good and was without a point. In the afternoon he didn't even try to preach a Christian sermon but gave us one from a Confucianist in Japan. He has spent about twenty years in Japan and is quite an authority on it. This was about some fool and a class of fools, and the point was "What we had come into the world for." It was better I thought than his morning attempt, but nothing much at that. He is a teacher or something at the Union Theological Seminary. Gene thinks it the best in the country, and says practically everyone goes there to prepare for the ministry. I disagreed, and he said his grandfather had founded it. I then said that it had probably changed a great deal since that time. That man getting up there and reading his text out of some book which didn't resemble a Bible in any way, just made me tired and fixed him for me. I thought how bad things are getting to be.

I don't know whether I told you about Mr. Weed or not, but anyway he was off nearly two weeks. His mother was expected to die any moment, but she didn't and has now recovered. As a result he is feeling mighty happy and thankful. In Bible Class tonight he read about the miracle of the wine at the marriage feast. Then he said that it was the modern idea that the man who believed in miracles was way behind the times. But he said things would happen in our lives so that we would *have* to believe in them. He said, "I have seen miracles within the last two weeks and believe in them." It was good that, after some of Dr. ——'s trash. I know you think the same way, and it makes me tired to hear all this talk against the old beliefs.

Mr. Weed is going to put the lights out in just a minute and I will have to say good night.—Your loving son,

WILLIAM

Happily for the boy's faith he was well-grounded in the Word of God, so that anything that seemed to him contrary to the truth awoke an energetic reaction in his soul. Looking back on these and similar experiences, he wrote to the Committee of the Chicago Avenue Church some years later:

I am very thankful for the teaching I received at the Moody Church and Institute before I was fifteen years of age, because it kept me firm in my beliefs in spite of opposition and criticism which I was not able to answer. The great truths of the deity of Christ, His vicarious atonement, and the inspiration and authority of the Bible had been indelibly impressed upon me. I was specially impressed by the testimony of our Lord Himself to this last matter, and was willing to wait until I could go to Seminary and be prepared to meet the critics on their own ground.

Hoping that the good work may go on and that many may be won to Christ and strengthened in the faith as I was—I remain, Very sincerely yours,

WILLIAM W. BORDEN

Debates, orations and the Class dance were absorbing as spring came again, not to speak of the war news from the Far East.

February 3, 1904

DEAR MOTHER—I have heard from both Mary and Marjorie and each says she can come. Mary said Miss Kellogg would chaperon her. It was the first I knew about such a thing and it might have made trouble. But it is all right, and I am all fixed now except to order more flowers for Miss Kellogg.

We have to get two sets of flowers, one for the dance on Friday night and the other for the show on Saturday night. I have ordered violets and bridesmaid roses to the amount of six dollars. Then we have to have a rig to go riding in, dramatic-club seats, etc., besides the fourteen dollars I spoke of in my last letter. . . .

Gene delivered his oration the other night, and it went off very well. In fact, all the orations so far have been remarkably good, and it's up to us who come later to do as well. As I have told you, mine comes Friday, the second speaker. I get scared off and on by spells.

I am very much interested in watching this war between Russia and Japan, and I suppose you must be. We rush over to the reading room after breakfast for a glimpse at the morning papers before going to study. The newsboy who sells papers here in the evening does a flourishing business, and you have to hustle to get one. Japan seems to be doing the Russians up on the sea. . . . I should think you might write to Huntingdon Wilson for news, although it would be rather old by the time it reached here.

The remaining letters for the year are missing—save one, which gives a last impression of Borden at The Hill. He graduated in 1904, receiving a grade of 83.6; standing fourth in a form of forty-eight boys of whom he was the youngest.

February 21, 1904

DEAR MOTHER—This morning we had Communion Service in the (new) chapel at eight o'clock. Mr. Speer and Dr. Cuthbert Hall conducted and it was very nice. Of course attendance was not compulsary; only a few were there. . . .

The Dedication Service was very good. Mr. Speer and Dr. Hall both made addresses.

It is after lights now, and I will have to say, Good-bye.—Your loving son,   WILLIAM

CHAPTER 3

AROUND THE WORLD

1904-1905. AGE 16-17

Something hidden. Go and find it. Go and look behind the Ranges—
Something lost behind the Ranges.
Lost and waiting for you. Go!

— R. KIPLING

THE WAR between Japan and Russia was still in progress when, in the summer of 1904, Borden set out on a journey round the world. He had graduated from The Hill at sixteen, and his parents felt that a year spent in this way would be well worth while before he entered college. It was no small responsibility Mr. Walter Erdman had undertaken in consenting to travel with him. Scholarly, brilliant, full of humor, recently graduated from Princeton University and Seminary, a more delightful companion could hardly have been found, but his chief recommendation in Mr. and Mrs. Borden's eyes lay in his fine Christian character.

"I remember our talks about William down in the pine grove at Camden," he wrote years later, "when you were wondering what sort of companion I should make for him, and I was wondering how I could measure up to your ideals."

He remembered also Mr. Borden's helpfulness when seeing them off from Chicago. Partly in boyish bravado, William prolonged his farewells, swinging on to the train when it was already in motion.

"William," called his father sharply, "don't do things like that! It isn't fair to Mr. Erdman."

37

"It was a word of caution that was not forgotten," wrote the latter, "save possibly on two occasions—once when he was clambering over the fortifications of the old castle at Ajmere, and once when his familiarity with nautical matters and the management of a yacht tempted him to climb thoughtlessly on the rail and swing from the halliards of an ocean liner. The Captain administered a sharp rebuke on that occasion. William called him 'an old stiff' in private—but he came down.

"It was inevitable that a boy of his physical endowments and active disposition should be on the whole more interested in doing than in seeing things, and one does not wonder that he was more enthusiastic over a swim in the phosphorescent sea before the shrine at Kamakura than in studying the wonderful lines and graceful bulk of its great bronze Buddha. He remonstrated with me a little for being willing to see it twice! One might have supposed that so active and independent a nature would be impatient of advice or restraint. Yet, excepting the occasions mentioned, his activity never gave cause for concern, and there was no time when he failed to accept suggestions or recognize the force of another's judgment."

It was a September day when the S.S. "Korea" put out from San Francisco. Fog hung over the Golden Gate, and the departure seemed a small affair compared with the outgoing of the transatlantic liners from New York. What Borden thought of it all may be seen from his unstudied letters:

Sept. 20, 1904

DEAREST MOTHER—We are off at last, and so far it seems quite nice, although in some respects a little speck disappointing.

We went down to the wharf quite early and our bags were taken up to the room by a lot of little Chinamen dressed in dark blue with a round black hat with a red top-knot to it. They were certainly very funny and cute. Most of them take the end of their queue and put it in their coat pocket. Our steward is a very nice Chinaman dressed like the ones I have just described.
. . .

The scene at the dock was quite queer, very different from the departure of an Atlantic steamer. Chinamen swarmed everywhere, and there were also a good many Japs mixed in. All the servants and sailors are Chinamen and they seem to be very competent. Some of them are comical in their appearance and actions and I enjoy watching them, especially the sailors about their work.

Our fellow passengers are mostly married people, in fact there aren't more than half a dozen young folk that I have noticed. The Chinamen are by far the most interesting bunch. There is an open space between the promenade deck and the poop where they congregate—fat, thin, old and young, some with gray queues and others with black. I watched them eating this afternoon with their chopsticks. About ten of them squatted around one pot of rice and a pot of some sort of meat. Each man had a little tin pan which he filled with rice. They ate by holding the pan up to the mouth and then shoving in the rice with their chopsticks, which they held in one hand. They picked up pieces of meat with their chopsticks and smeared them round in a common bowl of gravy. Several of these groups were scattered over the deck and it made a very queer spectacle.

Sept. 21, 1904

DEAR MOTHER—To-day we have gotten pretty well settled and have had a chance to look around a bit. Our chairs are located on the port side, near the forward end of the promenade deck. Our neighbours are a couple of young men starting out as missionaries. They are Jones and Gibb, and were on the train with us coming out to San Francisco.

Then there is a Mr. Lamb and his wife and little boy. Mr. Lamb is a classmate of Walter's, and he and his wife are going to the Philippines as missionaries. They are very nice and awfully jolly. Mr. Lamb and I got permission from the chief engineer and went all through the engineroom. One of the assistants showed us over and explained everything. He also took us into the stoking rooms of which there are five or six. It wasn't nearly as hot as I expected, in fact I don't believe it troubled the stokers at all. The stokers are Chinese and they work for seven dollars a month, rather small wages, isn't it?

Whenever they get hungry, they haul out a few coals, build a fire right on the floor and cook themselves some chow. It seems that there are a lot of Chinese on board who travel back and forth just to gamble. They certainly do it with a vengeance. To-day revealed five or six new games, and they were busy playing most of the day.

The colour of the water out here as it surges away from the ship is remarkable. It is a deep indigo blue and doesn't seem to be affected by the colour of the sky.

A day at Honolulu, where the water was like melted opals in coloring and clear as crystal, was welcome. Native boys, eager to dive for money, swam out to meet the ship, some of whom, scrambling on board, took-off even from boats on the hurricane deck. The Aquarium with its rainbow-colored fish, bathing, surf-riding, and a drive to various points of interest made the time pass quickly, until a fresh contingent of passengers came on board, wearing wreaths of flowers after the custom of the island, and the journey was resumed toward the setting sun.

Tuesday, Oct. 4, 1904

DEAR UNCLE FRED AND AUNT LAURA—I received the Round Robin to which you contributed so much and thank you very much for it. I often wish to be sailing (yachting) out here, where the trades blow steadily and the sea is comparatively smooth.

Going round the world may be quite a trip, but it isn't anything uncommon among these passengers. There are three or four who are on their fourth trip around, and several on their third and second. So we sink into insignificance. We have a couple of German and Austrian Counts and Countesses, an Italian doctor and also several German university men, one with scars on his cheek. Then there is an Admiral of the U. S. Navy and a Bishop. So you see we have quite a few celebrities.

We have only seen the smoke of one boat since we left San Francisco. The Pacific is quite large.

With love.—Your nephew,

WILLIAM W. BORDEN

His respect for the Pacific was further increased by encountering a typhoon before they reached Japan, as we learn from his journal:

> Strong breeze from the south-east and fairly big sea running. Life-lines put up on the lower deck and all awnings taken down. Wind developed to a gale in the afternoon. Hove to about seven and rode typhoon during the night.
>
> Rained hard early in the morning with the wind still blowing a gale. Engines started and kept at half speed from 5:30 A.M. to 4:30 P.M. Shipped big seas over the prow. Sea quieted down in the afternoon and full speed was put on.

Next day they were in Yokohama.

Japan was not the fascinating vision it would have been had they visited it in spring, when the cherry and wistaria are in bloom. Fall colors touched the hills with beauty, but it was more the people than the country that appealed to Borden.

Fifty years only had elapsed since Commodore Perry had effected, in 1853-4, the introduction of the Island Kingdom into the family of nations, and only thirty years since the famous Iwakura Commission had been sent out "to survey the world and cull its best for the future development of Japan," but what hadn't that brief period witnessed of progress along the lines of national education, representative government and facility of communication! Hundreds of miles of railway connected all the important cities of the main island, where previously there had been none. Schools, colleges and universities had sprung up in which tens of thousands were pursuing an up-to-date curriculum, and to the worship of the imperial line which had occupied the throne for more than two thousand years had been added modern parliamentary government, with a constitution granting liberty hitherto undreamed of in oriental lands.

Side by side with all this had gone territorial expansion and increase of prestige and population. The war with China concluded ten years previously had brought Formosa under the sovereignty of Japan; and the war with Russia still in progress had raised her to the first rank among naval and military powers. So it was a new Japan to which our travelers came, and yet the old was everywhere present, and the mingling of East and West was almost bewildering. In the fine station at Yokohama, for example, the clatter of wooden clogs on the pavement was deafening, and in the narrow oriental streets it was alarming to see children playing almost under the wheels of modern vehicles. One of his first letters was to his younger sister:

IMPERIAL HOTEL, TOKIO,
October 13, 1904

DEAR, DEAR JOYCE—I wish you were here to enjoy all the funny little people with their queer ways and dress. I know you would have a beautiful time. But as you can't see them, I will try and tell you about them.

I never saw so many children before as there are here in Japan. They seem to be everywhere, in groups of four or five and sometimes more, playing in the streets. None of the boys and girls that run around wear any socks, but they all wear queer little wooden clogs which they hold on with the big toe and the next one. I should think that they would keep coming off all the time, but they never do. The little girls all wear kimonos, something like Mary's only much prettier, some of them being all gold and red and purple. As soon as their hair is long enough, they do it up in a queer little bunch on top of their head just like their mothers. None of the girls or women wears any kind of hat, as it would muss their hair all up.

The boys wear the same kind of shoes and kimonos as the girls but their hair is fixed different. It is clipped quite short, in a ring all round the head. Then right on top a little round spot is shaved to make it look nice. The boys, or at least a good many of them, wear little soldier hats and look very cute.

Girls littler than you go around playing with a tiny little baby tied on their back. The baby hangs there in warm weather with its little bare feet hanging down and in cold weather is all bundled up so that you can only see the top of its head. The baby sleeps whenever it feels like it, and the little girl goes right on playing just the same. Do you think you could sleep while I was running around with you on my back? I don't. All the boys and girls seem very good. It is rare to see one crying unless it is very young or has been hurt. They haven't any toys to speak of, although there are plenty in the stores, yet they seem very happy and have a good time.

The newspaper men, not boys, go running through the streets shouting the news, with bells jangling at their waists to attract attention. They are mostly extras that are sold in this way, and the paper itself is about the size of this sheet I am writing on.

When it rains the people all carry big paper umbrellas, some of them very pretty. Some of the men have big straw hats instead of umbrellas, and sometimes a whole suit, or long coat, made out of this rice-straw. I shouldn't think it would be very dry or comfortable, but they wear them anyway.

With lots and lots of love,   WILLIAM

Their first railway journey was a short one, south from Yokohama to the shrines of Kamakura, about which he wrote to his mother:

October 9, 1904

At the station we took rickshaws and went first to see the Dai Butsu.[1] . . . We approached the statue by a stone walk through a very pretty garden, only there wasn't a bit of grass. On account of the trees we couldn't see the statue until quite close to it. It is a very impressive and remarkable piece of work considering it dates from A.D. 1243. Around the image foundation stones may be seen in the ground. These supported the

[1] Buddhism had been in Japan for four centuries before it could be said to have become part of the national life. This colossal image of Buddha (the Dai Butsu) was erected to commemorate the welding together of the alien faith, first brought over by Korean missionaries, with the indigenous cult of Japan. "The copper used in the construction of this magnificent image was to represent Shintoism while the gold was to represent Buddhism."

temple that once covered the statue. It has been gone a long time, as a result of tidal waves. . . .

From the Dai Butsu we went to another Buddhist temple on the top of a hill overlooking the sea. This was the temple of the Goddess of Mercy, and there were many small idols round the walls. One of them was all stuck-up with pieces of paper. These are prayers, and a string of them hangs near by to which the worshipper helps himself. After chewing it a while, he throws it—if it sticks, the prayers are answered; otherwise not.

Tokyo, the capital, and beautiful Nikko in the mountains north of it, were no disappointment. Through the kindness of a Japanese friend, they were permitted to drive through the grounds of the Palace, seeing something of the surroundings of the Mikado who was the hundred and twenty-second representative of his imperial line. No other dynasty in the world approaches such a record, and it was easy to understand the passionate loyalty of the people to a family which they believe to have been descended from the gods and which has given them such a succession of almost uniformly good rulers.

Parliamentary government had existed for only fifteen years —"a time, no doubt, of many thrills on the part of the people, far and near, who for the first time in the nation's history were taking part in the administration of national affairs."

NIKKO, Oct. 16, 1904

DEAR MOTHER—At present we are at Nikko, a beautiful spot up in the mountains. In the valley is a very pretty little stream and the mountains are covered with maples which are just beginning to change their colour. Well, I must go back and tell you what we did in Tokyo.

Last Wednesday we were shown through the Houses of Parliament by a very nice Jap. He took us into all the various offices and we saw the pictures of several presidents, etc. The room in which the Representatives meet is simple and not unusual. The House of Peers is much more gorgeous, especially the Mikado's office-room. This is beautifully fitted out with gold-lacquer screens and a cloth of gold over the desk. The Imperial box also is very fine with such things as silks and gold lace, etc. . . .

Friday we had a very interesting time. In the morning we went to the school where Mr. Hatta teaches and then went to call on a Japanese lady, Mrs. Fuki O. Kami. Her house was in the suburbs of the city in a pretty little compound. After walking through the garden we came to a very nice house with sliding walls made of rice paper. The maid greeted us on her knees and bumped her head on the floor at nearly every word. While we waited we were served tea and were then informed by Mr. Hatta that we were to be received at another house, as Mrs. Kami wished to treat us as very distinguished visitors. So we walked a short distance to another cute little house and after removing our shoes went in.

Walt had known Mrs. Kami in America, so we took the liberty of asking to be allowed to sit Japanese style instead of in the chairs offered to us. After we had talked a while (Mrs. Kami speaks very good English) the maid came on her knees pushing a tray with tea before her. There were also some small green and pink rice-cakes which we had some difficulty in picking up with chop-sticks, but which were really very good. We were informed that Mrs. O. Kami was quite rich, and that probably accounts for her two houses and also for the gown she had on. It was a kimono with very long sleeves. The cloth was a mixture of brown silk and old gold and it was simply stunning. . . .

In company with Mr. O. Kami they went to see some war-pictures.

We arrived at the theatre and checked our shoes, as everyone here does instead of leaving their hats and coats. The floor of the theatre was divided into little squares, about four feet each way, and in one of these we squatted. Between the pictures, tea and cigarettes flourished on all sides. The pictures themselves weren't anything special and we found the people more interesting.

A visit to the hospital enabled them to realize something of what the war was costing day by day.

We met two officers, both of whom had been fearfully wounded while fighting at Port Arthur. The first one, who spoke English very well, told us a little about it. He said they were so close to the Russians that they could hear one another talking and could throw stones across. Everything was very neat, clean and comfortable. The nurses looked nice in their white uniforms and high caps. We distributed flowers and books and towels which are appropriate Japanese gifts.

Of their journey westward to the former capital of the islands, lovely Kyoto, he tells in more than one letter. For they stopped by the way to obtain near views of Fujiyama, to enjoy the hot springs of a remote valley, and to climb passes from which the clouds lifted giving glimpses of the sacred mountain. After one climb,

"We had a hot sulphur bath," he wrote, "which was simply great! The Japanese tubs are made of wood and are about three feet deep and oblong in shape. Instead of climbing into them you step down. I think they are fine, and enjoy boiling in them up to my neck! I am afraid they will spoil me for any others."

To reach Nagoya they had to travel part of the way on a man-power railroad.

The car we got into was a perfect cube, measuring about five feet on a side. It was meant to seat four, but at various stages on the journey we had a number of fellow-passengers. Three coolies pushed us slowly up the hill and then jumped on while we coasted down at a terrific rate. Just why the car stayed on the track going round sharp curves I cannot tell, but it did, and that's the main point.

Kyoto palaces, gardens, temples and shops were of the finest, but they found, as Dr. Charles Erdman wrote on his later visit, that

"It is a city 'wholly given to idolatry.' Of course one will enjoy a visit to the grounds and buildings of the Mikado's palace; he will struggle against the temptation to bankrupt himself in the shops, which are the most attractive in the land, but his real concern in Kyoto will be with its countless temples. We rambled through acres of these, carefully depositing our shoes outside in the rain and walking in cloth slippers over vast expanses of polished floors and becoming more and more depressed by realizing the familiar fact that a proud modern empire, one of the five great powers of the world, is in the deadening grasp of false religions and degrading cults."

Of one of the temples at Kyoto Borden wrote:

November 5, 1904

The most interesting temple we visited was the Sangusanguido or Temple of the 33,333 gods. The building that contains this outfit is a shabby-looking place about four hundred feet long by sixty wide. The images all represent the same goddess, Kivanna, Goddess of Mercy. They are made of wood and gilded. Right opposite the entrance is a huge image said to be carved out of one willow-tree. On either side are five hundred idols, each about five feet high. They are arranged in ten rows of fifty, each row rising above the one in front of it. The images are meant to represent the eleven-faced-thousand-handed Goddess of Mercy, but they only have one face and twenty-one pairs of hands. I suppose it would have been too much work to make them all. The 33,333 are obtained by counting the small effigies held in the hands and in the haloes of the large ones. It is a very strange sight.[2]

In the midst of all he was seeing and doing, these were the

[2] A large per cent of the population of Japan . . . is to be found in rural districts. . . . "Scarcely any penetration has as yet been made by missionary forces into this rural area. Even near Tokyo there are large districts in which the missionaries are only as one to more than a million of the population. . . . To these farmer-folk, fishermen and boat-people, idolatry is a very sordid thing. It leaves unmet the real hunger of the heart."—*The Missionary Review of the World*, for October 1903.

things that went deepest. There is one picturesque letter on Japanese paper, six inches wide and seven feet long, in which he gives a detailed account of a display of national wrestling at Osaka, which they watched for hours. But there is another letter, written to his mother, that shows what his first contact with heathenism was meaning in his own life. He had been less than a month in Japan when he wrote:

Kyoto, November 3, 1904

I have received your birthday note with all the others, which was a very pleasant surprise. Your request that I pray to God for His very best plan for my life is not a hard thing to do, for I have been praying that very thing for a long time. Although I have never thought very seriously about being a missionary until lately, I was somewhat interested in that line as you know.[3] I think this trip is going to be a great help in showing things to me in a new light. I can't explain what my views were, but I met such pleasant young people on the steamer who were going out as missionaries, and meeting them influenced me. . . .

Walt has so many friends here whom we meet in nearly every city that I have seen a great deal of the work that is being done. While talking with them we learn of the work and the opportunities, etc., so that I realize things as I never did before. When I look ahead a few years it seems as though the only thing to do is to prepare for the foreign field. Of course, I want a college course and then perhaps some medical study, and certainly Bible study, at Moody Institute perhaps.

I may be a little premature, but I am beginning to think a little different. I don't know what you will think of this, but anyway I know you can help me.

With lots of love,

WILLIAM

[3] At the Hill School Borden had been chairman of the Mission Study Band.

CHAPTER 4

AROUND THE WORLD—*continued*

1904-1905. AGE 17

Christ has no hands but our hands to do His work to-day;
He has no feet but our feet to lead men in His way;
He has no tongue but our tongue to tell men how He died;
He has no help but our help to bring them to His side.

—Selected

CHINA MAY NOT HAVE the charm of Japan, but to Borden it appealed immediately. "I think I am going to like it better," he wrote, impressed with the strength and virility of the people.

SHANGHAI, Nov. 19, 1904

DEAR MOTHER—We are now in China and such a change! It is perfectly impossible to imagine how different it is. . . . This is the most cosmopolitan place I have ever seen, and yet we hear that Hongkong is even more so, but I can't see how it could be.

At the Bund where we landed we were immediately introduced to several very Chinese things. Of course the rickshas were nothing new, but the wheelbarrows! They are the queerest affairs I have ever seen. One wheel about two feet in diameter and a frame on either side for the load. The coolie has a strap from the handles which goes under his arms and over his neck. Four grown people is the most they carry and that is a pretty heavy load. The load isn't always balanced and of course that makes it harder yet. I think I would prefer to walk every time. The Chinese merchants go up and down the Bund in their carriages and practically every foreign resident has one, so that there is a continual stream of carriages, rickshas and wheelbarrows. There are several varieties of policemen but the most impressive are the Indians with their large red turbans, heavy braided beards and immense stature. Most of them are over six feet and some nearly seven.

We are staying at the Astor House which is very nice and is the place where you meet everyone, that is everyone who is travelling. We went over to the China Inland Mission and consulted Mr. Stevenson on our plans for China.

The plan worked out in Mr. Stevenson's study filled the time to be given to China in the most interesting way possible, and when the travelers left by river steamer for Hankow they were anticipating visits to Pekin and not a few other places. In his journal Borden noted:

November 20, 1904

Travelling all day up the mouth of the Yangtze, which is practically a sea, it is so wide. Immense reeds, fifteen or twenty feet high, grow along the banks.

November 21

Lots of fun to watch the steerage passengers all try to get in and out of the junks and up and down the narrow gangway of the steamer at the same time. The result was they got very excited, and all shouted and argued and pushed and shoved each other until I expected most of them would go overboard. But only one did, and he got out all right.

The river varies in width from one to six or seven miles. At times the current is very swift.

November 22

Arrived at Kiu-kiang about four in the afternoon. Two Chinese fell in and nearly got drowned, between the steamer and the dock. When they were hauled out, they went for each other and had a pig-tail pulling contest which was rather unique and interesting.

And in a letter to his father:

It took us four days to cover the six hundred miles to Hankow. On Wednesday morning we came in sight of the city, and while we were still several miles off a number of men came out in sampans and jumped on board while the steamer was going full speed. This is rather a dangerous proceeding and requires some skill. They were the representatives of native inns, eager to secure business.

At Hankow there is a difference of fifty feet in the depth of the water in summer and winter. Also the tide is sometimes felt up there. This would be the tide they had had at Shanghai two or three days previously. So there must be two or three high tides on the river at the same time, with as many low ones in between.

Hankow has a large foreign concession and a fine Bund, better even than Shanghai. The foreign and native cities do not overlap much. You just step through a gate from the concession and are at once plunged into the narrow dirty streets of the crowded Chinese city. Across the Yangtze is Wu-chang, a purely native city which is larger than Hankow. On the opposite bank of the Han River, which flows into the Yangtze at this point, is another city. The combined population of all three is about a million and a half.

But it is the unexpected that happens, and instead of traveling extensively in China, Borden was soon confined to a sick bed in a hospital. They did, however, get in two weeks in the Yangtze Valley, including a delightful time at Nanking where they were guests of Dr. Stewart of the American Methodist College. They had crossed the Pacific with these friends, and were more than glad to see again one bright girl who had had much to do with their enjoyment of the voyage. Borden missed the society of people of his own age, and it is safe to say that the Ming tombs did not suffer in interest through the companionship they had at Nanking. In this connection he wrote:

I have come to the conclusion that young people of either sex never travel out here and in fact don't exist! I almost feel as though we were breaking the rules. We have met scarcely any young people. There were two fellows and two or three girls on the *Korea,* no more. In Japan, none. However, we hope for better things as we reach more civilized regions.

All the early part of December, William was suffering from fever, and when they reached Canton it was found to be typhoid. This added seriously to Mr. Erdman's responsibilities, who was thankful to get him safely to the hospital on Victoria Peak overlooking the city and harbor of Hongkong. Happily the illness proved to be a mild attack and the patient was soon convalescent. On Christmas Day he was writing:

Although in bed, I manage to pass the time very well, reading a good deal, magazines, interesting books and my Bible. . . . We see a few American papers now and then, and I have learned most of the scores of the big games.

We stayed in Canton four days and saw a good deal and met some of the missionaries. Canton is a most interesting city, but I won't weary you with any more accounts of temples and the like. We were conveyed through the narrow streets in chairs carried by three bearers. They are quite comfortable. The streets with their busy throngs and open shops are always interesting. They vary in width from about twenty feet, in residence portions, to six or seven in business quarters. Sometimes they were so narrow that the chairs almost scraped both sides at once. I saw dried rats in great quantities hung up in the foodshops for sale, but no edible birds'-nests though we looked for them.

His love of yachting and boat life generally made him specially interested in the river population of Canton. He was accustomed on their own boat, the *Tsatsawassa,* to narrow quarters, but never had imagined that people could be born and married, live and die, rear their families and marry off their children, without ever having a home on shore. And so many of them!

HONGKONG, December 27, 1904

DEAR FATHER—There are some three hundred and fifty thousand boat-people in Canton I am told. They live in small *sampans* which line the river-banks about ten deep, and simply choke all the small canals. A boat perhaps twenty feet long will hold a family of six or seven. I couldn't see where they stowed themselves away, but they do it somehow. A great many keep chickens as well, hung out over the stern in a basket which serves as a chicken-yard. Some of the kids and women have empty cans tied to their backs to act as life-preservers if they should fall overboard. For one Chinaman will seldom rescue another, because the rescuer has to keep the rescued for the rest of his life, if he happens to want to be kept. And sometimes they will bargain with a drowning man before pulling him out! But to return to the river-people—they live and die on their boats, and are not allowed on shore by the land-people, who do not want their business taken away from them.

The work of the Y.M.C.A. in Canton had greatly interested him, as he wrote in that same Christmas letter, and he had been trying to take part in it a little.

I got into conversation with a young business man who said he was a Christian and made it a great point that he always went to church. The start of our argument was that he was railing at missions and saying they were no good, etc. Well I tried to defend them and we got deeper and he turned out to be practically an infidel not believing in anything the Bible said. I told him what I believed and he said I was young and didn't know better, that in a few years I would think differently. He couldn't have been more than twenty-five himself. I managed to quote a few verses to which he could not say anything but I didn't put up a very good argument as I got rather fussed and excited. I wished at the time that I knew my Bible better. . . .

This is my first Christmas away from home and my first one spent in bed. It is rather different from what I suppose is going on at 89.[1] But I am not kicking. As I lie here several thousand

[1] 89 Bellevue Place, his home in Chicago.

miles away, home seems pretty nice and I feel it would be fine to be there. But when I do get back, it will be nice to think that I've been out here. We may get home before the first of September by a good deal, but cannot tell just now.

That he was homesick was not to be disguised, but as he became stronger the desire to shorten their trip passed away. Java had to be given up and their plans for India curtailed, but what he and Mr. Erdman lost in this way was more than made up by the deepening friendship between them. Of those days Mr. Erdman wrote:

His Bible was always on his bed in the hospital, except when the fever was at its height. I remember finding him poring over the tenth chapter of Genesis one morning, with a new interest in its geographical and ethnological statements aroused by his first impressions of new races and men of other tongues. It was a little Bible with fine print, too fine indeed for practical use, but it must have become dear to him, for I have seen it since, open, on his study table at Princeton.

The voyage to India completely brought back his strength and he was eager for all possible excursions among the foot-hills of the Himalayas, at Darjeeling and elsewhere, and for opportunities not open to the ordinary tourist of shooting the spiral-horned black-buck when we were visiting friends in an isolated mission-station in the Central Provinces. His interest in the archæological and architectural features of the Orient was rapidly increasing, quickened by visits to the wonderful temples in South India and by the fascination of the Taj Mahal, and his imagination was stirred by the monuments of Egypt. In the closing months of travel, his growing interest in the achievements of man was manifested in what was to his fellow-traveller at least an unexpected appreciation of the art treasures of the galleries of Europe. But all the time, though one did not realize it then, he was being specially impressed with the spiritual destitution of the people of the countries we were visiting.

Sunrise over the Himalayas was the sight of a lifetime! Borden and his companion had been two weeks in India. They had left Calcutta the night before and had come up from the teeming plains of the Ganges by a mountain railway with a gauge of only two feet, through a dense jungle which did not lose in interest because "everyone said it was full of tigers and leopards"—a regular Mowgli jungle! It was misty when they reached Darjeeling and cold enough to make them realize that they were at an altitude of seven thousand feet. Few Hindus were to be seen, but in the crowded bazaar they found themselves surrounded by hardy mountain people, distinctly Mongol in appearance. There were Tibetans clad in sheepskins, from the land of mystery beyond the Himalayas; Nepalese and Bhutanese from the equally forbidden countries lying to the east and west, and enterprising merchants even from China.

It seemed a little strange, on leaving the railway, to have one's things carried up the steep hill paths by *women,* and at the hotel to have *men* chambermaids as well as waiters. But the women of Bhutan are said to be the strongest in the world. Barefooted, with large triangular baskets on their backs and the help of a strap that goes over the head, they carry the heaviest loads, apparently with ease. Men and children share the labor, carrying stone, wood, grain and what not, up the steep hillsides—sturdy, healthy, cheerful creatures, a contrast in almost every way with the enervated people of the plains. But nowhere in Bhutan, Nepal or Tibet was there a voice raised to tell these mountain races sunk in immorality, living in fear of demons and in dread of death, of the one and only Saviour.

The next morning was still misty, and they were not called at four A.M. to take the expected ride to Tiger Hill. But about six they woke to their first view of the highest mountains in the world.

To his father William wrote:

We looked right from the hotel porch, out across deep ravines filled with mist, at the mighty range of the Himalayas. The ranges we could see from the hotel were about forty miles away, and consisted of about ten peaks of which Kinshinjunga, twenty-eight thousand feet, was the highest. They were a solid mass of snow and towered above us clearly outlined against the blue sky. Our first view was very good but we had a better one next morning.

We got started a little after four, while the stars and moon were still bright, for Tiger Hill. This "hill," only nine thousand feel high, is about six miles from the hotel. I enjoyed the horseback ride very much although I nearly froze. We got to the top just as dawn began to break, and the effects of light and shade were wonderful. To our right was a perfect wall of snow-capped peaks about twenty thousand feet high, stretching away for a hundred miles. Directly west was the great range with Junga in it. Then more to the left was a line of foot-hills about eleven or twelve thousand feet high, wooded and without snow. Beyond these, when the sun got higher, we could plainly see the peak of Mt. Everest, a hundred and twenty miles away. With the glasses we could see very distinctly the sharp lines and great bare cliffs. We spent nearly two hours on the hill and enjoyed every minute.

Oh, the wonder of that mighty rampart beyond which lies Tibet! What words can paint the grandeur, purity and loveliness of its eternal snows, "shining in the dawn-light like some celestial country high above this lower world of human life and pain"? All around them at Darjeeling were touching evidences of the unsatisfied longing of hearts that search in vain for comfort amid life's mysteries. The faith of the mountain people is more simple and appealing than the heathenism of the plains.

It was at Madura, near the sandy, southern point of the Indian peninsula, that they had their introduction to the worship of Siva, whose mark—a horizontal smear—they had seen on so many foreheads. Imagine "a hot plain, a red road, shaded by the foliage of great overhanging trees in which monkeys were playing; the village folk coming home from the fields in the evening time; the village wells surrounded by women and girls with their water-jars; bullocks and buffaloes resting after the toils of the day, and the smoke of little wood or weed fires filling the air." In such surroundings they spent the night at a dak bungalow before visiting the great temple at Madura, one of the largest of the Dravidian temples of southern India. Covering a square twelve acres in extent, it dominated the surrounding country with its massive *gopura,* something between a pagoda and a pyramid, rising to a commanding height above each entrance. William's description of this place shows his reaction to Hinduism seen for the first time.

January, 1905

The Madura temple has five large *gopura* which are over two hundred feet high and four small ones. The outside of these structures is a solid mass of carved stone images of Hindu gods. Inside the wall is another enclosure with its *gopura,* and inside this is the sacred place which none but Hindus are allowed to enter. The rest of the space is taken up with bazaars, priests' quarters, etc. . . . The interior of the temple contains many images and corridors with wonderful stone monoliths. In the centre is the "Tank of the Golden Lilies," I am sure I didn't discover any appropriateness about the name. The water was covered with green slime, and yet pilgrims were washing themselves and their clothes in it as well as drinking from it. It is supposed to wash away their sins. . . . Of course we were not allowed to go into some of the inner chambers and I guess it was just as well, for the worship of Siva to which the temple is given over is the foulest thing imaginable.

The three principal Hindu gods are Brahma the creator, Vishnu the preserver and Siva the destroyer and reproducer. All the large temples we have seen and innumerable small shrines, are dedicated to the worship of Siva. You probably know something about this already—but if you don't I can't tell you, as it is too awful. The fact that this vile teaching is the most universal and popular thing in Hinduism is enough to offset everything that Hinduism may have done for the people, if it has done anything but degrade them.

It makes me tired to have a person who knows little or nothing about it say that these people are as well off with their religion as we are with ours, or rather that theirs is as good as ours. Five minutes' explanation of facts in any one of a dozen temples I have visited would disillusion such a person.

He would not put in plainer language the things these temples stand for—the deification of lust, the actual worship of symbols of vice, and the slavery of tens of thousands of women and girls "married to the gods." Around the temples in this part of India many monkeys gather and are looked upon as sacred. It was saying a good deal when one who knows the conditions wrote:

"Wealth and labour could not have been devoted to baser practices than the erection of the vast enclosures dedicated to Siva and Vishnu. Even the sacred monkeys are disgraced by association with indescribable vileness."

Another aspect of idolatry and superstition was seen when they reached Madras just in time for the annual festival of Juggernaut. It was impossible to describe it adequately, but Borden did the best he could under difficulties.

Feb. 1, 1905

Well I must hurry on to Madras. The city itself is nothing to see but we were fortunate in being able to witness the festival of the Juggernaut. This had always been a sort of unreal fairy tale to me until I saw it. We took a carriage about nine thirty P.M. and drove towards the native quarter of the city. On the way we passed groups of people all hurrying in the same direction, some on foot and some crowded into little bullock carts. The whole native population seemed to be centering on one point.

Immediately we entered the native city, it was all we could do to get the carriage through the crowds of people. Imagine the crowd at a parade at home, only dress them differently—men and women with red shawls about themselves, fakirs smeared from head to foot with ashes and dirt, making a ghastly combination, naked children and nearly everyone with some kind of a caste mark on his or her face. The street along which the procession was to pass was dimly lit up, adding to the weirdness of the scene.

Finally the approach of the car was heralded by the pushing of the crowds and a vanguard of men beating kettledrums and a number of men with torches. And then came the car itself, a truly wonderful sight, drawn by two long lines of men. It was a square shrine about thirty feet high on wheels. The whole thing was a solid mass of gilt and was brilliantly lit up by numerous torches. The men would raise a great shout and then pull the clumsy affair a short distance, stop and start again, and so on. Of course since the British Government came into power, the practice of people throwing themselves beneath the wheels of the car, to procure immediate transition to heaven, has been stopped. Nevertheless, I can easily see how a religiously fanatical people could, under the excitement of the moment, do such a thing. I was very glad that I had seen it all, and am sure I won't forget it for some time.

And now they were at Benares, the sacred city on the Ganges, which is much the same today as when Macaulay wrote, "It was commonly believed that half a million human beings were crowded into that labyrinth of lofty alleys, rich with shrines and minarets, and balconies, and carved oriels, to which the sacred apes clung by hundreds. The traveller could scarcely make his way through the press of holy mendicants and not less holy bulls. The broad and stately steps which descended from these swarming haunts to the bathing places were worn every day by the feet of an innumerable multitude of worshippers."

In Borden's letter to his mother it is interesting to get the point of view of a healthy minded boy among such scenes.

·February 6, 1905

Dear Mother—I was rather disappointed in Benares as a sacred city, it is too dirty, and its temples are comparatively poor and small affairs. However, it has interesting features, of which the ghats are foremost.

These ghats are steps or landing places which lead down to the Ganges. They are very numerous and practically line the whole water front. Some, in fact the majority, are bathing ghats for all classes of people. I mean there is a separate ghat for nearly every caste. There is only one burning ghat worthy of mention, and there all the dead of Benares are cremated. Benares is so holy that death within its precincts practically insures eternal happiness for the Hindu. The result is pilgrims come there simply to die. The best way to see these ghats is to take a boat on the river, which we did twice. In this way you get a very good view of everything. People are bathing continually in the sacred stream. They wash themselevs and their clothes in it, pray to it, drink it and throw their dead into it. It is quite a sight to see all this going on. The people bathe in their clothes, and many of them have no dry things to put on, and go away shivering in their wet garments. And it is cold here now in India. There is frost at night, and an overcoat is comfortable even during the day. It is really the strangest climate I ever met. I shivered all day, and then read in the paper that in the sun it had been 120° Fahrenheit!

But to return, we took a boat and went down stream for some distance, seeing people of all classes at their religious duties. . . . The burning ghat, though not a pleasant sight, was quite interesting. Several corpses were in the process of cremation when we saw it. The bodies are placed on piles of wood right in the open, and the ashes are thrown into the Ganges with people bathing not fifty feet off. The bodies are placed in certain positions according to the creed of the deceased, some with the head pointing east, others west, etc. All day long throughout the year the smoke of one or more pyres rises from this place. Another method of disposing of the dead is to weight the bodies with stones and drop them in mid-stream. We saw· several disposed of in this way.

"Holy" men and priests die, if possible, looking out over the river. As was passed down we saw an old man, a living skeleton, seated on the bottom step near the water with a friend propping him up. When we came back he was dead. He was one of the "holy" men. I hope you won't mind hearing about these things, but they are actual everyday occurrences and I couldn't well help seeing them.

The city itself is a dirty hole, full of beggars, fakirs and temples, with narrow streets in which sacred cows, donkeys and goats run around loose, getting in everyone's way. Right in the midst of this Hindu sanctum is the Mosque of Aurungzebe, the Mohammedan invader. He built this thing there just to insult the Hindus, and it is there yet, but his present followers have to enter by the side door as the Hindus have blocked up the main entrance. I have learned that, as a rule, any native with a beard is a Mohammedan, and those who have their whiskers dyed red have been to Mecca. Well this mosque has two tall minarets, one of which we climbed to get a view of the city.

The temples are disappointing. They are right in the crowded part of the city and are very dingy places indeed. We were only allowed to look in and not to enter, of which I was not sorry. Cows came and went with impunity in the Golden Temple, which was positively sickening even from the doorway. The "Well of Knowledge" was a foul-smelling hole into which everyone threw flowers and water. We didn't approach very close, though the priest wanted us to make an offering of flowers.

And here the millions come and go, still seeking to wash away their sins. The "sacred" cow is still the emblem, more than the emblem, the embodiment of the Hindu's highest hope, and if they cannot die by the Ganges, even scholarly men will send for a cow to be brought into the room and have the hairs of its tail spread over their faces, that they may breathe their souls away in the most sacred atmosphere they know.[2]

[2] There are temples like the temple of Vithoba, at Pandharpur, the great place of pilgrimage in the Deccan, where the cow is actually made an object of worship. The belief that the excreta of the cow have power to cleanse men from sin is well-nigh universal among Hindus.—From the *Report on India and Persia,* by Dr. Robert E. Speer, published in 1922, p. 152.

And *we* know that "God so loved the world that he gave his only begotten Son that whosoever believeth in him should not perish, but have everlasting life."

From Benares the travelers passed on up the Ganges to Allahabad, at the junction of that river with the Jumna— another focus of idolatrous worship, though at one time and for centuries under the heel of Moslem power. They reached the city as the annual Mela was commencing, when thousands of pilgrims were pouring in from far and near. For Allahabad is the site of "the greatest Mela in India, when more than a million devout Hindus pour up from all over the land to bathe in the mingling of the waters of the two sacred rivers. There is probably no religious spectacle equal to it anywhere else in the world. Under no other religion and in no other land could hundreds of naked men with matted locks and grotesquely daubed bodies be regarded as the highest embodiment of holiness, nor could such rites pass for religion and as acceptable with God."[3]

It was these fakirs who specially interested Borden, though the vast concourse of people, their absorption in their devotions and the sadness and weariness of many faces made also a deep impression. All the questions he wanted to ask at Allahabad found ready answers, for they were privileged to have as their escort a missionary who had been long in India. "You can learn more from a missionary in half an hour," he wrote with appreciation, "than you can pick up yourself in a couple of months of travel."

February 12, 1905

Dr. Lucas came in on Friday from his camp. He goes to the country and visits villages through the week. He has been out thirty-four years and knows a thing or two. He told us that the Tessul Dhar, a native official, had promised him an elephant

[3] From the *Report on India and Persia,* by Dr. Robert E. Speer, published in 1922, p. 54.

to use at the Mela. So Saturday morning we started off for the Mela grounds.

On the way we passed groups of pilgrims, some in bullock carts but most walking. Many of the men carried baskets in which Dr. Lucas told us they would carry back bottles of the sacred water to their friends far away, after getting a priest to seal it and mark it as the original article. Groups of women passed along the road chanting mournfully. All the pilgrims had the same sad expression on their faces—no trace of hope or happiness. They had been coming there and their ancestors before them, and yet were just as badly off as ever. But they keep on coming.

After some delay the elephant appeared and four of us clung to his back while he got on his feet, somewhat in the fashion of the camels at the World's Fair. From the back of this creature we had a splendid view of the sea of turbaned heads. The road leading up to the levee was lined with shops containing all sorts of things. Bottles for holy water, powder for caste marks, flowers for offerings, jewelry, shawls, etc. This levee, called a "bund" out here, was a good place to watch the approach of the pilgrims. They would come up the slope until they saw the river and then prostrate themselves in the dust and hurry on. I noticed that the women were much more painstaking than the men, who often did not stop at all. We rode with our elephant through the throng to the river bank, where we saw the crowds in bathing. It was cold and some of the poor beggars nearly shook to pieces in their wet clothes.

When we had gone as far as practicable, on account of the crowd, Walt and I got down and walked with Dr. Lucas to see the shrines, fakirs, etc. At the road sides were crowds of beggars with all sorts of deformities. Dr. Lucas explained that they consider any deformity a mark of divine power and consequently a holy thing. There were so many of these that a poor pilgrim could hardly be expected to offer something to all. But they would walk down the line with a bag of rice and drop a few grains at each place. In this way small heaps of rice and other food stuffs would collect in front of each one.

But the fakirs were the most interesting sight of all. I don't believe I have attempted to describe a fakir. He wears nothing but a loin cloth; his body is smeared or painted with ash-dust in such a way that it never comes off, but remains a dull grey color; his hair is long, and from sprinklings of ashes and more sprinkling of water, it hangs like pieces of half-inch rope. There were about two dozen of these men, but not all of them were self-torturists. However, there were about ten, either sitting or lying on boards full of spikes. To be sure the spikes were somewhat blunted, but it must have been very uncomfortable until they got hardened to it. There was one man sitting in a swing with one leg on the ground and his hands above his head. I noticed that his arms were very small and shrunken, and on inquiring we learned that he had held them up that way for seven years. The pain at first must have been frightful, but now he couldn't get them down if he wanted to and can only move his hands a very little. I had never expected to see anything like this. Dr. Lucas says that the British Government has put a stop to the worst of their self-torturing practices, and he told us some that he had seen which I won't repeat.

It is difficult for Westerners to enter with any understanding into the state of mind that produces such results. To see a man kneel or lie on his back in the blazing sun with his head completely buried in the ground, for a whole day at a time, would not impress us with a sense of his holiness or with any desire to worship him. But it is very different with those whose one hope for the next life is the accumulation of merit in this.[4]

[4] "The Hindu devotee," as Bishop Thoburn tells us, "flatters himself that he can by his penances of various kinds accumulate merit. The word penance to his mind conveys no idea of repentance, but solely that of a means of acquiring personal merit. In the next place he is possessed with the idea that matter is inherently evil, and that, since his union with a material body is the source of most of his misfortunes, he must make war on the body to liberate the soul. . . .

"No doubt a large number, of both sexes, choose a life of asceticism because they find it the simplest and easiest way of securing their daily bread. . . . But many of them show abundant evidence that they are sincere in their purpose, and persist through long lives of severe suffering and privation in faithfully following the course they have chosen."

At that very time there was in Bengal a woman who had been a fakir like the worst of those Borden saw at Allahabad. Having means of her own, she had visited all the most important temples in India, north, south, east and west, to try to escape the burden of sin. Her awful guilt was that her husband had died young, when she was only a child of thirteen, and of course it was attributed to some wickedness on her part in a previous life. To atone for this unknown sin and to obtain relief for heart and conscience she spent *seven long years* traveling on foot from shrine to shrine, facing untold hardship and danger; but the burden grew only heavier as time went on.

Then she determined to become a fakir. She had not suffered enough. She would give three years to self-inflicted torture, in the ways enjoined by the sacred books as pleasing to the gods. And this plan she carried out, though the sufferings she endured seem incredible.

For one period of six months she sat without shelter in the sun all day with five fires burning around her, the perspiration streaming from every pore. Even wealthy men would bring wood and keep the fires burning as an act of merit. With no clothing but a loincloth, her body smeared with ashes and her long hair with cow-dung, she was an object of veneration to the pilgrims, many of whom worshiped her as they fed the fires. At night she took her place in the temple, standing before the idol—actually standing on one foot with the other drawn up against it, from midnight until daylight—her hands pressed together in the attitude of prayer, imploring the god to reveal himself to her.

And then, to increase her sufferings, when the cold season came with frosty nights, she went down at dark to the sacred pond and sat with the water up to her neck, counting her beads hour after hour, till dawn appeared. Thus she called upon Ram day and night, with no response.

"If thou art God," she used to plead, "reveal thyself to me.

Reach forth and take the offering I bring. Let me see, hear or feel something by which I may know that I have pleased thee, and that my sin is pardoned"—but there was no sign, no rest, no peace.

When the years of her long endurance were ended, she went to Calcutta, cut off her once-beautiful hair and threw it into the Ganges as an offering, exclaiming:

"There—I have done and suffered all that can be required of mortal man, yet without avail!"

She had lost faith in the idols and had ceased to worship them.

"There is nothing in Hinduism," was the conclusion forced upon her, "or I would have found it."

Think of the privilege of bringing to such a soul the message of the love of God in Christ! Think of the joy on earth as well as in Heaven when the seeking sinner and the seeking Saviour met at last! That, indeed, is something worth living for, worth dying for, the glorious compensation of the missionary's life! And when the poor, tortured fakir becomes the Spirit-filled preacher, telling by lip and life the riches of redeeming grace, think of the wonder of that transformation.[5] Chundra Lela, Pandita Ramabai, Sadhu Sundra Singh—what witnesses these and many another to the power of the living Christ!

This was the brighter side to our travelers' experiences in India, for they did see and hear much of the transformation that is coming, slowly but surely, over the mingled peoples of that great land.[6]

---

[5] For a fuller account of this wonderful woman, see the brief biography entitled, *An Indian Priestess: The Life of Chundra Lela,* by Mrs. Ada Lee. Morgan and Scott, London, E.C.

[6] "India is being converted. The ideas that lie at the heart of the Gospel are slowly but steadily permeating the whole of Hindu society, modifying every phase of Hindu thought."—A prominent non-Christian judge, a native of India.

That Borden was thinking over these things is evident from his last letter from India. He had been writing to his sister at Vassar College about the native state of Rajputana—of Jeypore, the capital, with its wide streets, pink houses and fascinating medley of color, its magnificent horses, trains of camels, and the "Barbaric splendor" of its Maharajah, who kept elephants and tigers to fight in his arena. But it was Sunday, and he turned to other things.

Rajputana Hotel, Abu
February 26, 1905

Dear Mother—I have just been reading over some of your letters and enjoying them so much. I do not expect to get any more until we reach Cairo.

Walt and I have Bible study together every day when possible, and I enjoy it very much. He is able to point out many things that are new to me, and I am beginning to see what a wonderful storehouse of good things the Bible is. I pray every day for all my dear family. I also pray that God will take my life into His hands and use it for the furtherance of His Kingdom as He sees best. I feel sure that He will answer my prayer. It strengthens me to know that you are also praying for this.

I have so much of everything in this life, and there are so many millions who have nothing and live in darkness! I don't think it is possible to realize it until one sees the East. I know it is no *easy* thing to serve the Lord, but others have been enabled to do so, and there is no reason why I should not. Mark 10. 27.

Among the letters he had been re-reading was a sheet of

"It is the Christian's Bible that sooner or later will work out the regeneration of India."—The Maharajah of Travancore.

"It is a new heart that India requires, a transformation of life and character. Who can give that to India except a divine Saviour? Send us missionaries who are not ashamed of the Gospel of Christ, who are not ashamed of the Cross; men and women who are living in close personal touch with the Master; men and women who have sat at His feet. They will meet India's need."—Words of an Indian Christian. See "Jesus Christ in the Thinking of Asia" in *The Missionary Review of the World* for April, 1924, p. 252 ff.

paper he had carried with him all the way from Japan—not a letter, only a few verses in his mother's writing, sent to him for the birthday he had spent so far from home. All through college and seminary years he kept it. It was among his special papers to the last.

> Just as I am, Thine own to be,
> Friend of the young, who lovest me,
> To consecrate myself to Thee—
>   O Jesus Christ, I come.
>
> In the glad morning of my day,
> My life to give, my vows to pay,
> With no reserve and no delay—
>   With all my heart, I come.
>
> I would live ever in the light,
> I would work ever for the right,
> I would serve Thee with all my might—
>   Therefore to Thee I come.
>
> Just as I am, young, strong and free,
> To be the best that I can be
> For truth and righteousness and Thee—
>   Lord of my life, I come.

CHAPTER 5

COMING HOME

Summer 1905. Age 17

The meaning of being a Christian is that in response for the gift of a whole Christ I give my whole self to Him.

Alexander MacLaren, D.D.

Iт was not until they were in Rome that Borden seems to have received a reply to his special letter from Japan. His mother understood and rejoiced; his father wanted him to wait until he was twenty-one before committing himself to any decision as to his lifework. In the meanwhile the travelers had visited not only China, the Straits Settlements and India, but Egypt, Palestine and Asia Minor, and the chief treasure cities of Greece and Italy.

To his father, William wrote from Naples:

May 13, 1905

I have been enjoying myself more since we got into civilization again. . . . French is certainly useful here in Italy, although a great deal of English is spoken. I can understand French when not spoken at express speed, and some Italian, but the difficulty is to make oneself understood! It is really quite amusing. You ought to hear my attempts in Italian and French and English all at once.

I hope to have my Homer pretty well in shape by the time I get back, so as not to be bothered with it at Camden. I suppose you will be going up there soon. Have my golf clubs ready; I am longing for a whack at the ball. Have you any kind of automobile in mind which you prefer? I would like to know.

Please tell me a little about Chicago politics. How is Dunne? Whom did you vote for and what do you think about municipal ownership?

FLORENCE, May 28, 1905

We were nearly two weeks in Rome and saw a great many interesting things. I am curious to know how long you and Mother spent there on your wedding trip. There is an awful lot to see, isn't there? I wrote to Mother telling her about some of the places and pictures we had seen, but not nearly all. So I will tell you what we did and enjoyed most.

The afternoon of our first day we drove by the Colosseum, through the Arch of Constantine, around across the Tiber and back to our hotel, stopping at the Pantheon on the way. Horatius must have been a pretty good swimmer to cross the Tiber, if it flowed as swiftly as it does now. The Colosseum is very interesting, I think. We went all over it from top to bottom. They have excavated some since you were in Rome and have laid bare the old pavement outside the amphitheatre on the side opposite the Forum. There was a wooden model, a reconstruction of the original, which gave one a very good idea of what it must have looked like in all its glory.

The Pantheon, you remember, is the only building of ancient Rome in anything like perfect preservation. Its dome is very large and has a hole, thirty feet across, in the centre. The caldarium (hot room) of the baths was always made in this way, a dome with a hole closed by bronze doors in order to be able to control the temperature of the room. This hadn't struck me until Dr. Forbes pointed it out. He says that the Pantheon was really at one time nothing but the caldarium of the baths of Agrippa, son-in-law of Augustus.

Dr. Forbes, by the way, has been in Rome thirty-four years and is now the leading archaeological authority. You may have heard him lecture when you were here. We went with him three times and found him exceedingly interesting. The places we went to were the Palatine Hill, the Forum and the excursion to Tivoli and Hadrian's Villa. His talks were very interesting and instructive, given as they were on the exact spot where the events related took place. Romulus and Remus are facts and no longer legends. The legend of the wolf is explained by the fact that the wife of Faustulus was named Luca. Faustulus was one of the Sabines who lived by the Tiber, and his wife brought up Romulus and Remus. In the quarrel between Romulus and Remus, the two parties were led by Faustulus and Quintibius. The legend was that these two men were buried where they fell. Dr. Forbes has discovered their tombs seven feet below the level of the Forum of Caesar—I mean the Roman Forum, but at the period around A.D. As no one could be buried within the limits of Roma Quadrata this proves that the walls did not extend that far, and that the Forum was the battle-ground between the rival clans of Romulus and Remus on the Palatine and Quirinal hills. We were shown where Cicero delivered his orations and the spot where Julius Caesar's body was burned. It was exceedingly interesting, but I couldn't begin to tell you all about it.

I enjoyed the collections of antiques about as much as anything. My, but aren't there a lot of fine statues! I'm not sure which I prefer. As a group, I guess the Laocoön is about as good as any. I think I prefer Perseus with the head of Medusa to the Apollo Belvedere. And I certainly prefer the features and expression of Mercury. But then, I didn't have time enough to study them, although I did go to it two or three times. Now that I have seen the Marble Faun I must read the book, and shall when I find time. Undoubtedly, Rome excels in its collections of statues and antiques, but the pictures aren't in it with those here in Florence for instance. So perhaps I'm not all wrong when I say that I didn't care much for the pictures, while I did enjoy the sculptures.

I learned of two pictures, or rather a whole gallery which I hadn't visited, the Corcini. I wanted very much to see Van Dyck's Madonna and also Carlo Dolci's. But I made a mistake about the hour to which the gallery remained open, and consequently missed seeing them. I was very much struck by the prints, and may say they were the only ones which I really cared for. Carlo Dolci's is simply great, and it will be one of the first things I see if I ever get to Rome again. You may not remember the picture, but I have a fine carbon print of it to show you when I arrive.

Venice brought delightful relaxation.

June 1, 1905

We are now in the city of watery streets and gondolas, having arrived last night. After dinner we strolled over to St. Mark's, heard the band play and had some ice cream. I expect to enjoy our stay here.

It was warm June weather, and every day they had a swim at the Lido followed by afternoon tea, much appreciated after the sight-seeing of the morning, while evening was spent in a gondola, meeting friends, listening to music and watching the lights over the water. In the Doges' Palace they met an American party of seven young ladies with a chaperone who proved to be friendly as well as interesting, and they had already joined company with a Mrs. A. and her daughter, the latter a young graduate of Bryn Mawr under appointment as a missionary to India. So the week in Venice passed all too quickly, filled with many interests.

June 4, 1905

Mrs. A. invited us to go out in their gondola last night. It was simply great! The lights on the Grand Canal and the little dark Rios were a picture. We went way up to the north-eastern corner of the city, to the Three Bridges, and then out by the Guidecca and back down the Grand Canal. We lay alongside one of the singing barges and listened to the music for an hour or so. It was fine! I suppose you know all about it, for you and father must have enjoyed just such nights here together. I think I would like to come here on my wedding trip, if I ever have one. . . . Walt and I were remarking the other day that we had only met three American girls on our whole trip, until now. There's nothing like a real true American girl: French, German, English or Irish aren't in it!

In the midst of all this gaiety it is surprising to find how earnestly he was thinking about deeper things. From Rome he had written:

May 17, 1905

DARLING MOTHER—I am glad that you have told Father about my desire to be a missionary. I am thinking about it all the time, and looking forward to it with a good deal of anticipation. I know that I am not at all fitted or prepared yet, but in the next four or five years I ought to be able to prepare myself. I have been reading Mr. Speer's book on Missionary Principles and Practice. It is very good, in my opinion. He takes up the different kinds of missionary work, educational, medical and evangelistic, and discusses them with regard to the different countries. You may have read it, and if you haven't I think you would like it.

I don't think I want to go through a Seminary, but thorough Bible study is what I do need. As Dr. Torrey says, "It's much more important and profitable to know what God has to say on a subject that what men have to say." I would like some medical skill . . . enough so as not to be absolutely helpless and ignorant. But I really oughtn't to try and form plans of my own but let God do it for me, and then it's sure to be right. . . . I will be mighty glad when I can talk things over with you.

Lots and lots of love,   WILLIAM

And now amid all the charms of Venice:

June 4, 1905

I have just finished reading Mr. Speer's book. It has helped me a great deal. I especially noticed the two chapters he takes to the Student Volunteer Movement. He shows very clearly what the motto, "The Evangelization of the World in this Generation" means, and how perfectly possible it is, provided we pray the Lord of the harvest to send forth labourers. There is something inspiring in the project to me. It is something fine, something worth every effort to accomplish and which will repay us when we have done our duty.

When I got through reading, I knelt right down and prayed more earnestly than I have for some time for the mission work and for God's plan for my life, and also for His plans for the lives of every one of my family. Oh, Mother, do pray for me. College is so near and there will be such a lot of things to do, tremendous opportunities! pray that I may be guided in everything, small and great.

A month had been kept for England; but before crossing the Channel, a brief visit to Switzerland introduced Borden to real mountain climbing, which was to become his highest enthusiasm as far as personal enjoyment was concerned. Their first mountain was the Titlis, eleven thousand feet high, and with nails in their boots and a good guide they set out from Engelberg.

June 18, 1905

We walked that afternoon for an hour and a half to Trubsee. There we found a little hotel perched on the edge of a cliff, overlooking the town and valley of Engelberg. It was simply great, and after our walk a nice simple Swiss meal tasted pretty fine. We had our first glass of fresh milk since leaving America. Right back of the hotel rose the range of snowy mountains, some of them quite peaked, others less so. The Titlis is not peaked, but its summit is entirely covered with snow.

At 2.15 A.M. we arose and had something to eat. Two other parties, Germans, were going up also. After the first few minutes we left them and went on ahead, slowly but steadily, hardly stopping at all for an hour and a half. During that time we had been climbing up an easy sloping foothill and had crossed some snowfields. The snow at this altitude was soft, still we didn't sink in more than an inch or so. When we had rested a moment we hitched up, the guide taking the lead, I next and Walt last.

From there on it was all snow and quite a pull, but we reached the top in about an hour and twenty minutes, which was fair time. It was then about six and the sun was up and giving considerable warmth. We were very lucky in having a fine view of the mountains over towards Interlaken, Monte Rosa and the Dome in the distance, with the Jungfrau and many others nearer. It was worth three hours' hard work. I felt fine; the last stretch had gone very easily as I had gotten my stride and second wind. After we had eaten a little we started down, Walt leading and the guide last. We slid wherever we could, standing up and leaning back on our alpenstocks. It was great sport, and we laughed and shouted and had a fine time. After a bit the crust got thinner and we couldn't go so well, as we would break through and tumble over. We stopped only a few moments at the hotel to gather our belongings, and then went right on down to Engelberg, getting the nine A.M. train back to Lucerne.

In some ways the best was reserved for the last, for the travelers reached England in the midst of the London season, when the international championships were being contested in tennis, cricket and other sports. Paris had been delightful, and Borden had taken special lessons in a school for chauffeurs, learning to drive a car in the Bois de Boulogne. He had wandered through miles of pictures in the Louvre and had marveled at the glory of Versailles, a palace indeed! But the Anglo-Saxon in him rejoiced to set foot on British soil.

"What bliss to be back in a land," he wrote, "where people talk English!"

London, July 7, 1905

We have been having delightful weather here for a week and have enjoyed ourselves very much.

We went out to Wimbledon and saw some fine tennis last Tuesday. To-morrow we will go and see some of the finals which will be very good. Wednesday we went to the Henley

Regatta, at Henley on Thames. It was a fine sight. We got a canoe and paddled around among the crowd. The very first boat we went alongside had Barbara [a cousin] and her friends in it. It was rather remarkable considering that there were ten thousand people there. We only stayed for the morning races and returned to London about two. We saw the American eight defeated by the famous Leander crew.

Went to St. Paul's Cathedral the other day and climbed up to the whispering gallery and down into the crypt to the tombs of Wellington, Nelson and others. The Bank of England and Exchange are in that part of the town, so we visited them also. On the way back we went down a little court off Fleet Street and saw the Church of the Knight Templars, a pretty little old building. Oliver Goldsmith's Tomb was just outside. The most interesting thing we did was to take lunch at the Cheshire Cheese. This is the original Inn at which Dr. Sam Johnson and others used to meet, "Ye Olde Cheshyre Cheese."

In the afternoon we went over to Lord's cricket grounds to see the Cambridge-Oxford match. It was evidently quite a social event, as everyone was there and in their best. The field also was fine, but after watching the match for a while we had had enough of cricket and retired. To-day we spent our morning at the Tower which I found very interesting.

There were museums and picture galleries to see, the Houses of Parliament, Westminster Abbey and Hampton Court. There was boating on the Thames, coming home in the long summer evening by four-horse coach, shopping, calling on friends, and more than one visit to Shepherd's Bush where "the finest tennis in the world" was being played. And amid it all there was a new and deeper gladness, for to Borden had come perhaps the most vital experience of his life. *"I believe and I belong"* was henceforth to have new meaning. His own account of what took place is better than anything that can be said about it.

HOTEL RUSSELL, LONDON
Friday, July 7, 1905

DEAR MOTHER—I thought I would write you two letters this time, as I have several things to speak about. Last Sunday and Monday were a sort of Convention to me. I went to four meetings, every one of which was fine.

Sunday morning, Walt and I went over to Dr. Campbell Morgan's church, to hear Dr. Dixon of Boston preach. The sermon was very good. As I took notes, I can tell you all about it. One thing he said after the Scripture reading was, "Don't test the Bible by the book or the sermon; test the book or the sermon by the Bible. . . ." He is a man who preaches the Gospel, like Dr. Torrey.

Dr. Torrey, as you know, has been holding meetings here in London for five months. This last month or so they have been in a specially constructed hall on the Strand, seating about five thousand. Sunday was the last day of these meetings. Walt and I went in the afternoon. The hall was by no means full, but there were fifteen hundred I guess.

Dr. Torrey spoke about being "born again," and mentioned some of the foolish ideas people have about it. His sermon was meant to straighten things out. I know that my own ideas were somewhat hazy, and I wasn't at all sure about it. But I am now. The text was John 3:6, "That which is born of the flesh is flesh, and that which is born of the Spirit is spirit"— and Dr. Torrey gave five proofs by which we can tell whether we are "born again," born of the Spirit, or not. Every proof was a verse of Scripture. That's what I like, lots of the Word of God and little of man. The five proofs were very convincing and plain.

In the letter he could only state the points made, but in the full notes taken at the time he went more into detail. The proofs as he gave them were the following:

1st. I John 2:29. *"Every one that doeth righteousness is born of Him."* Righteousness equals such actions as are straight. Straight action is conduct that is conformed to a straight edge.

And the straight edge of life is the Word of God. Righteousness equals the practice of such actions as are conformed to the Word of God. Do we practise righteousness? If we do, we are born of God.

2nd. 1 John 3:9. *"Whatsoever is born of God doth not commit sin."* Sin is something done, a breaking of the law; and the law is the revealed will of God. Sin, therefore, is transgression of the will of God. "Every one that doeth sin, doeth also lawlessness: and sin is lawlessness." 1 John 3:4. The regenerate man does not wilfully and intentionally sin.

3rd. 1 John 3:14. *"We know that we have passed out of death into life because we love the brethren."* The brethren are all those who believe in the Lord Jesus Christ. Love for the brethren, positive and negative, is explained in verses 16-18. We ought to love to the extent of giving our lives—literally, if necessary—as God did for us. "Let us not love in word, neither with the tongue, but in deed and in truth," v. 18. Love for the brethren is a proof of rebirth.

4th. 1 John 5:1. *"Whosoever believeth that Jesus is the Christ is born of God."* Christ equals the Anointed One of God. Belief equals absolute conviction. Whosoever is convinced absolutely that Jesus is the Anointed One of God is born of God.

5th. 1 John 5:4. *"Whosoever is born of God overcometh the world."* A regenerate person has that within him which overcomes the world.

Summary: One who is "born again" practises righteousness; is not committing sin; loves the brethren; believes that Jesus is the Christ; overcomes the world. We cannot do all this by ourselves, therefore what are we to do? Answer, John 1:12. "As many as *received Him,* to them gave He power to become the sons of God, even to them that believe on His Name." So we have only to believe in Jesus and receive Him, and immediately we have power to become sons of God.

(The next thing to do is to use this power. W. W. B.)

Missing dinner at the hotel, Borden hastened back to the evening meeting. The vast hall, seated for five thousand, was filled to capacity, and a deep hush fell on the listeners as Dr.

Torrey gave his closing message. *Today versus Tomorrow* was his theme, and men were made to feel that they simply could not afford to put off the vital matter of salvation.

"To-day if ye will hear his voice, harden not your hearts" (Heb. 3.7).

"Boast not thyself of to-morrow, for thou knowest not what a day may bring forth" (Prov. 27:1).

The wise man accepts Christ today; the foolish puts it off till tomorrow.

Of his experience that night Borden continued in the letter to his mother:

> After this Dr. Torrey called for decisions. Fifty or sixty came forward and confessed Christ. Dr. Torrey told us to speak to those about us. I had an awful tussle, and almost didn't, for I thought the people around me were all Christians. However, I wasn't sure, and so decided not to be the foolish man of "to-morrow." I spoke to a lady next to me, and others, but they were all saved. However, I felt much better, and know it will be easier to do next time.
>
> In the After Meeting, Miss Davis sang the song, "I surrender all," and an invitation was given to those who had never publicly done so, whether Christians or not, to do so then. I stood up with several others, and we sang the chorus:
>
> > I surrender all, I surrender all;
> > All to Thee, my blessed Saviour,
> > I surrender all.
>
> Dr. Torrey then gave us a little talk on, The Way of Life. He also spoke on, How to keep on with the Christian Life when it is begun:
> 1. Look always at Jesus.
> 2. Keep confessing Jesus everywhere.
> 3. Keep studying God's Word, Matt. 4:4.
> 4. Keep praying every day, 1 Thes. 5:17.
> 5. Go to work.
> The first four I am doing and the fifth I will do.
> Well, when I got home that night I felt there was a difference.

You know the expression, "for Heaven's sake," that I have used so much. I knew it was wrong and yet I couldn't stop it. Before last Sunday I had been praying about it, but not very earnestly I am afraid, for though I managed to keep it from my lips, it got started several times. That night I prayed not only that my life might be controlled but my thoughts also, and I meant it. I expected a direct answer and got it the next day, and I have been kept in that matter ever since. I don't think I ever had any real definite experience like that before, and it has strengthened my faith. And now I am praying more earnestly about things for which we have been praying some time. . . .

You won't be able to get any answer to me about all this, but we will talk things over when I arrive.

A deep conviction that to accept Christ as Saviour means to accept Him as Lord was part of this experience, and a conviction leading to action. Personal work was the outcome. It was no easier for Borden at seventeen to witness for Christ than it is for other young fellows of his age. He was reserved by nature. But he had taken a step that must have consequences. In his journal he had written for that Sunday:

July 2, 1905

Fine address. I was greatly helped and surrendered all to Jesus at the invitation.

Surrender in his case meant not only giving up worldly amusements and indulgences, it meant taking on his Master's yoke, living with Him for others, always and everywhere. And it was very practical. Of the very next Sunday he wrote to his mother:

In the evening I started out to call on E. W. at the Coburg Hotel. I didn't feel just right about it, as I know you don't like us to make such calls on Sunday. However, I went ahead. Walking down Oxford Street, I came to a place where an outdoor service was being held. Something told me to stop and help, but I went on. I had almost gotten to the Coburg when I heard the singing of another group and after a few minutes decided to go back. So I did and joined the group. It was a Wesleyan Mission Band, holding a Gospel service.

After the meeting was over, I spoke to a young fellow and asked him if he believed in Jesus Christ. He said he didn't and didn't ever intend to. We stood on the street corner and talked until eleven P.M. He had evidently read some books written by a destructive critic, and I wasn't well enough versed to meet his questions in a way to convince him. He was a very nice young fellow, and gave me his address and said he would be very glad if I could convince him. I am going to get Pierson's *Many Infallible Proofs,* and try some more with him.

And he did, spending an entire afternoon hunting him up in Shoreditch, a very unattractive part of London. But the address proved to be fictitious. There was no such house or person to be found. It was a keen disappointment; but who shall say how much of blessing came to Borden himself—and to countless others—through his faithfulness in personal work which began with that full and glad surrender to Jesus Christ as Lord?

It is the surrendered life that counts, for through it God can work.

PART II

YALE UNIVERSITY

THE life that counts must toil and fight;
Must hate the wrong and love the right;
Must stand for truth, by day, by night—
    This is the life that counts.

The life that counts must hopeful be;
In darkest night make melody;
Must wait the dawn on bended knee—
    This is the life that counts.

The life that counts must aim to rise
Above the earth to sunlit skies;
Must fix its gaze on Paradise—
    This is the life that counts.

The life that counts must helpful be;
The cares and needs of others see;
Must seek the slaves of sin to free—
    This is the life that counts.

The life that counts is linked with God;
And turns not from the cross, the rod;
But walks with joy where Jesus trod—
    This is the life that counts.

A. W. S.

CHAPTER 6

FRESHMAN

1905-1906. Age 17-18

Wherewithal shall a young man cleanse his way? by taking heed thereto according to thy word.—Psalm 119:9

Thy word have I hid in my heart that I might not sin against thee.—Psalm 119:11

Borden's college mottos; the first he illuminated for his room at Yale, the second he wrote in full on the flyleaf of his pocket Testament.

It was at Camden that the reunion took place—the summer home on the coast of Maine which Mr. Borden had recently built. The golf links, bathing and yachting, delightful as they were, all took a secondary place compared with the renewed family intercourse and especially the times when William could be alone with his mother. College was drawing near, and there was more to look forward to than to look back upon after the first few days.

Is life anywhere on earth more real, more intense, more crowded with interest and full of opportunity than during the brief formative years of a college course? Into this absorbing life Borden plunged a month or so after his return to America. Yale with its fine old campus and still finer traditions was a new world to him, but one in which he was soon to take no unworthy part.

Yale, September 28, 1905

Dear Mother—I am here, as you know, and the crises have passed. Yesterday I took my Iliad examination and this after-

83

noon learned that I had successfully passed it. As this was my only condition, I am now a member in full standing of the class of 1909. . . .

On our arrival in New Haven, John [his brother] came up with me to this house, 242 York Street. My room is at the back and has a large bay-window in three sections, with an immense window-seat. As none of my trunks had arrived, I went over with him to his rooms in White Hall. He and George have a very nice suite, two bedrooms and a sitting-room. Things were in an awful mess though, as last year's occupants hadn't removed their stuff. We wandered around a while and met a good many fellows I knew. My trunks came in the afternoon, but I didn't unpack much, as the general opinion is that it is best not to do so until Thursday. John took M. H. and myself down to Mori's to dine. This is a little place—quite historic—where the fellows feed more or less. The tables have initials carved all over them, and in one room there is a special table on which seniors leave their trade marks.

After dinner I went back home and John left me. About 8:30 some sophomores came in and made me do a few foolish stunts which didn't amount to much. I sang them a song and attempted to "scramble" like an egg, a very difficult thing to do, I assure you! However, they went after a few minutes and I was left in peace for the rest of the night.

The next morning I passed my Iliad examination, and in the afternoon registered at Alumni Hall. There also we were assigned to divisions and given study schedules, etc. In the afternoon I went out and watched the football practice and while out there met Bob Noyes, a Hill fellow, who very kindly invited me to dinner. So that night, the "awful night," I dined with him and some other fellows, after which we went over to the campus to see the wrestling. Our dinner had taken us a long time, so we were late and the wrestling had already begun when we arrived. The seniors, without hats and with coats on inside out, were seated in a large circle with their torches on the ground in front of them. In the center were all the big "Y" men who were running the performance. I could only get a glimpse now and then of the doings inside, but the sophomores won the match by winning the third bout, the heavy weight, after the first two had been drawn.

After this the whole crowd adjourned to York Street and for a few minutes things were quite lively. Being peacefully inclined, we stayed up on the porch of 242 and looked on. Later, one of my visitors of the night before arrived, more or less drunk. There might have been something doing only Bob Noyes told him to leave me alone, for which I was thankful. I went over and slept with John that night, as George was putting up with someone else. So you see I have been well taken care of. I must quit now as there are lots of things to be done.

Oct. 1, 1905

DEAR MOTHER—This is Sunday evening and I have time to write you. I will take up the tale where I left off.

Friday morning our recitation began and I rather enjoyed mine. I don't think the work will be very hard. However I won't loaf just because it seems easy. . . . I am out trying for the freshman football eleven. As there are ninety-nine others doing likewise, there is a pretty good chance for your wish being fulfilled—that I should not make the team.

The opening of College has brought out all sorts of things. Nearly everyone uses a translation in his studies, that is in Greek and Latin. The great majority smoke, go to the theatre Saturday night and do their studying on Sunday. Rather a hopeless state of affairs! However, there are some fine Christian men in College and in my own class too, I believe. And I hope to be able to do something, by the grace of God, to help in the right direction. I am taking meals next door at a table with seven other fellows. One of these fellows only, besides myself, doesn't smoke and study on Sunday. I have only just met him but he seems like a pretty nice fellow. I must not criticise but rejoice that I am here in a position to give to others a little of what I have received. I am thankful for all the true teaching I have had from you, dear Mother, and Mr. Lombard, Walt and others. I know you are praying for me, so I don't have to ask you to. And there are others also. I just had a letter from Walt, in which he said that an old English lady in the Mission had told him that she had prayed for us every day for the past year. What a thing Christian fellowship is and what a power prayer! I wish I had that little poem you sent me once, about the ploughman at his work, praying, and the missionaries wondering how their words had such power, "because they did not see someone unknown, perhaps, and far away, on bended knee."[1]

This morning President Hadley preached in Chapel and gave a very good sermon for the opening of a college year. Only in impressing the necessity of having a fixed purpose in life and distinguishing between right and wrong, he neglected to say what our purpose should be, and where we should get the ability to persevere and the strength to resist temptations—things which seemed rather essential to me.

I forgot to mention the Dwight Hall reception which was held Friday night. The freshman class was invited to meet the President. I went and after we had all been introduced the President spoke and then others—the captains of the various teams and John Magee. The quartet also added to the entertainment and refreshments were served. It was a very nice informal gathering and I met a good many fellows. . . .

Oh, I nearly forgot about this evening's meeting! Dr. Henry Wright, son of the Dean, gave us a splendid address in Dwight Hall. It was the real true thing, and as he dealt with matters closely related to college life it was very helpful. . . .

Dwight Hall and Henry Wright were to have so large a part in Borden's experiences at Yale that it is important to

---

[1] The weary ones had rest, the sad had joy
    That day, and wondered "how?"
A ploughman singing at his work had prayed,
    "Lord, bless them now."

Away in foreign lands they wondered "how"
    Their simple word had power.
At home, the "Gleaners," two or three, had met
    To pray an hour.

Yes, we are always wondering "how?"
    Because we do not see
Someone, unknown perhaps, and far away,
    On bended knee.

understand their relation to the life of the University. From the recently published biography of Dr. Wright it is evident that he was in America very much what Henry Drummond had been in Scotland. His brilliant scholarship was almost lost sight of in his spiritual fervor, complete consecration and passion for winning men to Christ. He had a genius for friendship, and was young enough (twenty-eight when Borden entered) to be closely in touch with student life. He had taken his doctor's degree in classics and had already been two years on the faculty, of which his father was dean, as a tutor in Greek and Latin. He had also been General Secretary of the Yale Y.M.C.A. (1898-1901), and it was during that period of his post-graduate studies that he came to be a campus figure.

Dignified, kindly, a trifle shy at times, always eager to be of use, he grew into the hearts of faculty and students alike. "In connection with my own undergraduate days," said Prof. B. W. Kunkel of Lafayette College, "I look upon Henry's smile of greeting at the head of the stairs in Dwight Hall, as we came to the meetings, as one of the benedictions which helped me through the week."[2]

Dwight Hall, the home of the Y.M.C.A., was still, when Borden entered Yale, what Henry Wright had made it. It stood for a high type of scholarship as well as Christian manhood. From the Sunday evening services, often gathering hundreds, to the group meetings and personal talks in the little room on the top floor, it was the scene of much of the best work done in the University. And it was the inheritor of a glorious past. For the Y.M.C.A., organized in 1881, had not been a beginning so much as a culmination of Christian activity in the University. It had been "adopted as the best channel for the expression of the rich heritage of two centuries of Yale's religious traditions."[3]

[2] From *The Life of Henry B. Wright*, by George Stewart, Jr., Association Press, New York, p. 32.

[3] See *Two Centuries of Christian Activity at Yale*, by Henry B. Wright and others. Published in 1901.

Founded in the first instance (in 1701) as a college for training men for the ministry of the Gospel, Yale has always had a deeply religious basis, and has been visited in the past by many remarkable revivals of spiritual life. Under the mighty preaching of Whitefield, then only twenty-five years of age, the first of these took place (1740) and they have been repeated at intervals, so that we read of a whole series of revivals under the presidency of the first Dr. Timothy Dwight, continued through the lifetime of his devoted colleague, Professor Chauncey A. Goodrich. "As an undergraduate or instructor, the latter must have witnessed and was an important factor in all but two of the nineteen revivals that graciously visited Yale from the accession of President Dwight up to the Civil War."[4]

As far back as 1812-13 a revival swept the College which was distinctly a student movement. Several members of the senior class had been praying, mostly unknown to each other, for a spiritual awakening. Active opposition was expected from one student in particular, Elias Cornelius by name, and definite prayer was made for his conversion. Not long after, a sudden and complete change in this man made a great impression on the student body. He broke with evil companions and profanity, and soon was rejoicing in the consciousness of Christ's presence and power to save. "He led nearly twenty members of his own class to the Christian faith . . . and by his labours from eighty to a hundred of all classes were awakened to a new sense of their Christian responsibility."[5]

Another remarkable revival in 1825 was due to the prayers of a single individual of but little standing in the College. He invited members of the University Church of more influence than himself to his room and besought them to awaken others to prayer and effort for the conversion of those around them.

[4] *Ibid.*, p. 74.
[5] *Ibid.*, p. 68.

His earnestness was used of God, and a deeply spiritual movement was the result.

From the period of the Civil War to the visits of D. L. Moody, the control of the voluntary religious life of the University was passing more and more into the hands of the students themselves. Christian work by students for students, in time became centered in the Y.M.C.A., under whose auspices several revivals of more recent date had taken place, including that of 1900, when John R. Mott and Robert E. Speer were so powerfully used of God that no fewer than a hundred undergraduates professed conversion.

Five years later, with a new generation of students, there was need for all the prayer and effort centered at Dwight Hall, into which Borden wholeheartedly entered. John Magee, now a missionary at Nanking, was the Graduate Secretary, and it was not long before he discerned the intense reality behind the young freshman's spiritual life and convictions.

"The school is not a knowledge shop so much as a great assay of human souls," Professor Meigs of "The Hill" had written. Borden, at Yale, was being tested in that great assay, and was conscious of the same process in the lives of others. All around him it was going on—men making or marring their future. To him the Word of God meant so much in meeting the temptations of daily life and he was finding such strength in the companionship of the Lord Jesus Christ that he longed to share these great realities with others. So the purpose was forming in his heart of attempting to start a group for Bible study among those who would not avail themselves of the influences of Dwight Hall. The intimate correspondence with his mother continued:

SUNDAY, October 15, 1905

Just after chapel service this morning we had our class prayer meeting at which several of us spoke on the possibilities of the year. John Magee invited me to come to the Volunteer

Band at five this afternoon. There were about ten present and we had a very nice little meeting and time of prayer. There are some fine fellows here in the upper classes, I can tell you.

I have talked over the matter of my group Bible Study Class with Arthur Bradford and decided that paraphrasing Galatians is a little too strenuous for the sort of men to be reached. The object of these groups is to interest fellows who do not attend the Wednesday evening meeting in Dwight Hall, led by Dr. Wright. So I have been looking over methods of Bible study suggested by Dr. Torrey and decided upon Chapter Study as the best. You know the method, giving out questions to be answered. And I think John is the book to take, because it is written that men might believe that Jesus is the Christ the Son of God, "and that believing ye might have life through his name." I haven't spoken to the fellows yet but expect to do so this evening.

October 20, 1905

Am I busy? I will tell you what I am doing, and you can judge for yourself. To begin with I have twelve recitations a week to prepare, which isn't much, very little in fact.

Monday evening at 6:45, Freshman Religious Committee meets in Bill Barnes' room, Vice-President of Dwight Hall.

Wednesday evening at 6:40, the 1909 Bible Class meets in Dwight Hall, led by Dr. Wright.

Thursday evening at 6:45, our Mission Study Class meets. Herbert Malcolm, a member of the Volunteer Band, 1907 man, leads this.

And then Sunday. That day starts with Chapel at 10:30. Immediately after this comes our Class Prayer Meeting with which I have more or less to do and will probably lead at times. At five in the afternoon there is a meeting of the Volunteer Band, and at 6:40 a general meeting held in Dwight Hall. The preacher of the morning usually addresses this.

Besides these things, I intend to go down at least twice a week to the Oak Street Boy's Club.

Then I have been appointed chairman of a committee to promote interest and collect funds for the Yale Hall work here in

New Haven and the Yale Mission in China. . . .

My exercise, that is football, takes rather more time than I wish it did. . . .

I spoke to M. H. tonight about starting up a class in Bible Study. I approached him first as he is the key, so to speak, of a certain bunch of fellows I want to get at. He thought it would be a very good thing and said he would consider it. If possible I would like to have a first sort of explanatory meeting next Sunday. But I have my doubts about accomplishing this. However, a beginning has been made, for which I am thankful.

Please send me Dr. Torrey's *Vest Pocket Companion for Christian Workers,* best text for personal use. I have lost mine.

It was at one of those many meetings in Dwight Hall that Borden met his friend, the one who more than any other was to share his college life. Of that first meeting and his own impressions, Charlie Campbell wrote:

We were crowded together in Bill Barnes' room. Barnes was a junior at the time, Vice-President of the Y.M.C.A., and leader of the freshman religious work. Bill Borden was sitting on the floor with his back against the wall and his knees drawn up near his chin. I remember noticing him particularly. As we left the meeting he joined me and we walked back together to York Street. Bill told me then, as I remember, of his trip around the world and of his interest in missions. This was the beginning of the friendship which has meant so much to me.

About the early days of our acquaintance I would like to say a little, as they show one of Bill's finest characteristics, real democracy. I lived in freshman year in Pierson Hall, the one college-owned dormitory on York Street and not considered so swell as the private-owned dormitories. I not only lived in Pierson, but away up on the fifth floor. Anyone had to have courage to climb to the top of Pierson. My first impulse after meeting Bill and seeing his room at Garland's was to hold aloof. I felt he was too well off, and imagined he would not care to have much to do with me. How appreciative I felt and how drawn to Bill when I found him climbing up those Pierson steps, not once but often! And what times we would have! There was always the religious bond that drew us together; but Bill's spirit of fun was sure to show itself, and a good "rough-house" or game was in order. I think of one evening when we staged a complete track-meet in my room and Bill was the heavy competitor in all the events possible.

During this fall [1905] Bill went out for the freshman football team, and played very good ball. He did not make the team but came very near doing so. In fact in the game with Princeton freshmen he was told to warm up to go in, but time was called or something of that sort prevented.

It was well on in the first term when Bill and I began to pray together in the morning before breakfast. I cannot say positively whose suggestion it was, but I feel sure it must have originated with Bill. We had been meeting only a short time when a third, Farrand Williams, joined us and soon after a fourth, James M. Howard. These meetings were held in Bill's room just before we went to breakfast. The time was spent in prayer after a brief reading of Scripture. Our object was to pray for the religious work of the class and college, and also for those of our friends we were seeking to bring to Christ. I remember so well the stimulus Bill gave us in those meetings. His handling of Scripture was always helpful. From the very beginning of the years I knew him he would read to us from the Bible, show us something that God had promised and then proceed to claim the promise with assurance.

This group for prayer was the beginning of the daily groups that spread to every one of the college classes. From the membership of two at the start, the group in our class grew until it had to be divided in sophomore year, and by the end of that year there were similar groups in each of the classes. It was not passed down from the seniors to the juniors, but came up from the freshmen to the seniors. And very real blessing was given in answer to our prayers—quite a number were converted. I remember one with whom Bill worked very hard, a fellow with a scientific turn of mind who wanted everything proved. Bill must have looked down with joy from the Place to which he has gone when, some years later, this man came out brightly as a Christian.

Bill was always picking out the toughest proposition and going through thick and thin to win him for Christ. . . . His life, how true it rang! He came to college far ahead, spiritually, of any of us. He had already given his heart in full surrender to Christ—had really done it. He had formed his purpose to become a foreign missionary, and all through college and seminary that purpose never wavered. One can easily see the advantage this would give a man. His life was determined. We who were his classmates learned to lean on him and find in him a strength that was solid as a rock, just because of this settled purpose and consecration.

Unconsciously the young freshman was becoming a force in the best life of the University, but so unconsciously! To himself it seemed quite otherwise. One cannot but notice, in the letters to his mother of that fall and winter, the earnestness with which he was seeking to overcome inconsistencies and weaknesses.

October 29, 1905

My group work has not commenced yet, but I hope to get it going before long, by the end of the football season. Mr. Mott was here last Sunday and I had a few moments' talk with him in the afternoon. He wished to be remembered to you. This Sunday also he was here and gave us a couple of very fine talks—this morning on the required characteristics of leadership and this evening in Dwight Hall, a distinctly evangelistic meeting, something rather unusual for this place. Mr. Mott spoke very strongly on Sin, especially on "Be sure your sin will find you out." After his time was up he asked the fellows who wanted to learn how to deal with temptation to meet in another room. So we met, only about two-fifths having left, and there again he spoke very earnestly. . . .

YALE UNIVERSITY
Branford Court Memorial Quadrangle

The following Sundays brought a different experience. A preacher with an international reputation led the services, but to an earnest mind grappling with the realities of life left much to be desired.

November 12, 1905

Dr. ——— has been here for the last two Sundays, preaching in Chapel and talking in Dwight Hall in the evenings. He makes me tired, he's so smooth and subtle and pleasing to everyone. His talks are interesting in a way, but what he says merely amounts to human ethics. He takes texts simply "as pegs to hang his own thoughts on."

Perhaps the preacher did not realize what that hour might mean, as he faced the serried ranks in the college chapel. Had he had the vision of what lay behind in those hundreds upon hundreds of lives, the temptations and dangers, possibilities and needs, he surely would have wanted to give them more than just eloquence and ethics. Borden was having his own struggles.

December 3, 1905

I am at present a little discouraged about my Bible Class. . . . I find it very difficult to get started somehow, and am a little afraid of what may happen when it is started. There is a great deal to be done here and I don't feel that I am doing much of anything.

I am sorry to say that I don't even manage to keep up my own Bible study systematically, without breaks. I keep it up for a week or so, and then something happens and I miss a day.

In my opinion we get the saddest bunch of preachers you could scrape up in the U.S.A., and to-day we had one from Scotland who almost takes the cake. I think I'll live at the Moody Institute when I get back to Chicago. But seriously, I will go with you whenever there's anything to go to. You know I won't be going to dances, so I'll have lots of time.

The Christmas vacation was evidently a time when his

armor was buckled on afresh, and he came back determined
to put first things first in a new way.

January 14, 1906

It seems sort of nice and very natural to be back here again.
I am thankful to say that I have been enabled to get up every
morning, so far, in time to have Bible study and prayer before
beginning the day's work. I hope with God's help to keep it
up. . . .

The term has started well as far as sermons go. Mr. Speer was
here this morning and evening and gave us two very good talks.
In the morning he read a part of the tenth of Matthew, taking
as his text verses 32 and 33, the subject being "Confession and
Denial." He spoke on character as essential to strong manhood, and religion as necessary to character, and showed that
religion—Christianity—is a question of personal attitude toward
Jesus Christ. It is confession or—denial.

The Dwight Hall meeting as you know is voluntary, but
the room was packed, some fellows even standing, a thing
they wouldn't think of doing in Chapel. I guess there were
about five hundred present. There, too, he gave a very powerful talk on "Apart from me ye can do nothing," and "I can do
all things through Christ which strengtheneth me."

I have a regular night now for going to the Boys' Club. I go
down every Saturday with Charlie Campbell. He is a corker,
and I am glad I'm getting to know him.

This afternoon I had quite a time. I thought I'd study up
the question of *procrastination*. So I did, and as a result I felt
that it was up to me to go and speak to B.B. about Bible study.
Well, I went to his room about quarter of four and he was reading a magazine. I tried to start the subject and couldn't seem to
get up courage. I sat there for a solid hour scarcely saying a
word and didn't accomplish anything. I had a Mission Band
meeting at five, so I had to go, but I got B. to walk along with
me, as he was going that way, towards Dwight Hall, thinking
I might speak to him on the way. I didn't, however.

Ned Harvey led the Band Meeting and gave us a very good
talk from Philippians 1:6, 9 and 10. When he was through he

asked as usual whether there was anything special to be
brought up. I immediately thought of that verse in James,
"Confess your faults one to another and pray one for another."
I felt that I ought to confess. For a moment I hesitated, but I
was given strength to do so, thank God. I read the verse and
said that I knew that I must learn to save people here before
I could hope to do so anywhere else, and that I had had a good
chance this afternoon to speak to a fellow and had failed, and
that I wanted their prayers. I just managed to get this out before I was overcome with emotion and sat down. This evening
I had another chance at B. and finally managed to get on the
track by a roundabout way, still cowardly and fearful! The
result is that B. has said he will study with me. We haven't
arranged the details, but I have more confidence and faith that
through Christ I can carry out what is begun. Philippians 1:6,
"Being confident of this very thing, that He which hath begun a good work in you will perform it until the day of Jesus
Christ."

Get the Church to pray for me. I've only "begun." And
you may be sure I am praying for you, dear Mother, who
have done so much for me and for each member of our dear
family.

Another letter affords a glimpse into a very different side of
college life. The week of the annual "Promenade" had come,
and many of the students had visitors.

January 21, 1906

Chapel this morning was chuck full of Prom girls, naturally,
and also full of fellows, as many as could get in, who came
to "rubber." Mr. Speer preached a good sermon on distinctions
between right and wrong. After the service, according to college custom, the sophs all lined up outside and made remarks
about the girls as they came out, and yelled! It wasn't exactly
a Sunday performance.

However, we had a very nice little prayer meeting, fairly well
attended. The subject was Sabbath Observance. Various subjects,
studying, travelling, playing games, etc., were brought up.

Finally one of the fellows got up and reminded us of what Mr. Speer had just said—that if there was any doubt about a thing, it was pretty sure to be wrong, and it was best to give it a wide margin. It seemed to me that that just about hit the nail on the head. . . .

You probably know that fellows, a good many, go to the theatre and then afterwards go around and "pick up" chorus girls and usually come home drunk about one A.M. Well, one of the leaders of this sort of thing made rather elaborate plans for a spree. He invited a good many fellows, about thirty out of our class, each to chip in five dollars. The plan was to take the whole chorus of the play, the one that was here last night, and drive out to some dance hall and have a high old time. The way I learned of it was this—another fellow was asked who wouldn't go, and he came and told me, to see what we could do to stop it. He had been informed that they would have about ninety dollars' worth of punch. However, that's a mere detail. I didn't know any of the fellows at all well who were going, so couldn't do much. However, we saw a good many of the upper classmen, and the result was it didn't come off, for which I am very thankful. This is, of course, an extreme case, but it's an example of what sometimes happens. I heard someone in the hall, just this minute, say that there would have been about fifty chorus girls and seventy-five fellows.

That he was far from thinking himself better than other people comes out in many letters, but he was growing.

To-day hasn't been just as I would have liked. The morning sermon . . . was simply "sad." However, our little prayer meeting was better attended and a better spirit shown in it than ever before. I went off walking in the afternoon. Tried to find Bethany Mission and as we failed, kept on walking and didn't get back until supper time. Spent the early part of the evening in watching one of the fellows do tricks, and now it's late and B. is studying. So you see I have been pretty successfully "hindered," or rather I have allowed myself to be, for I confess I didn't make much effort, sort of shirked my duty. Oh yes, and I absolutely forgot about our Band Meeting, and missed that.

I don't know just what's wrong—but the fact is I've failed again. Guess I haven't fed upon God's Word enough, nor prayed enough. I *will* try again.

Your loving son,

WILLIAM

January 31, 1906

There is a group of men here in College, it might be called a personal-workers' group, which meets every Tuesday in Dr. Wright's room. James Howard, Charlie Campbell and I were chosen from our class. As Dr. Wright says, it doesn't mean any honour, it means work. . . . There are about fourteen in the group now. Dr. Wright first reads a short passage and says a few words. Then there is general discussion, each one bringing up his case, and then prayer. It is fine. We get to know some of the best men in college intimately. I realize here more than ever before that a man's *true friends* are his Christian friends. . . . I am sure these little gatherings will be a help to me and will accomplish great things here at Yale.[6]

February 18, 1906

I have only missed my Morning Watch once or twice this term. . . . I can easily believe that it is next in importance to accepting Christ. For I know that when I don't wait upon God in prayer and Bible study, things go wrong. The other night I had a fine chance to testify to that very fact, or rather to the fact that when I do pray and study, things go better, and I am sorry to say didn't make good use of it. I happened to mention to a fellow that I was nearly always up and dressed by 7:30, and knowing that I seldom went to breakfast before

---

[6] Professor Benjamin Wisner Bacon, who was then college pastor, spoke of these gatherings as the very "heart of heart" of Christian activity at Yale. "They were held in the little room under the eaves on the top floor at Dwight Hall, none being asked save the little inside group whom Henry [Wright] and the rest believed to be 100 per cent consecrated. You may be sure I felt it an honour to be with these heart and soul Christian boys. . . . Henry was of course always the leader, richest in experience, wisest in counsel, most indefatigable in effort. It was the very breath of life to him to be about his Father's business."

8:00 he wanted to know what I did in the interval. I don't think I was exactly ashamed or afraid, but I didn't reply as I should have done. I merely said in a vague way that I attended to certain things. Wasn't it foolish! I'm afraid it's one of my great troubles, not explaining myself. I know I've gotten into the habit of refusing to do things without saying why I refuse. I suppose the reason is that I feel that it would be like judging the fellows who are doing the thing, whatever it may be. However, in the future I am going to pray that I may be on the lookout for opportunities of confessing my belief and may stand for right against wrong. I'm sorry to say that I have done nothing with B. or any of the other fellows lately. . . .

In our Band Meeting this afternoon, there were only five of us; the point was brought out very strongly that "Except the Lord build the house, they labour in vain that build it" and "Apart from me ye can do nothing." We all felt our need of God's help and the necessity for greater consecration on our part. One of the fellows confessed that he wasn't wholly consecrated by any means, and I'm afraid I'm not. But I want to be. . . . Keep praying for me.

"I am keeping up my wrestling," he wrote to his father about the same time, "and like it very much. It certainly is a science! The last few days I have had to go easy because of a mat-burn on my arm—*i.e.,* the skin rubbed off and rather an awkward sore made."

"Yesterday I wrestled in the tournament and got beaten," he added a little later. "My class is 'middle heavy weight.' My opponent was about a head taller than I am, but the same weight. He is a senior and knows John. We had two bouts of five minutes each, and neither succeeded in putting the other down. So after the rest we went at it again, and this time were to wrestle till one of us was thrown. Well, after forty-nine minutes of rather strenuous exercise he succeeded in getting me down. I lost about three pounds in the process, but did not suffer any injuries and feel fine now."

CHAPTER 7

FRESHMAN—*continued*

1906. AGE 18

God has His best things for the few
Who dare to stand the test:
God has His second best for those
Who will not have His best.

I want in this short life of mine
As much as may be pressed
Of service true to God and men;
Help me to have Thy best.

—Selected

I F ONE WOULD UNDERSTAND the student life of America at its best during the last three decades, he should turn to the student conferences," wrote the biographer of Dr. Henry Wright; "for there are focussed the aspirations of Christian youth in its highest mood of dedication. . . . Among all the events of the college year making for emancipation of the spirit and dedication of life, he placed the student conferences first." In the middle and at the close of Borden's freshman year came two outstanding experiences of this sort.

The first was the Missionary Convention of the Student Volunteer Movement at Nashville, attended by over four thousand delegates. The Yale contingent was a strong one, and the way in which Charlie Campbell came to be included in it was a surprise to himself if not to his friend.

I was not one of those chosen. The last night before the delegation was to leave, I was in bed and almost asleep when a number of upper-classmen filed into my room. I believe Bill was with them. They told me that it was financially possible for them to take one more delegate, and wanted me to go. Of course, I went. I have always had a conviction that Bill was back of that. If not, it was at any rate the kind of thing he was always doing, while keeping out of sight himself.

What a time we had on that long train journey to Nashville! Bill and others of us would adjourn to the baggage car occasionally, to let off steam in games that usually came from his fertile imagination. One of his games went by the name of "hot-hand."[1] The man who was "it" must face the side of the car, with his eyes closed, supporting his head against the car. The rest would then group themselves behind him, and anyone was at liberty to take a whack. After each impact he had to guess who it was that had hit him. If his guess was correct, the giver of the blow had to change places with him; if incorrect, another whack was in order. Bill shone at this game, in both capacities! Then there would be high-kicking contests and other games, all in the rapidly-moving car.

And so we reached Nashville, full of life and spirits, where we separated for the different homes in which we were to be entertained. Those were the days of wonderful inspiration for us all. . . . If Bill was responsible for my going to Nashville, he was used of God to bring me a step further on in Christian experience, for it was there I gave my life to God in consecration for any work to which he might call me.

Among the speakers, secretaries of boards and visitors to the Convention, of whom there were hundreds, and the foreign missionaries representing twenty-six countries, one man stood out for Borden with a burning message. He was a man with a map. Charged with facts and with enthusiasm, grim with earnestness, filled with a passion of love for Christ and the perishing, Samuel Zwemer made that great map live, voicing

[1] Learned from watching sailors on a German steamer, on his trip round the world.

the silent appeal of the Mohammedan world. Two hundred millions of our fellow-creatures in the lands colored green on the map—two hundred millions under the sway of Islam, held in a bondage than which none on earth is more relentless, more deadening, and to its womanhood more degrading—what a challenge to the Christian Church! From China to the west coast of Africa and from the steppes of Russia right down to Zanzibar stretched that great sweep of green, sparsely dotted here and there with centers from which Christian light was spreading. Yet, as Dr. Zwemer showed, never before had there been such open doors for the evangelization of the Moslem world. *"The hour is ripe"* was the burden of his message, and he sustained it with startling facts.

Making full allowance for all that was being done by missionaries in Moslem lands, the speaker pointed out country after country, province after province, still absolutely without the Light of Life, as far as their Mohammedan population was concerned. Some had no missionaries at all, such as Afghanistan with its four million Moslems; some had missionaries among their heathen races but none for the followers of the prophet. In China, for example, with fifteen million Moslems, not a single missionary was set apart for their evangelization. Yet the door was no longer closed to the inland provinces in which most of them are found.

When the door opens [Dr. Zwemer urged] we ought to press in, sacrificing our lives if need be for God, as the Moslems did at Khartum for their Prophet. If the call voiced by those who have already spoken moved us deeply, coming from Persia, from Turkey, from Egypt, from India, if that was a call from God, what shall be said of the mute appeal of the *seventy millions of the wholly unevangelized Moslem world?* Shall we stand by and allow these seventy millions to continue under the curse and in the snare of a false religion, with no knowledge of the saving love and power of Christ, not because they have proved fanatical and refused to listen, not because they have thrust us back, but because none of us has ever had the courage to go to those lands and win them to Jesus Christ?

Of course it will cost life. It is not an expedition of ease nor a picnic excursion to which we are called. . . . It is going to cost many a life, and not lives only, but prayers and tears and blood. Leadership in this movement has always been a leadership in suffering. There was Raymond Lull, the first missionary to the Moslems, stoned to death in Algiers; Henry Martyn, pioneering in Persia with the cry, "Let me burn out for God." We who are missionaries to Moslems to-day call upon you to follow with us in their train, to go to these waiting lands and light the beacon of the love of Christ in all the Mohammedan world. Did he not live, pray, suffer for Moslems as well as for us? Shall we do less if the call comes? Let us be like those Scots of Bruce who were ready to falter until that man on the white charger took the heart of Bruce in its casket and swinging it round cried out, "Oh, heart of Bruce, lead on!" As he flung it toward the enemy and bore down upon them you could not have held those soldiers back with bands of steel. Say not it is the appeal of the Mohammedan world or of the missionaries— it is the call of the Master. Let us answer with the shout, "Oh, heart of Christ, lead on!" And we will follow that cry and win the Mohammedan world for Him.

More Moslems in China than there are in Persia; more Moslems in China than in the whole of Egypt; more Moslems in China even than in Arabia, home and cradle of Islam, and *no one* giving himself to their evangelization—little wonder that with a nature like Borden's the facts demanded a response. "We do not plead for missions," Dr. Zwemer is wont to say. "We simply bring the facts before you and ask for a verdict."

If thou forbear to deliver them that are drawn unto death, and those that are ready to be slain; if thou sayest, Behold we knew it not; doth not he that pondereth the heart consider it? and he that keepeth thy soul, doth not he know it? and shall not he render to every man according to his works?[2]

2 Proverbs 24:12.

Borden went back from Nashville committed in heart to that great enterprise, should the Lord confirm the call. He did not say much about it, but from that time his most intimate friends knew that he was definitely considering work among Moslems in some unoccupied field.

On the return of the Yale delegation, reports had to be given in various meetings, and he wrote about one particular Sunday:

March 26, 1906

DEAR MOTHER—Yesterday was a rather strenuous day and I'm glad it's over. Our prayer meeting was well attended and the fellows did very well. One fellow's testimony was especially good. He said he had gone down there [Nashville S.V. Convention] believing that foreign missions were useless, but that he had come back ashamed of himself and thoroughly convinced that they were doing good. Another of the fellows gave a brief sketch of the Student Volunteer Movement. Another told a little about Medical Missions. Harold Stokes spoke on The Inadequacy of the Non-Christian Religions. I followed, on The Adequacy of the Christian Religion, and told the story Dr. Leary of Malaita told us; also I made things personal and hope I hit somebody. Charlie Campbell spoke last on Responsibility, and did splendidly. I am indeed thankful for the way God helped us.

In the evening Ken Latourette, a senior, Charley and myself, spoke at the Calvary Baptist Church. I tried to say too much, as I only had ten minutes, got balled-up and did rather poorly. However, the other fellows did very well, and as I came in between it didn't matter so much. I'm afraid there was a little pride and ambition inside. The three of us speak again Friday and Sunday evening next, and I'm going to be more careful.

Took some exercise to-day for the first time. My marks for this term are all A's except Greek, which is C; my general average is A. We have to pick our courses for Sophomore year soon, and I will send a book giving courses of study so that you and Father can look it over. . . .

Wish I were in Lakewood with you, but——
Lots of love, your son,

WILLIAM

He did not mention, in connection with his Greek, something that came out in a letter from his friend, Ken Latourette, now Professor of Missions at Yale.

My first recollection of Bill is in a Greek class in which we both recited to Professor ——. Dear old Professor —— was a rare scholar and a splendid Christian gentleman, but he had a quick temper and at times was subject to queer dislikes. For some reason I could never account for, he seemed totally to misunderstand and thoroughly to dislike Bill. For one who prepared as conscientiously as did Bill, it was very galling to be systematically, openly and unjustly berated. Although very indignant, he never retorted in any way, and I cannot now remember that he ever spoke of the experience, except when someone else mentioned it, and then he said only a few words of apology for Professor ——.

Just at this time the course of life in the University was arrested for Borden and his more intimate friends by the sudden death of one of their classmates. How much it meant to him may be seen from the following letter:

April 1, 1906

There was a fellow in our class, from Ohio, who was very bright in his studies but who came here with no reference for moral character. The Faculty let him in hoping it would be all right, but it wasn't. He got in with the wrong bunch and led a fast life. Last Monday he was taken sick and removed to the Infirmary. It was found that he had pleurisy, pneumonia and water on the heart, the last being the most serious.

Now I had been meaning to try and get hold of this fellow, but had never done anything. Few of us knew his sickness was serious until Wednesday, when it was rumoured that he was dying. Charlie, Bill Williams and I went to the Infirmary, to find out for sure. We were told that he was unconscious and not likely to live out the day. Immediately, we came back here to my room and *prayed*—there was nothing we could do. This was about two o'clock. He died at three, and I don't know whether he regained consciousness or not. . . . It's an awful lesson to me, and should make the whole University stop and think. Yet, already the thing is being forgotten.

The class decided to send flowers for the funeral and to wear mourning buttons for a month, and Borden as chairman of a committee for the purpose was to draw up a resolution to send to the family.

I appointed the committee, consisting of three of his most intimate friends, and Charlie. We did what was to be done, and it was but little. Now, Charlie and I want to get hold of three other fellows, who are all fast themselves. I went up to see them the other night, and found them playing cards with poker chips on the table and the door locked!

And yet, it is not hopeless. Charlie has been working with a fellow who was about the same as these. Formerly he avoided Charlie, but now he looks for him. I can see a change in his face already. I do hope and will work hard and pray for these fellows, one of whom by the way may be rusticated for six weeks. It's awful—the need for Christ here at Yale! I am thankful for our Personal Workers' Group, for our Volunteer Band and for *friends* like Charlie and others.

The current of his thoughts was changed a few days later by an unexpected visit from his parents. It was early in April, and everything was tingling with the new life of spring. To John and William it was a special pleasure to show their father the college campus, and the joy of those hours was unshadowed by any premonition of coming sorrow. Strange to say, it was only a week later that William was writing from Chicago, telling of the grief of their homecoming.[3]

Friday, April 13, 1906

Father and Mother were east about a week ago and had a fine visit with us. First they went to Vassar and heard the

[3] A letter to Dr. Henry W. Frost of the China Inland Mission.

debate, in which Mary did very well. This pleased Father immensely. Then they came on to Yale, and John and I had a nice visit with them. It was the first time Father had visited either John or myself at school or college. After leaving us they went down to New York, got Mary and went to Lakewood. There Mary spent a day or two with them and had a fine time. . . .

Back in Chicago, Father was perfectly well apparently, and had nice visits with most of his near relatives and friends. Saturday evening last he was taken sick, and on Sunday became critically ill. It was then we were summoned. Mary got here Monday evening in time to see him, though he was unconscious. John and I arrived on Tuesday morning, three or four hours after he had passed away.

William was only eighteen, but from that time he took more than a son's place at his mother's side. With him, love was a matter of deeds rather than of words, and in the midst of his college work he made time to write to her daily, with few exceptions. What that correspondence meant, keeping him in touch with all that concerned her, bringing the strong comfort of his sympathy into her aching loneliness, only a mother's heart can understand. If it cost some sacrifice, some moments of weariness after the strenuous day, the letters never showed it. They were always cheery and tender, and frequently contained charges not to reply unless she felt equal to writing.

April 21, 1906

DEAR MOTHER—I haven't much to tell you this evening, but just thought I'd write a little note to send you my love. . . . The weather continues pleasant and I can literally see the leaves grow from day to day. . . . I will try and write often, but don't you try to.

April 24, 1906

Tuesdays are always my hard days, that is, busy ones, as you can easily see when I tell you how my time is occupied.

I get up about seven, dress, have my Morning Watch, which I like to call my "breakfast" for "man doth not live by bread alone, but by every word that proceedeth out of the mouth of God"—go to breakfast and then Chapel. From eight thirty until four in the afternoon my studies keep me busy. From four to five I try and get in an hour's practice (piano) and at five we have our meeting for personal workers. After that, supper and study until nine, when my Bible Study Group meets for about an hour.

This has been the program today, so you see that until now, 10:30 P.M., I have been kept moving. But I sort of like it; it's just about enough.

Farrand brought another fellow down to my room tonight for our Bible Class. He is sort of an earnest-minded agnostic, and we hope to get hold of him as well as the others.

April 28, 1906

This afternoon Jim Whittaker and I went off on a glorious horseback ride together. We went way out in the country and then struck down to the Sound and came back to New Haven along the shore. The air and everything was fine and I enjoyed it immensely.

May 3, 1906

We had an examination in Ruskin and Byron the other day in which I am quite sure I did well. Also my standing in Analytical Geometry is nearly as good as in Trigonometry. In fact everything goes well but my Greek. I somehow find that hard and tiresome and don't seem to make a great success of it. But I'm going to work hard these *few*, for they are few, remaining weeks and see if I can't get as good in it as in my other subjects.

May 4, 1906

At our last group meeting I asked the fellows what they thought about our present method, and the majority were for continuing it. Some of them are doing work outside (Bible Study). . . . I gave Tom the name of Dawson's book, *Mod-*

ern Ideas of Evolution, and think he will get it soon if he hasn't already done so. I have gotten my sceptical friend a little bit interested on the evolution theory, and may be able to do something with him.

May 5, 1906

To-day was the day of the track games and the old Hill distinguished herself by winning the meet with a margin of ten and a half points. I saw Mr. Sweeney and the fellows, most all of whom I knew. It was fine. . . . After supper Farrand and I went over to Charlie's room and had a good rough-house. It was real interesting and amusing. I have to relax Saturday afternoon and evening, but now I'm going to do a little work for Monday.

To-morrow being Communion, we don't have any prayer meeting. I think I'll try and get in a little more Bible study and have a few talks with fellows. . . . Mother, I know you're tired. I can see it in your handwriting. You've got to get rested and strong. So don't try and write or exert yourself unnecessarily in any way.

May 9, 1906

I am rather enjoying my track work and as Johnny Mack, the trainer and coach, condescends to say a word now and then, I'm almost getting a "swelled head," but not quite. I suppose if I work hard, after two or three years I may be some good. I am working with both shot and hammer, each weighing sixteen pounds.

May 12, 1906

To-day, Yale distinguished herself in many ways. They easily won from Princeton in Track, won the Inter-collegiate shoot from Penn, beat Holy Cross in Baseball, 10-7 I believe, the Freshman Crew beat out the Columbia Freshmen, and the Freshman Ball team was also victorious. Quite a day, was it not? I relaxed all right!

May 13, 1906

Charlie has just been in and told me some very encouraging things about his work with certain fellows. The more I see of him and the better I come to know him, the more I see to wonder at and admire. He's taught me more than one lesson. A fellow said to me the other day, "It would be a mighty good thing for the College if there were a few more fellows like Charlie Campbell." He's as near perfect as anyone I have ever known. If I'm to be up at six (for their early prayer meeting) I must go to bed. Lots of love.

May 15, 1906

This evening we had our little Bible study group, seven fellows being present. We took up the fifth chapter of John which has important teachings on the Divinity of Christ, the Second Coming and the Resurrection, the Authority of the Old Testament, etc. We had an interesting and I hope a profitable time.

I have a good many openings now which I ought to make use of. You know I said Charlie had taught me a good many things. Well perhaps two principal ones are to have patience and not to waste time. I was up in his room the other day and when he had finished what he was doing he said, "What useful thing can I do next?" With such an example, and there are others, I guess there's hope for me.

May 17, 1906

Thank you for the book, *God's Image in Man,* which arrived to-day. . . . As I was up at a quarter to six and have been going pretty well all day, I am a little tired. However, it is early yet, and I have my work ready for to-morrow, so I expect a good rest. I'm sorry, but I haven't anything much to say. I love you very dearly and am looking forward to the time when I shall see you.

May 21, 1906

We have just celebrated Omega Lambda Chi to-night, which is a rather strenuous proceeding. First we all—the whole college—danced around hippity-hop, finally ending up at the campus. Then there was a race between the sophomores and freshmen. After this we had a tug-of-war. Nearly the whole college tacked on, seniors and sophs at one end and juniors and freshmen at the other. We just walked it over to York Street when somebody foolishly tried to take it into Pearson Hall. Then the sophs got it going and we couldn't stop them for quite a while. Had an awful scrap which finally ended up on Chapel Street. I have a small piece of the rope. . . .

But there is something more interesting to tell you. As things have worked out it seems almost providential that I stayed here. For Saturday night Farrand and I went down to Savin Rock, one of those "rotten" summer resorts. They have a lot of merry-go-rounds and such amusements, but also saloons and dance halls. We went to the dance hall and found a mess in the saloon. A lot of college fellows in various stages of drunkenness with a lot of loose women, also more or less drunk. It was positively disgusting. I am thankful to say there were no fellows from our class there.

But there was a fellow there who had been expelled from Hill, whom I knew. He is living here in New Haven, tutoring. Well, I watched him and spoke to him after I saw him go to a couple of these women. But he wouldn't come away. So we just literally followed them and got on the same car as they did to return to New Haven. There's no use describing that ride. Finally his girl got off alone and said "Good-night" very distinctly, for us to hear. I went and spoke to the fellow and he was mad as thunder and a little under the influence of liquor. After a block or two he slipped off and was starting back. I spoke to him but he wouldn't stop, so Farrand and I had to use a little physical force to restrain him. . . . We *had* to stop him. Of course he was very obstinate, but after about half or three-quarters of an hour we won him around and he walked home with us. We said everything we could think of and prayed when we got home. He's in with an awful bunch and I don't know just what to do. But we know that "with God all things are possible."

Charlie has been working with a fellow most of the year. His boast was that he'd broken every commandment but one. As he isn't in jail, I suppose that one is murder. Well, Charlie and I prayed that he might get a talk with X. The other day his uncle died and on returning he nearly went off again (that is to the bad) but went up to Charlie's room instead, and he was there alone. Charlie told me how hard it was, how he beat around the bush, and prayed. But thank God, he won out, and had a fine talk with X, who has decided to give Christ a chance in his life. Charlie and I prayed and took Christ's words, "Him that cometh unto me, I will in *no* wise cast out." I feel convinced that X. is started all right, and what's more I think he's going to be a power. For he is a skilful debater and if he found Christ he could have a strong influence. It's wonderful, isn't it, and glorious!

Sunday I had another talk with S., my sceptical, indifferent friend, but accomplished very little apparently. The preacher was fine I thought and very helpful.

This morning we met again at 6:30 and had a fine time of prayer.

May 23, 1906

This afternoon I went down and called on my friend whom I was with at Savin Rock, the other night. He was tutoring, but came down and saw me. Later we went to the ball game together. I had hoped to bring him to the Bible class and then maybe have a talk afterwards, but I couldn't do this. However he isn't mad at me and I'm going to see him again.

May 24, 1906

This was Tap Day, rather an interesting event to witness for the first time.[4] On the first stroke of five o'clock the tapping began, and continued for about three-quarters of an hour. Tapping is rather a misnomer, for they hit the men most tremendously and rush them off to their rooms. B.C. went Scroll and Keys and B.B. was the last man tapped for Skull and Bones. Bill Barnes also went Bones. This is a great honour, as it means he is head of that Society for next year. It's all very

---

[4] The day when the senior societies make known their elections—the most coveted honor in an undergraduate's career. Skull and Bones, Scroll and Keys and Wolf's Head are the senior fraternities. As, collectively, they only take in about forty-five new members each year, the large majority of aspirants is necessarily disappointed.

well in a way, but they make entirely too much of it, it seems to me.

Well as a result of this excitement I haven't done my work as I should, and must get busy now.

May 25, 1906

We have only a week and a half more of recitations now. It is hard to realize that freshman year is nearly over. I have seen nine fellows to-day about Bible study next year, and all have expressed their willingness to join a group. S., my sceptical friend, is one of these, and a fellow who doubts the immortality of the soul is another. I think it is going fine.

May 28, 1906

Farrand is working now with a fellow who has been going with women. He is the son of a Presbyterian Elder, and says his father would be simply dumbfounded if he should hear about it. It's pitiful and awful. I keep hearing things, and am beginning to realize that it's much more widespread than I had supposed.

May 29, 1906

We have just had quite a time with a fellow. Charlie, Farrand and I were walking along when a man, a town fellow, came up half-drunk and spoke to us. He swore, as they always do, and Charlie asked him if he knew who Christ was, whose name he had just spoken. Well, this started things and I brought him up to my room and we talked things over and prayed with him. He was quite deeply touched once or twice, but wouldn't take any definite action. However, we saw him home after having filled him up with water so that he didn't want any more liquor. He was quite intelligent and said he would come and see us again. We did what we could and are trusting God for the rest.

May 30, 1906

To-day we have had a holiday. In the morning Mitch, Jim, Whitaker, Farrand and I went off for a horseback ride. The horses were frisky, the country beautiful and the air fine. . . . In the afternoon we went down to the harbour and got a motor-boat, which I ran, being the only one who had had much experience with engines. We had some good fun and I enjoyed being on the water, the first time since last summer. Altogether it has been a day of pure sport, and I guess it has done us all good.

Borden's freshman year came to a wonderful climax in the Yale Summer Conference that followed Commencement. Debarred from the Student Conference at Northfield on account of its early date that year, they arranged for a gathering of their own under the leadership of Dr. Henry Wright, availing themselves of the grounds and buildings of the Hotchkiss School at Lakeville, Conn. One feature of the conference was a special course of training given to men who were to be leaders of voluntary groups for Bible study in the following year, for Borden's plan of small separate groups was to be extended to all the classes. A canvass had already been made, and out of Borden's class alone more than a hundred and fifty men were reported as willing to take up regular study in this way. This meant the preparation of a large body of leaders, who were keen to get all they could from the full program of the conference.

Half the substantial reporter's notebook Borden had had with him in London is filled with jottings from this Lakeville Conference, showing how very much it meant to him. Even in those full days of meetings, sports and personal work—for he was leading one of the daily groups for Bible study—he found time to write with the same loving thoughtfulness to his mother.

July 3, 1906

Whom do you suppose we had with us Sunday? S. D. Gordon! Before breakfast a few of us met in Henry Wright's room for prayer—our personal workers' group. Afterwards we met with Mr. Gordon. At 10 A.M. he gave us a talk on Power. It was wonderful. I will tell you more about it later. In the afternoon, down by the brook, he spoke on John 7:37-39 in his quiet way.[5]

Monday our regular Bible study groups started. The subject was Jesus and the Father. Beginnings are all hard, and possibly this was a hard subject to draw the fellows out on. . . . Today the subject was Jesus and Sin, a splendid one indeed, and we all got along much better. In my group is a Chinese nobleman's son. I'm not sure but that he is a Viceroy's son. He is one of our classmates, and is interested, as is shown by the fact that he is here.

In the course of study on Student Summer Missions, Henry (Dr. Wright) is outlining for us ten studies on Traits of Manhood. We had "Honesty" this morning, and it was splendid. I must get some boys together as soon as I get back to Camden.

Charlie and all the rest are here, and it's fine! I am rooming with Farrand and think he may come to Camden with me. . . . Charlie, I am afraid, can't come. I must close now, as I am to play on The Hill team against the Grads. Until just a moment ago I forgot that you were praying for me. The recollection has given me strength.

I am remembering you. Don't be lonely.

In his notebook Borden had written after Sunday's talks:

Say "No" to self, "Yes" to Jesus every time. A steep road—hard work? But every man on this road has One who walks with him in lock-step. His presence overtops everything that has been cut out. . . .

In every man's heart there is a throne and a cross. If Christ is on the throne, self is on the cross; and if self, even a little bit, is on the throne, Jesus is on the cross in that man's heart. . . . If Jesus is on the throne, you will go where He wants you to go. Jesus on the throne glorifies any work or spot. . . .

[5] "If any man thirst let him come unto me and drink. He that believeth on me . . . out of him shall flow rivers of living water." Rivers, Jordans, but clear as crystal. The proposition of the world is *into,* turning man into a Dead Sea. The proposition of Jesus is *out of.* Note that *out of.*—From Borden's notes.

If you are thirsty, and He is enthroned, *drink*. Drinking, the simplest act there is, means taking. "He that believeth on Me, out of him shall flow rivers of living water. This spake He of the Spirit." To "believe" is *to know,* because of His word. How shall I know that I have power to meet temptation, to witness for Him? Believe His word: it will come.

Lord Jesus, I ʾke hands off, as far as my life is concerned. I put Thee on ʾ ʾ throne in my heart. Change, cleanse, use me as Thou shalt choose. I take the full power of Thy Holy Spirit. I thank Thee.

May never know a tithe of the result until Morning.

CHAPTER 8

SOPHOMORE

1906-1907. AGE 18-19

His lamps are we,
To shine where He shall say:
And lamps are not for sunny rooms
Nor for the light of day;
But for dark places of the earth
Where shame and wrong and crime have birth;
Or for the murky twilight grey
Where wandering sheep have gone astray,
Or where the lamp of faith burns dim
And souls are groping after Him.

ANNIE JOHNSTON FLINT

WAS IT ONE RESULT of the step taken at the Lakeville Conference that in sophomore year Borden was drawn into most unexpected and fruitful work for others? The Living Water was flowing out in new, unlooked-for channels.

But first he had to face the fraternity question which had been causing him a good deal of exercise of mind. There were five junior (Greek letter) societies at Yale, as well as the three senior fraternities already referred to in Borden's letters. Unless a man had been elected in sophomore year to membership in one of the five, the senior societies would as a matter of course pass him by. Each of the junior societies received thirty new members annually, and as with the senior fraternities, the greatest possible secrecy was observed in all their proceedings. A fraternity man would "keep still" if his society were even

117

mentioned. It was this secrecy and the exclusiveness of the system that troubled Borden, whose uncle had been one of the founders of Wolf's Head, of which his brother was a member. "He could have had anything here that he wanted," wrote Dr. Kenneth Latourette in this connection. But, though feeling no less than others how hard it would be to be shut out, Borden had his misgivings. His friend Charles Campbell recalls:

> Shortly before College opened, Bill asked me to come to Poughkeepsie[1] to talk over the society question. He invited James M. Howard and E. F. Jefferson at the same time. The discussion centred about such questions as these: Could we as Christians go into a secret society? Would such action harm or help our work for Christ? It was a new thought to most of us. We had taken the society system very much for granted, and had never questioned whether it was right or wrong for us to join one of the fraternities. But Bill took nothing for granted. He was a servant of Jesus Christ, and everything must be tested and bear the stamp of Christ's approval before he would enter upon it.
>
> The element of secrecy was one of Bill's difficulties with regard to joining a fraternity. As a Christian he felt that he should not go into anything that he did not clearly understand beforehand. Then he feared that the fraternity system led to the forming of cliques in the college. He did not wish to be set apart from the class. Further, Bill did not wish to have anything come between him and God. He had given himself wholeheartedly to Christ, to be His follower pure and simple, and he wanted that relation kept always real. Therefore he felt he had no right to vow allegiance to any secret, man-made organization.
>
> This attitude is entirely comprehensible to the thoughtful Yale man who thinks back to his freshman year and remembers how certain men lose their heads and set out to make a fraternity as the be-all and end-all of existence. I remember Bill's telling

---

[1] A place on one of the most beautiful reaches of the Hudson River, where Mrs. Borden had taken a house to be near Vassar College in her daughter's senior year.

me of one classmate who said that he should consider his college course a failure unless he made Delta Kappa Epsilon among the first ten elected. Happily such insanity does not continue long after the verdant stage. This man, as I remember, never made Delta Kappa at all, but another fraternity in its second election, and I am sure he did not, as a senior, think his course a failure—certainly we, his classmates, did not.

The discussions at Poughkeepsie brought out much that was to be said on both sides, but no definite decision was arrived at. The first fraternity elections would not be given out until a month after college reopened, so Borden and his friends went back with the question more or less unsettled. The position this little group held in the estimation of their classmates is seen in an interesting light as the letter continues:

A short time before the fraternity elections were given out, the class elected the "Deacons." At Yale, during our time, each class chose four men at the beginning of sophomore year who acted as deacons in the University Church and were charged with responsibility for the religious work of their class. The day of the elections, Bill, Jim Howard, Pop Jefferson and I prayed that God would guide the choice, so that the right people should be appointed. As it turned out, the four of us were chosen! We always used to laugh about that—it seemed so like praying for ourselves.

Soon after came the first elections to the junior fraternities. We had talked together many times since the visit in Poughkeepsie, and had discussed the society question from every point of view. I think Bill talked the matter over with Henry Wright and one or two others, and of course with his mother. The final outcome was Bill's decision to go into no society. The others of us decided to join if we had the opportunity.[2] Bill adhered to this decision all through his college course, never joining a secret society, though he did join the Elihu Club, a non-secret organization, at the close of his junior year.

[2] All three were among the first elected.

That the decision cost him a good deal is evident from letters to his mother:

October 3, 1906

Last night I had several callers—two bunches of Psi U men, one of Delta K.E., one of Zeta Psi. But as I'm not worrying, it didn't bother me, and I was able to study between their visits. I knew most of them.

October 6, 1906

I have had more ups and downs in the last day or two than I've ever had before, I think. Nothing very serious to be sure, but annoying. Just at present I'm recovering from a down. Your little notes are a great source of comfort and enjoyment. I am going out to get some exercise now, throwing the hammer.

October 18, 1906

Well, I guess I wanted to go in a good deal more than I realized. . . . I have not slept much the last few nights I know. The question yesterday resolved itself into this: Are secret societies a good thing—from the Christian standpoint, of course? I cannot feel that they are either good or necessary, therefore I cannot go into one and lend them my support. I hope that God will bless Jim and Jeff and Charlie and use them mightily, but I cannot see my way clear. It is settled.

He felt like a different man, he wrote as soon as this decision was reached. "Busy and happy" was his next report. The sacrifice had been great, greater perhaps than anyone realized, but the reward was great too. Far from losing influence by not being a member of a fraternity, Dr. Kenneth Latourette stated that "as a matter of fact he had more influence with his classmates in his senior year than ever before." He had more freedom also, and more time to give to his work as a deacon and in other spiritual ways. And this meant much, as it proved, in connection with unexpected developments.

It was on his nineteenth birthday, the first of November, that

John Magee, the graduate Secretary of the Y.M.C.A., stopped him in Dwight Hall and asked for a few minutes' conversation. There were matters in which he needed help that he felt Borden could give.

New Haven, a seaport town midway between New York and Boston, was a place where vagrants of all sorts were apt to congregate. Work was to be had on the docks, and it was a halfway house for tramps and hoboes moving from one city to the other. It was also the location of the county jail, from which prisoners were constantly being discharged with no one to give them a helping hand. For while drinking saloons and infamous resorts were to be found in abundance there was no Rescue Mission with its doors always open to those who needed succor. This state of things appealed to John Magee from a double point of view. He saw the need of the down-and-out; he saw also the possible influence of such a mission upon the college community, as a witness to the living, saving power of Christ. And he believed that Borden would see and feel it too.

"For," as a modern writer has well stated, "there is an empiricism of religion which is worth attention. It challenges the sceptic to explain both the conversion of the sinner and the beauty of the saint. If religion can change a man's whole character in the twinkling of an eye, if it can give a beauty of holiness to human nature such as is felt by all men to be the highest expression of man's spirit, truly it is a science of life which works and one which its critics must explain. . . . Let the sceptic bring his indictment against the lives of those who attribute to Christ alone the daily miracle of their gladness."

What could the unbeliever make, for example, of a man who had been the terror of the worst ward in New York, the river-thief who would not have hesitated, as he said himself, "to cut a man's throat for a five dollar bill, and kick him overboard," who was sentenced to fifteen years' hard labor in Sing Sing when he was only nineteen, and came out to sink ever deeper into drunkenness and sin, with no power to break his chains—until Christ met and transformed him? Yet that man was Jerry McAuley, who established in his old haunts the first of such Rescue Missions, and was a means of temporal and spiritual blessing to thousands.

What would the skeptic do with the educated, able man of business, entangled in the meshes of the drinking habit, sinking from depth to depth of misery, until his friends, home and wife all gone, haunted by crimes he had committed—a hundred and twenty forgeries against one man alone—tormented with the horrors of delirium tremens, there was nothing before him but the jail or suicide, and he had chosen the latter? Yet that man was Samuel H. Hadley, McAuley's successor in the Water Street Mission, and like him an apostle of the lost. Truly "if any man be in Christ Jesus he is a new creation."

Knowing such facts as these it was little wonder that Magee and Borden began to pray that a similar mission might be established in New Haven, for the sake of the University no less than for the unfortunate. To his mother Borden wrote:

November 1, 1906

John Magee is trying his best to do just what we have wanted done—to develop the evangelistic element and spirit here at Yale. As you may know, Dr. J. W. Dawson is to be here for a week in February.[3] The present head of the McAuley Mission in New York is a college graduate who went down, down, and was converted about two years ago, Edward C. Mercer. They had him at Princeton recently, and John has been enquiring to see how it went down there. He found that it was fine, and he is going to invite him here to speak at Dwight. That's just what I've been hoping for, and I think you have too. John is really a corker and is doing a lot.

He had me up in his room to-day to speak about the need

[3] A well-known writer and preacher who had had remarkable experiences in revival and midnight meetings.

for a good City Mission here in New Haven. . . . The plan is to get a suitable building in the down-town district and have a real Rescue Mission, run by a man from Water Street, or some such place, and a few picked men from the University. . . . It would be great!—just the thing to take a few sceptics down and let them see the Spirit of God really at work regenerating men.

November 8, 1906

Last night I went over and saw Magee. Mr. Skinner and old Brother Martin (converted drunkards) met with us, and we talked over plans for the City Mission. I tell you it was inspiring to hear those men talk! . . . We decided to pray over the matter for a week and see what would develop. I hope to go to the prison with them a week from Sunday. They go once a month. The prospects for the Mission are very bright, and I feel sure we shall have it, if it is the Lord's will.

Meanwhile his classroom work was not neglected. At the close of freshman year Borden had discovered that his marks were not up to Phi Beta Kappa standard, and he decided to change his habits of study. Previously he had gone on the method of studying up for each recitation just before it came. Now he set himself to prepare a day ahead, and never retired for the night without having all his preparation completed for the following day.

"It was a hard method to live up to," commented his friend Campbell, "and showed his strength of will. Think of what it meant on Saturday to get all Monday's work out of hand. For Bill never studied on Sunday. He would work till eleven or eleven-thirty at night, but not later. Then he could sleep quietly, and be ready for whatever calls upon his time might come. It meant much in his mental make-up and when it came to examinations."

"I figured up yesterday where my time went per week," Borden wrote early in sophomore year, "and found that about thirty-five hours are wasted somehow. I am going to see if I can't systematize, so as to get the most use out of them."

That he must have been successful in this effort is evident from the amount of work he was able to get through in addition to his studies as the year went on. The daily prayer groups were still kept up, as he wrote to his mother in December:

> You just *must* come to New Haven and meet these fellows, J. B. and B. R. especially. The latter is the latest addition to our group and is growing every day. It is interesting that out of our bunch of eleven, eight should be A men, one B and two C; a pretty good showing I think.

The responsibilities of Class Deacon were taken seriously by the four friends. It seems that the office, which is much respected, dates back to the founding of "The Church of Christ in Yale," in 1756. Up to that time the students and faculty had attended the old Congregational Church on The Green, but it was felt that a different style of preaching was desirable from that suited to the usual mixed assembly. Much opposition had to be overcome, but ultimately the University Church was organized on Congregational lines. As in that fellowship the officers are not elders but deacons, the term "Class Deacon" was adopted to designate the students chosen by the undergraduate body as their representatives in church affairs.

In Borden's time they held their meetings weekly, a committee of twelve men, four from each of the sophomore, junior and senior classes, charged with the spiritual interests of their fellow students.[4] These meetings were times of sincere prayer for help and guidance, and resulted in "strong friendships that

---

[4] "The verdict of men most in touch with life on the campus is that the morals and tone of the undergraduates are unusually high and clean, and steadily improving. That such is the case is largely due to the presence year after year of this small, earnest body of men, elected by the classes, but connected with and under the control of the Church, to lead the Christian work and set an example of manly living." From *Two Centuries of Christian Activity at Yale.* Chapter on "The Class Deacons," by S. H. Fisher, p. 208.

gave a certain sense of unity to the religious life in the college."
Borden and his friends had been already on the Freshman
Religious Committee, and brought to these new opportunities
the same earnest aggressive spirit.

And all the while, Borden was writing just as frequently to
his mother.

October 21, 1906

Charley, Jeff and I got together to-day and divided up the
class (consisting of about three hundred men). The plan is
for each deacon to have a quarter of the class as his parish and
to *know* every individual man. It will take time, but we believe it will pay.

October 24, 1906

Things are going to hum this year, or I'm very much mis-
taken. We deacons meet with Joe Twitchell, '06, the College
Y.M.C.A. Secretary, every Wednesday evening. He is very
amusing in his impetuosity, but very frank and good-natured.

December 10, 1906

You will be pleased to hear that X. is getting on very well
in every way (the classmate who formerly boasted that he had
broken every commandment but one). He leads a Sunday
School class and has a Phi Beta Kappa stand in his studies.
Rather a contrast with last year!

Had my first exam. to-day, Physics. It was very hard.

Have received six Christmas invitations. Guess I'm still in
society!

Sunday, January 20, 1907

We have had a fine time to-day, and I feel like singing the
Doxology. . . .

You remember I told you that the first meeting of our Bible
Class with the new teacher wasn't much good. Well, Wednesday we had an extra good prayer meeting at noon, and had
faith. The result was we had a *fine* meeting that evening, though
not many fellows were present. Charlie and I spoke to Mr. C.

afterwards and said that we were behind him in prayer. He was very nice, and we feel confident for the future.

My Mission Study class went very nicely on Thursday.

I am thankful to say I have been doing a little more real work for Christ. I asked N.S. to go and hear Gipsy Smith, and he said he would if possible. I also wrote to M. T., following up our talk at Camden. D. W. was on my heart, and I wrote a pretty plain letter to him. This is about all my long-distance work.

With F. I haven't done much more, but the door is open. My work with S. is going finely. After our Bible groups to-day, which went very well, I had the best talk with him I've ever had. He's nearly there, I believe.

Charlie's work is going well. He has a new group started to-day (Bible Study) among some seemingly impossible fellows. He is getting hold of perhaps the brightest man in the class, who is also one of the most dissipated. . . .

This afternoon and evening though were the best. At Band Meeting a Mr. Smeet from China spoke to us. He was filled with the spirit and gave a wonderful message which stirred Ken and me deeply, and we are going to work more for volunteers out of 1909. The evening service had a fine message for us too. Everything is leading up to the meetings Feb. 3-9, in answer to prayer.

Here on my floor things are going badly. The fellows play cards a great deal—most of it is gambling, and on Sunday too.

January 25, 1907

Things have been moving here in a great way. We went over our class again among the group leaders and made a new canvass. Charlie and I each took a hard bunch of fellows, and after a little prayer went *trusting* in God. The way opened up wonderfully, and we each have a new group started, mine of four men, his of ten. Charlie has three groups now, and I two beside my Mission Study Class. So we are busy—with our studies and exercise.

Yet at this very time they were planning for the rescue work which early in the new year took shape as The Yale Hope Mission. The visit of Dr. Dawson and Mr. Mercer could hardly have been more opportune, demonstrating the power of Christ and the need in men's lives for such a Saviour.

February 10, 1907

I have just come from the last of our special services, and it was fine. . . . The meetings have had a great effect. Mr. Mercer's talks have opened men's eyes to the evil of the "social glass." (That was what ruined him, while in the University of Virginia.) "Shef" has been moved as never before and is ripe for the reaping.[5] Every man in the University must be reached! . . .

I just want to say right now that any day in which work is not done for Christ is wasted. Moreover, I'm a fool for letting such days be—for they are *not pleasant*.

It was a welcome development therefore when, a few weeks later, the Rescue Mission was opened which provided new opportunities for the work he and others were learning to put first in their lives. Much of hope and prayer lay behind the modest beginning, of which Charlie Campbell wrote:

A room had been rented in a cheap hotel in just the right quarter—the room which has been used ever since for the meetings. It had hideous dark red paper in those days. Later on, Bill bought the entire building, and we now have downstairs dormitories and shower baths, and a place in which clothes can be fumigated, as well as a good, inexpensive lodging-house upstairs, known as the Hotel Martin.[6] For two dollars a week a man can have a room to himself, a little home.

But we had no such helps in those early days and did the more ourselves in consequence. I can remember distinctly how we carted hymn-books in my suit-case down to the hall for that first meeting. The handle of the suit-case broke, and we had to hoist it upon our shoulders and carry it through the

[5] "Shef," or Sheffield, was the scientific department of the University with over a thousand students.
[6] After "Daddy Martin," greatly beloved.

streets! Bill was heart and soul in it all. It was great to see him in those meetings—so earnest in his presentation of the truth and in dealing with those who came forward for prayer. Afterwards, he would often take men around until he could find a place for them to sleep, and pay the lodging-house charge himself so as to avoid putting temptation in their way by giving them money.

It was the sixteenth of March when this beginning was made, and before the month was over Borden was writing to his mother of a man from Water Street who was coming to live on the premises and take charge of the growing work.

Mr. Bernhardt was a graduate of the University of Georgia and did post-graduate work at Vanderbilt. He rose to the position of cashier in a big southern Express Company. Then, through gambling, he got into debt. This led to stealing, first a little, then more, then a large sum and he was caught. Result—five years in a southern prison which he found to be "a literal hell." He went in a comparatively innocent boy, and came out "a fiend." He could get nothing to do, so he deliberately became a professional criminal and was before long an international character. One of his sentences was, "work in the mines under the lash for *three and a half years, never seeing daylight*"!

In all, he spent over twenty-two years in prison. After the last term he "lost his nerve" and determined to be a man. He travelled eight thousand miles in search of employment, without success. At last, stranded in New York, he was about to commit suicide. On his way to the river he heard singing from the Water Street Mission and turned in. Nothing happened that night or the next, but the third night the great change came. I cannot tell you all about it—but he is a Christian now and no mistake!

His present job is clerking in a cheap Bowery hotel, but he is always ready, Mr. Mercer says, to go anywhere and speak for Christ. His ambition is to get into rescue work and devote his whole time to it. This is the man we have asked to come and take the Yale Hope Mission. All he wants is a clean place to sleep, three meals a day, decent clothes and some money in his pocket to "help the other fellow." Sixty dollars a month he says is too much, in addition to board and lodging, so we are to give him fifty.

Bernhardt was no disappointment. Many a man on the Yale campus as well as on the streets of New Haven had reason to thank God for his coming.

"The Yale Hope Mission is booming at present beyond all expectation," Borden wrote at the end of the month. "Bernhardt began last Sunday and that evening eight men came forward, several of them in dead earnest. I was unable to go down last night, but Magee told me that seven more were seeking salvation. Bernhardt is fine, and is taking hold of the work wonderfully."

CHAPTER 9

UPPER CLASSMAN

1907-1909. AGE 19-21

It takes great strength to bring your life up square
With your accepted thought and hold it there:

It is so easy to drift back, to sink,
So hard to live abreast of what you think.

C.P.S.

IT WAS CHARACTERISTIC of Borden and of his friend Campbell
that they did not room together either in junior or senior
year. But they were on the same floor in White Hall and had
what they valued most, the opportunity of being helpful to
others. With lively recollections Campbell wrote:

In the selection of quarters for junior year, Bill had chosen
a room in White Hall on Berkeley Oval, just off the old college campus. Malcolm B. Vilas of Cleveland was his roommate, a boy of fine character who had taken a positive Christian stand at the Lakeville Conference at the close of freshman
year.[1] Next door, I lived with Louis G. Audette, and across
the way were two other classmates, Sandford D. Stockton and
Frank Assman. It was a great combination, made up of very
different types, and what times we did have! Every now and
then we would get rid of superfluous energy in a big rough-
house. We would nag at Bill until we had him roused and then
something would be doing. Around that room he would go like

[1] The suite occupied by Borden and Vilas, a study and two bedrooms, was
on the fourth floor of White Hall (number 380) with an open outlook toward
the Yale gymnasium and West Rock.

a tornado, crushing all opposition. It was a sight to see him really roused. He was a fellow of unusual physical strength and knew how to use it to advantage. I found that the best way to treat Bill when he went at me was to give right in. This seemed to mollify him, while resistance only spurred him on to greater efforts. We used to have many a tussle, but he was altogether too strong for the average man, and with his knowledge of wrestling was more than a match for any of us. We would laugh at him because of his strength and call him a "brute."

The activities in the religious work went along much the same. There were the Bible groups, the mission study classes, the daily prayer groups, the Wednesday evening Bible classes, the Volunteer Band meetings and the Yale Hope Mission, all of which occupied Bill's time. The last named was specially absorbing for Bill this year. I believe he took one night a week at the Mission, conducting the service.

In our Christmas vacation (junior year) Bill went with Mrs. Borden and Joyce to the Lake Placid Club in the Adirondacks. It was a beautiful winter with several feet of snow on the ground in the mountains. Bill and his mother with their wonted hospitality decided to have a house-party. So invitations came to Isabel Corbiere, Mary Abbe and three of my sisters, with Mac Vilas, Bill Roberts, Lou Audette and myself. All but Mac Vilas were able to accept, and we arrived on New Year's Eve.

How crisp the mountain air was as we drove up in sleighs from the station and started in for a glorious party! We cast off all thought of work and settled down to healthy outdoor sport. Bill was in the thick of it. We would all dress up in our warmest old clothes and go out to the toboggan course. The snow was soft and all kinds of stunts were possible. We spent a good deal of time trying to go down the hill standing on the toboggans. Four or five of us would get on one toboggan, standing up, and would then launch out. There always came the time when one would lose balance and upset the rest, and away we would go head first into the snow. It was fine healthy sport, and Bill was right in his element.

Over on the road, coasting on the bob-sled was possible, and near the Club was good skating. One day we all ploughed off in the deep snow and climbed a little mountain near by. Every night we would turn up tired, healthily so, and ready for the biggest kind of dinner and the soundest sort of sleep. Bill simply revelled in good fellowship and sport such as this, and it did one good to be with him. He made an ideal host and always saw that his guests had a good time.

Few letters are available for junior and none for senior years, as Mrs. Borden, who was at that time in very poor health, was living in New Haven to be near her son, but the recollections of classmates tell a good deal. The last of his own letters follow that Christmas in the Adirondacks.

January 13, 1908

DEAR MOTHER—Things have been moving here since we came back and I am very thankful.

I believe I wrote you that we had gotten our prayer group started. It has been going nicely so far and will continue so I'm sure. Our mission study work promises very well indeed, not only the group I spoke of, but all the others. We shall have about twice as many men as we have had before.

Well, Saturday, things began to happen. Mr. and Mrs. Asher (Saloon Evangelists) conducted a union meeting of the missions in town. Charley and I prayed that it might be the right kind of meeting and then went to get some fellows to go. I got the whole of my last year's group, the tough bunch, and they stayed until the invitation was given. The meeting was fine, and Dr. Dawson who was here last year contributed not a little to its success.

Afterwards, I talked with a man until eleven, and hope to be able to help him more. On Friday Charley got a fellow he is working with to go to one of the Chapman meetings and I went to the Mission, and as the fellow who was leading (Bernhardt being away) didn't want to give the invitation, I did it. About eight men came forward and I conducted things as best I could. I feel very hopeful about some of them and that we've got a most important work on our hands.

As it's late, I'll reserve the rest, and best, for to-morrow. Lots of love, WILLIAM

January 14, 1908

I think you will be interested in my report of Sunday's happenings. The evening service was led by Dr. Dawson and was one of the most remarkable I've seen here yet. He spoke on the Price of Perfectness, from the rich young ruler passage, and put in very straight to the fellows. At the close he gave an invitation for all who wanted to follow Christ (I've forgotten just his words) and about twenty responded.

Right after I went over and saw a fellow named B., one of those I'd had at the Mission the night before. I started right in —having found him alone providentially—and we talked for about two hours, with the result that he finally decided that he would take Christ and try it. There are three others I want to get after.

January 20, 1908

Had a very nice group meeting which I didn't deserve, as I had expected the "Prom" to be more attractive. After it was over, S. spoke up and said that he was practically a Christian, believing almost as I did. He is (or was) the sceptical fellow I've been working with for months, since freshman year in fact. I expect to see him come out openly now in a very short time. It is wonderful.

"To him that hath shall be given" was certainly true in Borden's case, for one upon another, even in junior year, responsibilities came crowding upon him. The Student Missionary Union of colleges in the Connecticut Valley held its annual conference at New Haven that fall and Borden was chairman at all the meetings. Months of preparation lay behind the success of the gathering, and all the responsibility for speakers and arrangements had been on his shoulders. Stephen W. Ryder, a classmate who helped him, wrote:

As a stenographer and typewriter, I often took his dictation of letters to his friends. I specially remember quite an extensive correspondence which devolved upon him as chairman of the Connecticut Valley Student Missionary Conference. His apologies, his thoughtful explanations and general care to avoid misunderstandings, his desire to please, encourage and inspire others often impressed me. He sought no subterfuges or excuses, nor dealt in flattery to serve his ends. There was always frankness and sincerity in his letters.

* John Magee among others was impressed with the organizing ability Borden showed in handling this undertaking.

Bill was busy enough with all he was doing in College to take the time of any ordinary man. But he seemed to have little difficulty in running this Conference, in spite of the large amount of work connected with it, of which I had had experience. It was held in New Haven that year (1908) and I remember hearing a number of people remark on Bill's ability as a presiding officer. He was a regular John R. Mott, and had everything at his fingers' ends, everybody knowing just what meetings were to be held, and where, through his conciseness and clearness. All his correspondence beforehand, tentative programmes, bills, etc., were kept in such orderly fashion that he never had to waste time looking for anything.

This same ability in handling affairs came out in our work together in the Yale Hope Mission. Bill gave a great deal of attention to it, though he did not let it interfere with his other work as far as I could see. He went down to the meetings a great deal, and might often be found in the lower parts of the city at night—on the street, in a cheap lodging-house or some restaurant to which he had taken a poor hungry fellow to feed him—seeking to lead men to Christ.

Yet his studies were not neglected, for in February of junior year when the list of those who had made Phi Beta Kappa was announced, Borden was one of thirty chosen, and when the society organized a little later he was elected president for the coming year. In this connection Charles Campbell recalled:

At the Phi Beta Kappa banquet, which came late in the winter of 1908, Bill as president of the society took the lead. The Phi Beta Kappa banquet is perhaps the finest of the yearly banquets given at Yale. Many celebrated men are invited from other colleges and most of the best known professors of the University itself, so that the dinner is quite an affair. I have a pleasant recollection of the dignified way in which Bill presided and made the opening address. It was a striking illustration of the maturity and balance of the man.

Borden's college activities were summarized in the Yale Alumni Weekly as follows:

He was president of Phi Beta Kappa. In athletics he was active in football, baseball, crew and wrestling, rowing on the winning, 1909. club crew in the fall of junior year,[2] and playing on the winning Philosophical and High Oration baseball team and on the Phi Beta Kappa team. He served on the Class Book Committee and on the Senior Council. Elected a Class Deacon, he devoted himself largely to religious work. He was unwilling to join any fraternity or secret society, because he feared that it might set him apart from the body of the class. He accepted, however, an election to the Elihu Club.

Not a little additional work was entailed by his election to the Senior Council, with its special relation to the faculty, and by his duties as a member of the Senior Class Book Committee.

"Bill was keenly interested in doing his full share of drudgery for the good of his class," wrote a fellow-deacon. "I remember going into his room frequently when he was summing up class-statistics. He spent hours collecting from the blanks the votes for individual preferences. Often he would pause for a rest, and joke about some bright answer to a question."

2 "One of the events of the regatta on Lake Whitney," wrote Mr. C. Campbell, "was a race between the four class crews. This was won by 1909, Bill's class. I have before me the cup awarded to him for his part in this race. It is inscribed: 'Fall Regatta, 1907, Club Championship, won by 1909. W. W. Borden, Number four.' "

His own standing, when the Class Book appeared, was third in the vote for "the hardest worker," fourth among "the most energetic," ninth among "the most to be admired," and seventh in the vote for "the one who had done most for Yale"; this in a class of close upon three hundred.

But it was in the small, intimate meetings of the Student Volunteer Band that Borden was most himself, as Stephen W. Ryder recalls:

> It was there the flame of his spiritual life seemed to glow most brightly. There reserve was thrown aside; he was among those who were in sympathy with his life-purpose. His presence in the Band kept the spiritual tone right up to concert pitch. . . . It will always be an inspiration to remember him there, in his true element.

And Dr. Kenneth Latourette:

> Of course the outstanding thing in one's memory of Bill is his missionary motive. He was so sane and unpretending about it, and yet it was so completely a part of his life. The memory of it and his courage to carry the gospel to unreached fields is a constant rebuke and inspiration to me. He had the Pauline spirit. I recall how he quoted him, about not wanting to build on another man's foundation (Romans 15:20, 21). The steadfastness of that purpose of Bill's had no small part, I am sure, in bringing the largest Volunteer Band in Yale's history into the days of his college life.

The same friend touched the secret of the power of that life when he wrote:

> How easy Bill was to pray with! He was a jolly fellow—loved a rough-house; delighted to get hold of a man and crack his ribs! He could be jolly with the rest, and when the crowd was gone it would be just as natural for him to say,
>
> "Come into the bedroom and let us have prayer together."
>
> There was no sense of incongruity about it. I remember very vividly—how could one ever forget—those times of prayer,

when just the two of us would kneel down and take to God some of the problems we were facing. Bill was so simple in his prayer life, so natural, so trustful! He was the easiest man to pray with I have ever known.

Prayer was to him his most important work, as well as the breath of his life. He had a card-system for recording prayers and their answers in connection with individuals who were on his heart, and a loose-leaf note-book in which he listed subjects for prayer in groups, one for each day of the week. To take in the meaning of those notes even for one day is a revelation of the depth and thoroughness of the prayer life they represent, reaching out to the ends of the earth. It helps one to understand the statement made by his most intimate friend, Campbell:

> Through all the time I have known him, when there has been opportunity, we have never parted without going on our knees and praying for God's work.

It is easy to see how much this friendship must have meant to the two who were in every way so fitted for and worthy of each other.[3] But there was nothing exclusive about it, any more than about Borden's religion. "Bill was to me the rarest Christian spirit I have ever known," was the estimate of one now on the faculty—and yet he was so very human too!

"No picture of Bill at New Haven would be complete," wrote Jefferson to another of the Class Deacons, "without the old slouch hat he used to wear so often. Remember it? It was of brownish grey, pointed at the top, torn on the side, and with a large convenient hole used to hang it up by. One time I set

---

[3] "Campbell prepared for Yale at Kingsley School and at the Montclair Military Academy. He got a Philosophical Oration appointment and is a member of Phi Beta Kappa; a member of the University track team for the last three years; he won his 'Y' in the pole vault in the inter-collegiate meet, sophomore year. Elected a Deacon, sophomore year, his chief interest in college has been Dwight Hall, of which he is president. He is an active Bible group leader. He served on the Class Day committee. Zeta Psi. Skull and Bones."— From *The History of the Class of 1909, Yale College.*

fire to Bill's hat. When he discovered the flame he was suddenly active to rescue the treasure and punish me for my presumption." The hat, it may be added, was not discarded even after this fiery ordeal.

Mac Vilas, his roommate for two years at Yale, spoke of him as "a Christian, first, last and all the time"; but he was interested in recalling details that showed that he was not narrow in his sympathies, and that socially as well as physically he was an all-round man.

In the letter he wrote accepting an invitation to be usher at my wedding, Bill spoke about not being a social light, etc., but we were delighted with the way he entered into the spirit of the occasion, and I believe he had just as much fun as the most frivolous of the rest of us. I mention this because it shows that his social instinct was strong. Here were a dozen or more young men and women, and Bill was simply one of us. All the girls told Helen that he was most entertaining and attractive to them, and they were girls used to meeting all sorts of men.

Bill also went to the 1909 Tea at our Junior Prom., with Helen and me and my aunt, who chaperoned Helen, and was very much at home on that occasion. I had a good time, too. Bill was not slow at the "fussing game," as his taking girls to the inter-collegiate matches also indicates. I, personally, was very happy to see this trait in him, and if it had not been there to a considerable extent our Cleveland "social butterflies" would never have enthused over him as they did.

Bill's interest in business affairs was something I frequently observed. He read the *New York Times* regularly at College, and also took and read the *Wall Street Journal*. I know that he was fairly conversant with the stock quotations from day to day and that he followed the big financial developments eagerly. How he could go the *Wall Street Journal* was a mystery to me. I think Prof. Emery's lectures in economics had something to do with starting his interest in those things.

Bill was very reticent about mentioning his financial affairs to me. In fact, I don't remember ever asking him a single thing about them, as I considered it none of my business. This reticence was, to my mind, another indication that he would have been a shrewd business man. He was able to keep his own counsel, to say little but think and work hard. Bill seemed to pay considerable attention to his Chicago business affairs, for he corresponded a good deal with Mr. Spink (I used to see the printed envelopes), and I remember his mentioning several business trips to Chicago. . . .

As to his wrestling, you know what a bull he was and how hard he wrestled and rough-housed. I remember in senior year one night, when Jeff was holding Lou and Frank at bay easily, how Bill just for fun rushed in, grabbed Jeff by the legs and tossed him back on his couch without much effort. You were there, I am sure. How thankful I am for those happy, happy days together, Charley! Len Parks can also witness to Bill's physical prowess and athletic enthusiasm. They used to wrestle together quite frequently, and Len was no slouch, but he couldn't throw Bill. He told me once that Bill was a "regular bear," and that though he didn't go in for fancy holds, etc., he was the hardest man to tackle in the whole gym. Len, I believe, threw even Bill Goebel a few times, but not Bill Borden.

Bill was also a loyal rooter for the teams at Yale. He attended practically all the games and meets, as I recall it. I remember well how he stood on Derby Avenue, between the bridge and the lower entrance to the track and baseball field, on the day in November, 1907, when we had the first cross-country run with Harvard. As we came up the little rise on Derby Avenue, before entering the gate, there was Bill, who had come down to meet us runners. When he saw that I was in the lead, he let out a most encouraging yell! Perhaps it was partly surprise—and I wouldn't blame him if it was. You and all the other fellows may have been there, I don't remember about that, but Bill's enthusiasm for and interest in his room-mate I can never forget. He had come down a little further than most of the fellows to give his encouraging support.

I believe I am right in saying that Bill was elected to every class office for which he was nominated, and I well remember one stormy class-meeting—we could scarcely hear ourselves speak—when a word of suggestion from him brought order out of chaos, and showed very clearly the quality of the fellows' respect and admiration for him.

Others also recall characteristics which impressed them:

No matter if some said he was too religious, or others that he was too narrow, or that he was heavy, there was one thing nobody at Yale ever questioned—that was that he was *strong*. He was red-blooded and he had the punch. He played hard and he studied hard and was intense in his religious beliefs. When he bucked the football line, every ounce of his hundred and seventy-five was back of him. When he was elected to the presidency of Phi Beta Kappa he received the highest scholarship honour in Yale. There was power written all over him. You either followed him or you let him alone. . . . I can vouch that he was the strongest religious force in our class at Yale.[4]

He certainly was one of the strongest characters I have ever known,[5] and he put backbone into the rest of us at College, who were interested in the same things but did not have the strength he had. There was real iron in him, and I always felt he was of the stuff martyrs were made of, and heroic missionaries of more modern times. Our point of view differed on many things; but it was always refreshing to discuss matters with him even if we disagreed, because I knew so well his strength of purpose and consecration. I had complete trust in him as a man. . . . He never seemed to lose his vision for a single instant. . . . Among many fine qualities, the supreme impression he made upon others, it seems to me, was that of moral rectitude.

Bill was the great example to me of one who seemed to realize always that he must be about his Father's business, and not wasting time in the pursuit of amusement. . . . He was a man who had very high ideals and lived up to them; who impressed his sincerity upon you by his daily life among his fel-

---

[4] Max Parry, a leading member of the class of 1909.
[5] John Magee, writing from China.

lows, no matter how restricting his beliefs might be. We disagreed about some things, and I thought Bill narrow, but as the years pass I am beginning to see that his perspective was the one which I am only just reaching. But I want to say that even when I disagreed with him, there was never a moment that I did not respect him for those same beliefs and the way in which he lived up to them.[6]

In his sophomore year we organized Bible-study groups and divided up the class of three hundred or more, each man interested taking a certain number, so that all might, if possible, be reached. The names were gone over one by one, and the question asked, "Who will take this person or that?" When it came to one who was a hard proposition there would be an ominous pause. Nobody wanted the responsibility. Then Bill's voice would be heard: "Put him down to me."

Thus he got together a group of the hardest to reach, the least attractive, and worked for them faithfully. In a house in College Street he had three of his incorrigibles, anything but promising material for a Bible class. I remember one meeting of the group when only one man was present, while another listened through a half-open door into the next room. But Bill held on, glad that they gave him the opportunity.

His rugged yet simple faith in Christ as Saviour and Lord, and in the Bible as God's inspired Word, is a tonic to me, for one, whenever I am tempted to drift into barren doubtings or a purely intellectual attitude toward our faith. But with all his convictions as to the futility of higher criticism and his distrust of the so-called new theology, I cannot recall hearing him speak unkindly, or even frequently, of the many who preached it to us from the Yale pulpit or lecture desk. He was always the Christian gentleman.[7]

There never was a time during those years when Bill was not looking for the opportunity of doing personal work.[8]

Joe Twitchell's remark in our Deacons' meeting one night was interesting, as showing something of Bill's idea of personal

[6] Farrand Williams.
[7] Professor Kenneth Latourette.
[8] Charles Campbell.

work. Joe said, "Bill hunts up the worst skunk in College, and goes after him."[9]

One of the passions of his life was for righteousness. He had indeed that "hunger and thirst" we read about in Matt. 5:6. His prayer-life was full of petitions that illustrated this, and his actual living illustrated it too.

I remember, in this connection, that after we had finished our final examinations in College we had a four days' interval before Commencement, and Bill with a few others of us ran up to his place in Maine and attempted to sail his boat down to New Haven. We had head-winds all the way, and could do no better than reach Cape Cod and put in to Hyannisport in time to take a train to New Haven. As we walked up the streets of Hyannisport, where Bill had spent a summer as a boy, he remembered that at the close of that vacation he had gone away owing some shopkeeper in the place a few cents. He had forgotten all about it, but it came back to him as we walked up the street that day, and he must needs find the little shop and pay the debt, that he might be straight with the world. That was his nature all through. If he found anything wrong with his life, he set to work to make it right.

But there is another characteristic of Bill's that I want to speak about, that is his great loving heart, which always seemed to me his richest and rarest quality. There were many, perhaps, who, seeing him in a casual way busy with the work he had to do, set him down as severe and unapproachable. We knew that the very opposite was true. He had one of the most affectionate, lovable natures of any man I have ever known. No one who visited in his home could for a moment doubt this. But I mean more than family love. He had a way, for example, when walking with a friend, of putting his arm over his shoulder as they talked. I can feel the great loving touch of his arm about my shoulder now.

After graduation we attended Northfield again, sleeping in a tent as before. For two summers, at least, Bill waited at table during the Conference. He never did this if there was a man needing the job to help to make expenses. But if the coast was

[9] E. F. Jefferson, Class Deacon and famous Yale first baseman.

clear, on would go the waiter's apron and he would do the work, getting nothing to eat himself until the crowd had left the dining-room. He never told me why he did this. It may have been partly to keep friends company who had to wait for monetary reasons. But I always felt it went deeper than that, and that Bill was trying to be among us as "he that serveth."[10]

Just one more picture from the Yale Hope Mission, from one of the early converts:

I came in here on the twenty-seventh of March, 1908. I was on a drunk and hadn't much use for religion. I'm not going to tell the worst part of my life, but I was a rambler all right— a down-and-out bum. There was only three states in the Union I hadn't been in. I had heard of the Mission, same as a good many of them do. I knew it was the only thing that would save me from booze. Well, I went out, that first night. I had a Christian mother, and I got to thinking of her and I came back. That was the twenty-ninth of March, and that night Bill was here and he spoke to me. Bill was a great personal worker. He always believed in getting right down and talking to a man. If Bill had anything to say he gave it right out. I know the gist of what he said to me that night.

"What are you going to do about it? Can't you see where you've missed the road?"

He would tell you to hope again; tell you of the God who'd made the universe and held you in the hollow of His hand and could help you if you'd only ask. That's the way he talked. He was one good boy. I could never forget him as long as I breathe—no, I never forget him. And he barely twenty that night I first knew him! He was at Yale College here then, and Louis Bernhardt was superintendent of the Mission.

I went forward and kneeled down and Bill came and kneeled down beside me, and he explained as much as he could the power of Jesus Christ, and how it was only Him who could help me. I never drank from that night to this, never felt like

10 Charles Campbell. The reference is to Luke 22:27.

it—never felt like it, from that twenty-ninth day of March to this—and before that I was drunk most of the time. I had been drunk all that winter. Bill was a great man to watch you and not say much, but just ask how you were getting along. Well, after I was converted I come every night—didn't miss a night after that for seven weeks.

It's all fresh in my mind yet. I got work, too, soon. I got a job on an ice-wagon. That was one of the greatest tests on the booze question that a man ever got. I was boss of the team that year, and went back and was boss again the second summer. I was boss sixteen or seventeen months altogether. I hadn't worked only three weeks when they put me in charge of the team.

I saw Bill right along those times, except in his vacation; then he was in Europe. And he wrote me a letter. After some time I went back to the shop, and then I was foreman in the New Haven County Jail, where I'd served time in a cell. About two years after I was converted I was remarried right in this building, right up-stairs. I think Bill sent a letter that he couldn't come. He knew I was going to be married. He met my wife and family—seemed tickled to death, too, to meet 'em. We've got a home now in Yalesville, Connecticut, and a big garden, plenty of land, lots of chickens, and a piano in the house—makes quite a change from when I first came to the Mission drunk, with no prospects but whiskey! There's not been a day since my conversion that I haven't had money in my pocket, not a day from that day to this. God has wonderfully blessed me.

After my conversion I was baptized and joined the Church. If Bill hadn't opened this Mission I'd been dead. My old chum who was once on bums with me, he'd never have been converted if it hadn't been for this Mission. We was holding prayer meetings at different houses. They'd come in drunk sometimes. Then I always took 'em after the meetings and gave 'em a talking to just before they left. Told 'em about this work here at Yale Hope Mission. There's no time in a drunkard's life when he don't have serious thoughts. When he drowns his conscience in booze, he's tearing away from the voice of God,

I think. Well, someone asked my chum to come when the meeting was at my house. He said he would if Jack Clark would lead. He knew that what God did for Jack Clark He could do for him. There was about twenty-four there and I led, and that night Whitney Todd, my chum, was converted. He lives right in Yalesville now and is foreman of a shop. He's got his wife and children with him, and he's always got his hand out to the man that's down. So you see you cannot trace what Yale Hope Mission's done by what you see lying around. Not till the books of Heaven are opened will you know what Bill Borden done by opening Yale Hope Mission. . . .

He was great at individual work. As a talker, he'd hasten through his address and get to work with the men, always aiming to get close to the man he was talking with—always with his hand on his shoulder. He didn't believe in talking over people's heads, but tried to land right on his man and bring his thoughts right home. He would interest you quicker than the ordinary man, because he had a more sympathetic way to start in. He seemed to reach out and win you. I watched him from night to night, and always, as soon as the invitation was given to come forward, he would be off the platform and right down among the men, and he'd urge them to accept a better life. He was always sympathetic, and he never went at a man in the same way twice. He had a habit of putting his hand on a man's shoulder, and they'd most always break down when he spoke to them.

I never knew a feller just like Bill. I'd like to get a hold of one of his pictures. Seems to me if I saw one I'd 'most try to steal it. I never knew a feller like him. He was a gentleman in every sense of the word, and a Christian through and through. That was first and last in his life. He enjoyed life, and people who came in contact with him, seeing his happy spirit, would say, "Why, life is worth living after all."

Why, the way he came amongst us, you would never think he was a man of wealth, and he always dressed so plain. He had a peculiar way, very interesting to me. He wouldn't tell you anything about himself, but he had a way of making you talk and tell things. It seemed to be his whole object, to know how I was and about my life so as he could help. It couldn't seem possible a man could be so humble and yet so-great. He could talk to anyone, didn't matter who they was. And he'd get down with his arms round the poor burly bum and hug him up.

Never knowed his like in this world. I know he must have done for hundreds just what he done for me. He was always trying to study into the lives of men, to see how they'd work out and how he could help 'em.

It was Professor Henry Wright who said, "It is my firm conviction that the Yale Hope Mission has done more to convince all classes of men at Yale of the power and practicability of Christianity to regenerate individuals and communities than any other force in the University."

CHAPTER 10

VACATIONS

1906-1912. Age 18-24

No duty could overtask him,
No need his will outrun;
Or ever we could ask him
His hands the work had done.

J. G. WHITTIER

BORDEN LOVED THE SEA, and was at home on it and in it. Most of his vacations during student years were spent at Camden, Maine, where he almost lived on the white-sailed *Tsatsawassa*. Talking with the captain of the yacht one day, who knew and loved him as did few others, Mrs. Borden remarked:

"You at any rate must have seen him off duty—off his guard."

"Mrs. Borden," was the unexpected reply, "William was never off his guard."

It was a true word, for in spite of all the good times, in the midst of them indeed, he was as steady in his higher allegiance as the needle to the pole. This comes out in the recollections of those who played as well as worked with him.

"There were few things that Bill liked better than to don his canvas jeans and jumper and sit behind the tiller of his yacht in a spanking good breeze," wrote a medical-student friend. "Many a pleasant sail I have had with Bill, and many a time we have been together in sloppy weather. One well-remembered summer we took a cruise down the Nova Scotia shore, and there is no time like a cruise for getting to know one another. Bill was our skipper and an ideal one, but he didn't stop at being in charge. There were few meals we ate that he hadn't cooked. Life on the boat was full of joy from beginning to end with Bill to keep things going.

"One morning we were becalmed in the middle of the Bay of Fundy. It was a hot sultry day, and we had been talking about sharks. Suddenly Bill said: 'Sharks or no sharks, here goes!' And he was overboard in a moment, swimming round the yacht.

"One learned in those days more of the secret of Bill's life, that his strength lay in his prayer-life. No matter what the weather might be, he would always hand over his trick at the wheel and go below for his times of quiet. I remember him distinctly one very rough day, with the boat standing on her beam-end, coming below and climbing up on his berth and losing himself in his God."

"The time I came to know him best was on the cruise we had in August, 1911," wrote Mrs. Henry W. Frost, who had chaperoned a merry house-party on the yacht. "I cannot think of an instance during those seven days of good thorough testing in close quarters, when William did not put everyone's comfort and pleasure before his own. He was captain and steersman, steward and cook for a party of ten hungry people, and well he did it. It was something more than the salt sea air that made his coffee and tea and corned-beef hash and pancakes so popular.

"Between times he was ready for any game. Stretched out in the cockpit at dominoes, his hearty laugh rang out with any success that was achieved.

"On Sunday we went to morning service ashore, and in the evening as we finished our meal and had a sing, with perfect naturalness and simplicity he led in a brief prayer service. It was always a pleasure to me to have him conduct prayers. His Scripture reading, while reverent, was so natural and his prayers so direct and simple, conveying the feeling that God was near and real."

Many were the happy days at Camden that Mr. Charles Campbell recalled.

Three weeks of one summer and the larger part of another I was with Bill Borden. That time, spent largely out of doors, opened my eyes to Bill's real self even more than had close association with him at College. At Yale I had learned that he was a rare man to work with; our weeks together in his summer home showed me that he was a rare man indeed to play with. At College I knew, as did all his friends, the strength and intensity of the serious purpose of his life; our happy, every-day comradeship at Camden taught me more of his very human and lovable boyishness, and his enjoyment of outdoor life and play. There was no mistaking the fact that Bill liked to sail, that he liked to swim, play tennis and golf. His laugh was always the heartiest, his enthusiasm the most contagious, and his delight at doing well the most evident.

One of our sailing trips was from Camden to Beverley Farms, on the Massachusetts north-shore. We had hardly rounded the lighthouse at the entrance to Camden harbour when we realized that a stiff breeze was blowing. A few hours later, with Monhegan Island astern, we were facing the full force of the open ocean. By six P.M we were off Portland and, with wind and rain-storms becoming more frequent, held a consultation as to whether we should run for shelter. Just then a coaster, which had been wallowing southward, emerged from a squall, her top-sail and top-mast gone, and, changing her course, ran for Portland Harbour. That decided Bill; but his decision was that, having started for Beverley, to Beverley we would go. Through the stormy night that followed, Bill was quiet and self-possessed, and I remember that when he took his turn at the wheel his strength and confidence seemed an assurance that all would be well. Serious though the situation was, Bill could laugh when he sang out to us at midnight that the lines with which we had been towing our power-dinghy had parted, taking pleasure in fighting the battle out with only our own resources to depend on.

Some of my most vivid recollections of Bill cluster round those different sailing trips. They range from the above experience to the spectacle of Bill in rough weather, seated in the cabin, calmly disposing of quantities of grapenuts and condensed milk. Great was our secret admiration for one who could perform such a feat at a time when the rolling of the boat had put some of us *hors de combat*.

I remember one evening anchoring off Bar Harbour about seven o'clock. By the time all was ship-shape the sun had set and the riding lights were shining from all the boats in the harbour. Before getting supper, Bill suggested that we have a swim. The air was chilly, and the black water rippling by with the outgoing tide looked colder than I had ever seen it. But overboard we went, swam a few strokes, took another dive, and were out again and dressing. The splendid reaction put us in the best of spirits as we prepared supper. I can see Bill now, hustling round that cabin, whistling, singing, just full of the joy of living.

It was at that same time, I think, that we sat on deck talking of another trip when we had put into Bar Harbour after sailing the entire preceding night. We had anchored at about the same spot, and as soon as possible had turned in for a little sleep. Before long we had wakened to find the boat dragging her anchor and almost upon the rocks. I can feel Bill's hearty slap upon my back and hear his laughter still, as we recalled how we had had to hustle to get out of danger.

Of another sort was an experience one day off the Massachusetts coast. We had been watching a school of whales blowing at some little distance. A few moments later one of them came lazily to the surface, not a hundred feet from our fifty-foot yacht. In some alarm one of the party called to Bill, who was at the wheel, to keep the boat off. His response was to edge in a little nearer, with—"Oh, let's have a good look!"

He was brushing up his Greek, the summer of our graduation from Yale, with a view to the entrance examination at Princeton. Out in the yacht he would often go below and plug away at Greek. He did a great deal of studying aboard his boat during the years I knew him, and was a past-master at making the odd moments count.

One day we sailed over to Eagle Island to take part in some races that were being run there. The wind was very light, and we came to the starting-line just after our race had begun. There was no time to report to the judges and no time to put the tender ashore. Bill managed everything. We just hauled the tender up on deck and went after the boats that had already started. All through the race Bill was captain, giving his orders and making every point to get the most out of his boat. We were heeled far over most of the time, as a good wind had sprung up. It all resulted in our crossing the winning line well in the lead. We were not allowed the victory, because we had not reported beforehand, but the winning was just as real all the same.

Sailing and tennis with Bill were always great fun, but the best hours of our visits were passed in quite another way. Before going to Camden a friend had wonderfully opened the Bible to me, giving me a new insight into its content. I mentioned this to Bill, and he at once suggested further Bible-study together. It had been good to play with him, but to join him in the one thing nearest his heart was worth incomparably more.

And it was not only to his guests that Borden's life meant much during the summer vacations. Many residents in Camden and the vicinity looked forward to his coming, and through his friendship some found the Friend who transforms life from within.

Among those was the gardener, a valuable employee of the family, who had fallen under the power of strong drink. Mrs. Borden had done all she could to help him, but without success, and one day when she was away from home he was found intoxicated near the house. Next morning he sent a note to William saying that he was ill and could not come to work, a situation which was explained by Melanie, who had found him—the children's former nurse. Waiting only to get her to pray with him about the visit, William set out to see the gardener. But when he reached the house it was only to be told that he did not feel like seeing anyone that day.

"I know the reason," William said to the gardener's wife, "but please ask him to let me come in."

The talk that followed resulted in a transformation that brought blessing to the whole family. For the man himself a new life began that day, and months later William was writing from College:

"J. is a constant source of joy and thanksgiving to God, is he not?"

But of all his Camden friends it was Captain Arey who knew Borden best and to whom his life meant most. The following recollections are given just as they came from his heart:

I've known him ever since he first come to Camden, and that must have been about nine years ago. If anyone showed on their outside the happiness of being a Christian it was Mr. Borden. When he talked it just seemed as if you could feel his earnestness.

When we two was out alone—we went all the way to New Haven alone once—I have seen him kneel for perhaps an hour at a time and never lift his head. The villagers loved him, everybody loved him. He was so noble-looking! When he came up in the spring, he always shook hands with everybody. All the summer-people don't do that. If 'twas a stranger or a fisherman, didn't make no difference. He always spoke to everybody, like as if he wanted to, and shook hands with them.

William was a nice hand to sail a boat. You didn't need no one else when he was along. I used to be afraid he'd fall in the water, at first. He was always singing and jumping around. He'd climb away up the riggin' and get into the row-boat behind. He did everything well he tried to do. He was so strong, too! When he'd go out and work at the riggin', I'd be afraid he'd break the sail, he was so strong. Sometimes he'd steer and sometimes he'd help with the sails, but he was an expert on the boat. He could take a chart and go anywhere with it. Of course, he'd studied into it and learned it. It didn't seem hard for him to go through with anything he undertook—it just seemed easy.

One awful good feature he had; if the boat wasn't fixed up quite as it ought to be, perhaps if ladies came aboard and the brass wasn't cleaned, I'd tell him about it, and he'd smile and say it was all right. He never spoke a cross word to me all the time I was with him.

He lent me two books by Gordon, *Talks on Prayer* and *Talks on Power*. We have a Young People's Meeting in the Baptist Church here. After the summer in London when he was converted, he would sometimes lead our prayer-meeting. If I had the job, I'd get him to do it for me. Others did too, for they liked to hear him. He could always hold the audience. Sometimes the young people are a little noisy at their meeting, but they was still when he spoke.

Sometimes he'd tell us he was going to be a missionary— seemed to think he was mapped out for it. If 'twas worldly pleasure he'd wanted, he could have had everything. But he was so much different from others! All his pleasure seemed to be in going about doin' people good. The last summer here at one of meetings he said he was going to the Mohammedans. He spoke about the National Bible Institute one night, but I don't remember just what he said.

If we was out all night on the boat, he'd roll in the blanket and sleep on deck. The others would be in the cabin. There might be a bed to spare, but he'd take the deck. He liked it better.

One summer here, he and Mr. T. held open-air meetings. They'd begin right in front of the hotel, about 7:30, and get the crowds sort of interested. They had a little organ and would sing. William could sing quite well. He had a strong voice. Then they'd go into the Opera House, which they'd rented for a while. Sometimes it was crowded full. The last two evenings they'd have after-meetin's, and many stayed. After the meeting was opened—in the Opera House—anybody could speak. Many did. The superintendent of the mills spoke one night, and sometimes ministers would come and speak.

It was blowin' awful heavy one night—dark and rainy. Two other fellers was out with us, his friends. About two o'clock in the morning, the bran' new boat we was towin', the steam-launch, rolled over and sunk, the rope parted. I remember what he said.

"The boat's gone," he called down to the other fellers. "We can go faster now!"

Lots and lots of boats that night that was about as big as the *Tsatsawassa* was wrecked—that is, the sails were torn and the spars broke, so that they had to be towed in. The storm commenced about eleven o'clock. James Perry and another of William's friends was with us. I don't think any of us slept. I know I didn't, and I know William didn't. It was about six o'clock next morning when we got into Beverley Farms and anchored (after a record run of nearly two hundred miles in eighteen hours). When all was made safe, William said:

"Now we'll have family prayers, and give thanks for gettin' in."

He always had prayers for us every mornin'. Whoever was on the boat, we always had prayers and a blessin' at table. Sometimes she'd be so keeled over that we'd be standin' up, but that didn't make no difference. We always had a blessin'. If we was in port Sunday mornin', we'd go ashore to church. Perhaps I'd stay aboard—someone had to be there. But before he'd go ashore, he'd have prayers with me on the boat. He was always thoughtful, that way, of others. If he'd been my own brother he couldn't have used me any better.

Once he and Mary was out, and a fog and heavy sea came on. We couldn't get back to the landing stage, so they went to my house and stayed all night. He just said so natural-like to my wife:

"Have you anything to eat? We didn't get much supper! Can you give us some milk and cake?"

My wife went to all the meetin's. She likes him, too. He wasn't like one of the summer people! I'd be awful glad to have his picture, so'd my wife.

When he and I'd go out alone sometimes, I'd ask where he'd like to go.

"Anywhere," he'd say, "so as to get out where it's quiet."

And he'd go down into the cabin with his Bible or some other book and study all the time we was out. It might be three hours or so. And when we'd come in, he'd seem to be kind of refreshed in his mind.

He always read the Bible before turnin' in at night. It didn't matter who was there. If I was alone with him, he'd read it to me and explain it. Yes, he was jolly and he was happy in the work he was undertakin'.

A group of later recollections, running on into Princeton years, come from the family of his College friend, Sherwood Day. The Days were fortunate in having a camp of their own, tucked away on the low shoulder of a mountain overlooking Lake George. William loved the spot, close to that exquisite expanse of water, and loved still more the Christian fellowship recalled in the following letters from Mrs. Day and two of her daughters, Bryn Mawr students:

> In the very first conversation I ever had with Bill, we discovered that we both believed in the inerrancy of the Bible, and I can feel yet the hearty grasp of his outstretched hand as we laughed in serious sympathy over our common orthodoxy! That was the summer he joined us at Shelving Rock. I had hesitated to invite him, because it was real camping, and I fancied he might need some conveniences which are no longer considered luxuries but necessaries. I soon learned, however, that comforts were easily dispensable with him, and that no change of surroundings interfered with his habitual walk with God.
>
> That same summer Harriet was with us. You remember how she dubbed him "the Parson," but you cannot know the amused little smile with which he responded to her fun. They too frolicked together so much that I remember Sherwood's saying: "I wish the College fellows could see this side of Bill!" We knew that he went in for athletics and outdoor life, but until then it seemed as if even they were *serious* undertakings. But with Harriet the playful side was brought out, and we were so glad to know the *boy* under the manly exterior.
>
> . . . .
>
> I, too, loved his standing simply and firmly for the eternal verities of our faith. That staunchness of his, after all his thought and study, has meant much to me. And I have learned much, too, from *the way* Bill stood for truth. We always noticed that

the more earnest he became, the lower, not the louder, he spoke. When others in argument would raise their voices, he would grow more quiet and speak more low, with the result that everyone listened.

I recall one day a somewhat heated discussion of the suffrage question. We finally got down to Genesis, Mother basing her plea against it on the teachings of that book, upon which one of our pro-suffrage guests denied much belief in Genesis, anyway. I don't remember that up to that point Bill had said much, but somehow, the first thing I knew, he was talking along and the other guests were listening. We all listened. Much that he said was beyond us. We did not know enough to follow it fully. But the impression was made that there is such a thing as a deep scholarly conviction as to the authority and inspiration of the book (Genesis) and that the speaker was no unthinking conservative, but an intelligent believer in the Bible.

I do not know that he convinced the friends in question. They did not talk long. But he did what I felt at the time was perhaps more needed, showed that we could hold to the old views in these matters, after thinking. Real certainty and security in the truth *is* unruffled when the attack comes. He was so sure, as on that occasion, of what he believed—Him whom he believed—that he did not get excited and loudly insist on his opinions. He could wait to say what he *knew*. And the more you knew him the more sure you felt that, keen and active as his intellect was, that knowledge was the result of no mere theological training, but of personal experience, and prayerful Spirit-guided study of the Word of God.

The thought of him always challenges me. I mean that one knew that he was holding himself and always would hold himself to what he felt to be best and highest. He would not stoop to petty excuses or take advantage of loopholes for self-indulgence. Here at camp he was up early for his Morning Watch as regularly as, I am sure, he must have been at the Seminary. I can see his testament coming out of his pocket now! As surely as he carried that Testament he carried his religion. You felt he would never be one to want a vacation from religious duties. They were not "duties" to him. It was just *natural* to him to take that morning hour for fellowship with God, and he bore its imprint all through the day.

It was always an opportune time with Bill to speak of the deepest things, because with him they were the realest things. His spiritual life affected all his living, the heartiness and wholesomeness of his fun as well as his religious activities. . . . If there arose in his mind a doubt about the rightness of something, he put the doubtful thing aside at once. For example, he became much interested in a card-game someone was playing here in camp and took some share in it. Then, one day he would not play it any more, and you knew he had questioned the rightness of his taking such a keen interest in the game and had shut down on it immediately. It was this steadfast turning from doubtful things that gave him, I think, the atmosphere of separateness that was part of his power.

And then, I suppose, this single-mindedness in his spiritual life was the secret of that fixity of purpose which took him straight along whither he had set out. What Bill started, you might be quite sure he would finish. From the room in which I write I can see where a limb has been cut off a tree, high up from the ground. He cut it off. Someone had expressed a wish that the dead limb might go, because it looked like an ugly clenched fist, and he set out to do it. The ladder was not long enough and he had to prop it up—it was on a steep hillside, and almost dangerous to do so. He had to hang on with his right arm and saw with his left, in an almost impossible position. I can see him doing it now, sawing and resting and sawing again, but sticking at it until the limb fell.

One other thing I want to speak of, but I don't quite know what to call it. It was something that made you feel that everything would be all right as long as he was around. It was partly, I suppose, his consideration for others.

When, one evening last September, we ran down to the Sagamore, to take him there to get an automobile for Lake George, he discovered that we had no flashlight in the launch with which to examine the engine if necessary. He insisted upon giving us his, one from his travelling bag, because he felt we ought not to be without it. And as we started home, leaving him there on the dock, he called out to Rosalie and me—novices at running the engine—not to forget about an oil-cup, I think it was, that it was important we should attend to.

He was such a one to rely on! And it seemed to me that His Lord's spirit of service had so permeated his life that it not only led him to set his face to the field of greatest need, but meanwhile made his life full of *little services*, day by day, that many would not see the occasion for. It was easy to see his force, his devotion to Christ's cause, but it was only after having him around that you began to appreciate what a Christlike man he was.

· · · · · · ·

A kindness he did in a New York station is one of the things I have recalled repeatedly. We were going out to take a train, when I noticed that he had dropped behind, and turning, I saw him helping a very poor immigrant woman who was struggling along with many bundles and a baby in her arms. How well I remember, at camp, how he used to stand near the kitchen door and watch for a chance to be of use. We often said that the table was never cleared so quickly as when Bill did it.

And what a help he was in some German I had to do (for an examination at Bryn Mawr)! The days at camp were pretty well filled with picnics, canoeing, swimming, etc., and it was not easy to make time for study. He was anxious that I should finish that German reading. If a thing had to be done, it was his way to do it and then put it from his mind. When there were a few minutes before it was time to start on a picnic or other outing he would say: "Can't we get some of that German done now?" I do not know how I should ever have 'tackled' it without this encouragement. His help during the few days he was there gave me, so to speak, "a running start," and I was able to finish it in the required time. . . .

But with all his seriousness there was abundant playfulness and love of fun. He had an inexhaustible store of tricks, which kept us entertained many an evening. I remember specially a spelling-game called "Ghost" which he enjoyed immensely.

And one other thing about Bill—his instant and full obedience to the will of God. There never seemed to be any conflict in his life between duty and pleasure, for the moment he saw what his duty was, he did it. There was no procrastination about him. If the thing was hard to do, it made no difference. Feelings were out of the reckoning. "Obedience irrespective of feeling" was, perhaps, the strongest thing about his life.

One of the most vivid memories I have of him is as he sat before our open fire at camp one Sunday evening. We were all there singing hymns, and the only light was that of the fire which shone full on his face. How earnest it was, and with what joyousness he sang the hymns he loved best! "O Love that will not let me go" and "In the secret of His presence" were among his favourites. But it was not the firelight only that brought that light to his face. These lines come to me as I recall the scene and especially that look of joy and calm:

> "Beautiful now his face had grown,
>   But the beauty was something not his own;
> A solemn light from that blessed land
>   Within whose border he soon must stand."

"His ideals and ambitions were so great," wrote Elsa Frost, then a young nurse in a hospital, "that anyone who knew him at all could not but be influenced by them, and to us who counted ourselves friends of his they were much more.

"My most vivid remembrance of William has not to do with any football game or sailing, but with a Communion Service we all attended together at Camden. I somehow think of him most often then—not that he did or said anything to fix it in my mind, but just that he seemed to be so in the spirit of the service. When at times I am tempted to wonder whether the end in view is worth all the work and struggle, just to remember the separations and hardships he was facing is enough to start me on again."

PART III

PRINCETON SEMINARY

Many crowd the Saviour's kingdom,
  Few receive His Cross.
Many seek His consolation,
  Few will suffer loss,
For the dear sake of the Master,
  Counting all but dross.

Many sit at Jesus' table,
  Few will fast with Him,
When the sorrow-cup of anguish
  Trembles to the brim:
Few watch with Him in the garden
  Who have sung the hymn.

But the souls who love Him truly
  Both in woe and bliss,
These will count their very heart's blood
  Not their own but His!
Saviour, Thou who thus hast loved me,
  Give me love like this.

—Selected

CHAPTER 11

STUDIES AND HOME LIFE
1909-1912. AGE 21-24

*The purpose of his life had been "to turn many to righteousness."
. . . The Bible was the source of all his power. He learned it, he
loved it, he lived it. It made him what he was. And I am hearing
from all parts of the world testimonies from men and women who
were drawn to give their lives to the Saviour through his teaching.
That is a noble purpose to live for, is it not?*—Written of the
Rev. Prebendary Webb Peploe, by his widow.

BORDEN'S LIFE AT PRINCETON was strenuous almost beyond belief, for in addition to his studies, many outside claims
were crowding upon him. He was now of age and had considerable share in the management of large financial interests.
His mother had come to live at Princeton, partly in order that
his younger sister might see as much of him as possible. Their
home was a center of hospitality, and as Mrs. Borden was still
far from strong, upon William devolved the keeping of household accounts as well as a host's responsibilities. His studies
were absorbing, even more so than he had anticipated, and the
pressure of other interests was not allowed to encroach upon the
time they demanded. All this meant a heavy program and no
little exercise of self-discipline.

He had decided upon taking the full course at Princeton
Seminary largely on account of questionings that had disturbed
his mind during his senior year at Yale. When urged to return
as graduate secretary of the Y.M.C.A. he exclaimed to a College friend:

"Gee whiz! I want to pull out for a while and see where I am. I must take time for thought and study rather than rush on in the same sort of activities."

So honest and earnest a nature could not be satisfied with uncertainty in the most vital issues. Three years of close mental application was a price he willingly paid for the strength that comes from knowledge and settled convictions. He was at the same time enlarging his missionary outlook by a special course of study for his Yale M.A. This had been gone over in detail with Professor Harlan P. Beach before leaving College. Professor Beach wrote:

> The ground covered was enough Arabic to secure the degree if offered alone, and in addition a broad course of missionary reading, mostly having to do with the science of missions, Mohammedanism and missionary biographies. He was duly entered as a graduate student with permission to pass his examinations at his convenience. Had he done so, he would have covered more than even the best Master's Degree men are required to take. "Factors in Missionary Efficiency" was the theme decided upon for his thesis.

Borden did not share the view expressed by some Student Volunteers that it will be time enough when they reach the mission field to study missions. Even amid the pressure of College and Seminary life he was following out a steady course of missionary reading, which made him always interesting and helpful at the Band meeting and gave definiteness to his prayers. There was nothing half-way about such a preparation. It was deep and thorough-going.

"Thus Bill entered upon three years of busy, happy life at Princeton," wrote his friend Campbell. "The studies were absorbing and the social life congenial. He was a member of the Benham Club, the oldest eating club of the Seminary. He played most of the games, but was especially fond of tennis. He was a leader among the Student Volunteers and was always present at the early morning prayer service of the Band each Wednesday.

"In addition to the duties and pleasures that centred about his life in the Seminary, Bill had many responsibilities outside Princeton itself. In the fall of 1909 he had been made a trustee of the Moody Bible Institute in Chicago. In the spring of 1910 he was appointed a delegate to the Edinburgh Missionary Conference by the China Inland Mission, and in the fall was made one of the directors of the National Bible Institute of New York City. He also became a member of the North American Council of the China Inland Mission and of the American Committee of the Nile Mission Press.

"It is easy to see that the calls on his time would be many. Few men of his age could so well have handled the duties that pressed upon him from all these quarters. His singleness of purpose helped him and gave such direction to his life that no one, even among his nearest friends, saw anything but a quiet, consistent, unhurried doing of each task that came. Almost every month he went to New Haven to look over the work of the Yale Hope Mission. The unusual feature of his relationship to all such organizations was that he was never satisfied with merely giving generous financial aid. In addition, he always gave time, thought and counsel, usually conducting a service at the Mission when he went to New Haven. New York, New Haven and Chicago trips succeeded one another, and still he never seemed to neglect his work, though he carried a much heavier schedule than the average man. More than this, he stood very high in scholarship.

"Life at Princeton was brightened by the happy home influences that surrounded him. The Borden home was hospitably open to all. Students, missionaries and prominent lay workers were frequent visitors. The tennis court, back of the house, was the scene of many hotly contested games. In spite of his busy life, Bill never neglected his body. He made it a point to get an hour's exercise daily if it was possible. How his eyes would light up at the prospect of a good game of tennis! Back he would come from a class, hustle into tennis clothes and then out to the court. He was never more than an average tennis player, but he played hard all the time and gave his opponent plenty of work."

It is interesting to see from letters written only a little later the impression Borden made upon members of the Faculty during those full years at Princeton.

"I never saw, perhaps, a finer example of *mens sana in corpore sano,*" recalled Professor Brenton Greene. "I used to think as I saw him from my study window dashing down Library Place on his bicycle to the early morning recitations, 'that man is so strong and so sane that his prospect of life is better than that of any other student in our Seminary.'

"His memory was as wax to receive an impression and as marble to retain it. He had the happy faculty of seeing at once the gist of a question and going straight to the point. Yet he never relied on this power, but used every means at his command. Rarely if ever was he absent from the classes, and I cannot recall a single instance of inattention on his part. As might have been expected, he attained the natural result. He became distinguished as a scholar. . . . I well remember my deep regret, the feeling of positive loss, at the time of his graduation, when I read his last paper, knowing that I should never have another from him."

"No student has exerted a greater personal influence over me than did William Borden," wrote Professor Charles Erdman. "This was due both to the fact of our intimate friendship and to his peculiarly strong and impressive personality. His judgment was so unerring and so mature that I always forgot there was such a difference in our ages. His complete consecration and devotion to Christ were a revelation to me, and his confidence in prayer a continual inspiration.

"He had doubtless inherited unusual gifts, but these were developed by the most careful and persistent discipline, requiring great determination and fixity of purpose. . . . There was much in his life to tempt him to less strenuous work, to lure him to self-indulgence and content with imperfect achievement. There was also the test of resolution that comes from apparently conflicting duties. His responsibilities were great, his days crowded with a multiplicity of demands. Neither social duties, however, nor filial duties, nor the duties of Christian stewardship were allowed to draw him from the supreme duty of preparation for his chosen work. The strain of unremitting application was relieved by a keen sense of humour and a delight in the society of relatives and friends. His friendship was one of the most stimulating with which I have been blessed."

"It was as his teacher in Church History that I knew him best," said Dr. John de Witt. "His fidelity, high intelligence and rare grasp of the subjects brought before him made on me a deep impression. But it was his spiritual ideal of life, his absolute loyalty to it, the sound judgment he showed in actualizing it, not only in the choice of his work and field, but in the details of daily activity and the simplicity and sincerity of his character, that led me not only to respect but to reverence him. I have had a few students among the many I have taught who have distinctly called into action this feeling of reverence, and he was one of them."

A like note is found in not a few other letters from men of experience and Christian standing. Dr. Henry W. Frost, for example, Director in North America of the China Inland Mission, invited Borden, when only twenty-two, to a seat on its Council. They had been in correspondence for years, and Dr.

Frost, who knew him intimately, felt no hesitation in asking him to become one of the burden-bearers at the heart of the Mission, sharing the prayer and faith as well as the problems of those responsible for its direction.

"The disparity in age was seldom noticed," he recalled. "There was an equality of mind which made him one with those with whom he was associated. None could help noticing the freshness of thought and enthusiasm of spirit characteristic of youth, and the Council rejoiced in these. But they were not accompanied by immaturity of judgment. When he spoke, it was evident that he was thinking carefully and broadly. He was a constant illustration of the fact that it is no vain thing for a man, even a young man, to obey the injunction, 'If any of you lack wisdom let him ask of God.' Christ, through the study of the Word and through prayer, was made unto him 'wisdom.' His advice, therefore, was sought by not a few who, in the average case, would have gone to the man of more years. And he seldom failed of help. If he did fail, his eagerness to be of assistance made him a greater help than the average man would have been, though more wise through experience."

Borden's love for the faith principles of the China Inland Mission was strong and growing. He owed not a little in the deeper things of the spiritual life to his friendship with Dr. Frost, whose love for him was almost that of a father for a son. William had long consulted him in matters of importance, and especially as to his prospective relations with the Mission. In this connection, Dr. Frost continued:

The first time William Borden spoke to me about offering himself to the China Inland Mission was while he was in his sophomore year at Yale. He had already come to feel that his work should be in China and desired to put himself in a position to reach that land. But I felt he was then too young to come to a positive conclusion as to the country in which he should serve, and I advised him to postpone considering the matter.

At the end of his university course he again consulted me about going to China. Once more I advised him to defer the decision, and urged him to prepare himself further by taking the seminary course at Princeton. This he did, with credit to himself and to the Seminary.

Toward the end of his studies at Princeton, he again offered himself to the Mission for work in China. This time I was persuaded that God was indeed in the matter of his application. But to further test him, I asked if he had considered offering himself to the Presbyterian Board rather than to us. He replied that he had; that he highly esteemed the Presbyterian Board, but that there were three reasons why he was more drawn to the China Inland Mission—firstly, on account of its inter-denominational character; secondly, because of its emphasis upon evangelistic work; and thirdly, because it held the personal and pre-millennial coming of Christ. So at last we considered his application and accepted him for service in China.

This was only ten days before Borden's graduation from Princeton, so that he had already been for more than two years a member of the Council. It was an unusual coincidence when his case came up for final consideration and, as a candidate, he had to be asked to withdraw while the Council proceeded to accept one of its own members as a probationer of the Mission.

But all this took place gradually, while the busy years at Princeton were passing on. During his first summer vacation from the Seminary, Borden went to Europe, as we have seen, representing the China Inland Mission at the Ecumenical Missionary Conference in Edinburgh (1910), where he was the youngest of two thousand delegates. It was there that Mrs. Borden learned for the first time that his decision was taken to give himself definitely to work for Mohammedans in China, if that proved to be the Lord's will. Miss Annie Van Sommer had arranged for a gathering of representative workers from Mohammedan lands at the house where she was staying. Dr. Zwemer was chairman, and Mr. (now Canon) Gairdner and Dr. St. Clair Tisdall, all from Cairo, were there. In order to introduce people to one another, Dr. Zwemer asked each to rise and give his or her name and field. When Borden's turn came, he mentioned without hesitation as his prospective field the Mohammedans of Northwest China.

That was a full summer! The missionary gatherings in Edinburgh were followed by a brief visit to Norway with Mr. Robert P. Wilder, who was then working among students in England and on the Continent. Of Borden's stay in their Norwegian home Mr. Wilder wrote:

> He took a real interest in our home-life and all our doings. He helped the children to learn to ride their bicycles, running by each of them in turn. Mrs. Wilder specially remembers how, when a box of aerated water had come by train and she was thinking of sending to the station for it, we saw to our surprise William Borden coming up the steep hill with the box on his shoulder. . . . He and I had long talks over God's Word and work, frequently pausing to pray about the matter we were discussing. He seemed never out of sight of the Mercy Seat.

A week in the Engadine gave Borden the conquest of the Piz Pallu and the Piz Julier as glorious memories, and a few days at Lucerne brought delightful fellowship with Mr. and Mrs. Charles Campbell, who were there on their wedding journey.

> He joined us in Lucerne. There were also a young Irishman and his bride in the same Pension, and for several days we five had a great time! We went to the Glacier Garten; went rowing on the lake and swimming in it, and altogether acted like a bunch of kids. Our afternoon teas were a wonderful mixture of assorted cakes and unlimited cups of tea.

Three weeks in Hanover were given to intensive study of German, and opened Borden's eyes to threatened dangers. To Dr. Frost he wrote:

Hanover, July 20, 1910

Only to-day I read in a London paper "Unity of Christendom
—gigantic task! Twenty-four American Episcopalians have undertaken to bring about a union of Christians all over the world
—Protestants, Greek Catholics, Roman Catholics, everybody, everywhere!" Things are certainly rushing to the climax. I wonder
what will come next?

People talk about peace in Peace Congresses, but in reality here
in Europe they are preparing for a great struggle I believe.
. . . How wonderful that we have "that blessed hope" to
look forward to, "the glorious appearing of our God and Saviour
Jesus Christ"!

On the voyage home he was deep in Arabic with a view
to the advanced course he was taking in that language and
Aramaic. "I spent most of my time in London buying books,"
he wrote to his friend Campbell, "and am taking home a small
library of theological and Oriental literature."

Back in Princeton he threw himself as before into all the
religious and other activities of seminary life. Letters from
many of his classmates might be quoted, but the following
from the Rev. James M'Cammon, now a missionary in China,
will suffice to give an impression of his influence.

His thoroughness, especially in his studies, was evident to us
all. He kept up his work from day to day, so that he was not
"rushed" as many of us were when examinations came round.
So well did he have his knowledge in hand that long before the
three hours' period for an exam was over he would have finished
his paper and handed it in, to the plaudits of his fellow-students.
It was my habit to look in on a class-mate in Alexander Hall
daily, and there, two or three afternoons in the week, I was sure
to find Bill Borden and his friend, Mr. Fowler, doing extra-cur-
riculum work on Arabic. On one such occasion I discovered that
they had formed the project of making an Arabic Concordance
of the Bible, and had actually begun work upon it. I had known
of their studiousness before, but this more than astonished me.

He was one of the most faithful attendants we had at the Y.M.C.A. and Student Volunteer meetings in the Seminary. He took his turn in leading such meetings, and his messages were of a devotional and missionary character that evidenced thorough preparation of mind and heart. One term he undertook to go through the Reports of the World's Missionary Conference which he had attended in Edinburgh, giving them in the form of a résumé week by week. Those talks I shall never forget. His mastery of the facts was astonishing. He gave us in clear, condensed statements, from carefully prepared notes, a synopsis of each of these Reports, bringing out the spiritual bearing of the facts dealt with. It was a remarkable evidence of his knowledge as well as zeal in connection with foreign missions. . . .

He was a convinced believer in the personal and pre-millennial coming of our Lord. He looked for that glorious Advent as the hope of the Church and the only hope for the world. I often had conversations with him on this subject, and the extent of his knowledge and intensity of his convictions left their mark on my mind. One of my most prized possessions is a book on the Lord's Coming he once gave me as we were talking together.

Another conviction that dominated his life was that the Bible, from first to last, is the inspired word of God. To him it was the Book of books. He had not only an intellectual grasp of its teachings such as one may get in a theological seminary, but he had the spiritual understanding of it which only comes through prayerful and devotional study in humble dependence on the Spirit of God. . . .

The secret of William Borden's life, as it seems to a fellow-student, was his belief in the sufficiency and abiding presence of the Lord Jesus Christ. For this was more than a belief, it was with him an experimental reality.

This reality and the strength he derived daily from his study of the Word of God made him feel intensely the drift away from these things in modern university life, a subject upon which he had written to Mr. Wilder, as leader of the Student Volunteer Movement, in the hope of inducing him to return to America:

Princeton, January 29, 1910

The spirit that prevails is this: in all scientific studies Darwinian evolution is taught, often anti-theistically, and seldom is any attempt made to harmonize it with the early part of Genesis, for example. Ussher's chronology is still the cause of trouble, in the light of geology, etc. But these are the least serious issues. Much more serious is the general agnostic atmosphere pervading everything and deadening all convictions, those as to sin and truth included. In line with this, a broad spirit of tolerance is insisted upon, especially in matters of religion, and any and all are branded as narrow who dare think otherwise. That word "narrow" is one of Satan's deadliest weapons, it seems to me; for most people would apparently rather be shot than be called narrow. Thus it is even as Christ predicted—the broad way to destruction is thronged, but few are climbing the narrow way that leads to life.

When we come to distinctively Christian and religious matters, the situation is even worse. "Practically everyone" believes that the Bible is full of contradictions and errors, etc., etc. Even earnest Christians seem to feel that it doesn't matter. The New Testament fares little better than the Old at the hands of critics, and the supernatural is expunged from both. And against all this scarcely a voice of any authority is raised in protest, from within the ranks. In the women's colleges things are even worse, as I know from my sister who was at Vassar and from a recent conversation with one of the Y.W.C.A. secretaries, who is firm in the faith and alive to the situation.

In spite of everything the work of the Y.M.C.A. goes on, men are really won to Christ, and many good workers are sent into active Christian service. But it is *in spite of* all this.

Now the leaders, I feel, do not all of them by any means see the real tendency of this modern teaching, especially of the Biblical teaching, which in the name of Christianity really discredits Christ and the Christian faith. Either they do not clearly see the issues, or if they do, they seek to compromise. This is evident from the kind of speakers approved of, and still more so from the Bible teachers and teaching that are popular. There is tremendous zeal and energy among many students and leaders here, and my only desire is that they should find the truth. Dr. Zwemer sees all these things clearly and has helped a lot, but now he is going, and as far as I know there is no one with a theological training (which is almost essential, to enable one to see the real issues) who can take his place and help to keep the student movement pure, strong and evangelical. The need is tremendous and the opportunity immense. I should like nothing better than to get into the fight, right here in the American colleges, should the Lord close my way to the foreign field.

One other word I would like to add. The teaching about the kingdom of God is entirely with the idea that it is gradually to be brought in by our making the world better. This of course fits in with the socialistic ideas of the day, but hardly with Scripture! And here again, in the college world scarcely a voice is raised in support of God's Word.

I do hope you will come and help. I feel sure it would mean a better quality of work here, and a better quality of really equipped men for the work abroad. And I would like to add a word about the China Inland Mission, which I am only beginning really to know and with which you doubtless are better acquainted. What I want to say is that if you join yourself with them in some capacity, you will have a praying constituency behind you such as no other organization I know of would afford.

CHAPTER 12

WIDER ACTIVITIES

1910-1912. AGE 22-24

And evermore beside him on his way
The unseen Christ shall move,
That he may lean upon His arm and say,
"Dost Thou, dear Lord, approve?"

H. W. LONGFELLOW

IT WAS THE SUMMER of 1910. Borden was leaving for Europe to attend the Edinburgh Conference, and on the steamer, amid all the bustle of departure, was engrossed in conversation with a friend whose acquaintance he had recently made.

"I want to help you in the work you are doing," he said quietly, "and will send you a hundred dollars a month for the next year. If you will come to my cabin I will write the first check now."

"We went down," Mr. Don O. Shelton recalled when that friendship had become one of the most precious in his life, "and he wrote the check and gave it to me. When I reached home I found it was for two hundred dollars. 'He is going abroad,' I thought, 'and has made it for two months this time.' But exactly one month later came another check for two hundred dollars, and again the following month, two hundred. 'He is giving it all in six months,' was my conclusion. But when he returned at the end of the summer he continued to send two hundred dollars a month through the entire year.

"I was learning to know Will Borden, one of whose characteristics it was always do better than he promised, more and not less than he led you to expect."

Needless to say, this was when he felt his confidence to be well founded, as in the case of The National Bible Institute under the leadership of Mr. Shelton.

Twenty years of work in the Y.M.C.A. and in Bible Conferences had convinced this earnest evangelist that something new and different in the way of approach was needed if the multitudes who never darken a church door were to hear the Gospel. He had given up a promising career for no other reason than that he realized the Christian man's responsibility for a situation such as we have around us today. More than half the people in the United States, as he well knew, are outside the membership of any church. Seventy-five per cent of the young men are bowing down to gods of wealth, lust and pleasure, and are worshiping them alone.

"Of what value is it preaching to empty seats," he questioned, "when the people who ought to occupy them are in crowded tenements or on street corners or in the parks, and do not hear the faintest whisper of the message?"

The outcome, after much prayer and consideration, was a simple, earnest effort on the part of businessmen, chiefly, to reach the crowds in the city of New York. It was on a June day in 1907 that the first meeting was held at the busy hour of noon. A low platform under a tree in Madison Square Garden was all the equipment, with a little organ and a group of singers to lead familiar hymns. The speakers were businessmen, the language was that of the newspaper rather than the theological hall. But the results were amazing. It was no unusual thing to see three hundred men listening with riveted attention through the daily half-hour, and very soon other noon meetings had to be commenced—and a School for Lay Evangelists, to meet the need of training for such work.

"The people hear the Gospel gladly," Mr. Shelton was writing a few weeks later. "In Madison Square Garden more men have assembled daily to hear the message than gather on Sundays for any Protestant church service in Greater New York, with two or three exceptions. And what representative throngs we have! Workingmen from near-by buildings, clerks from offices, boot-blacks sitting on their kits, street cleaners, messenger boys, police officers, contractors, well-to-do businessmen, drunkards, the unemployed and discouraged, editors and professional people, all listening with the same interest. The attention is so close at times as to be pathetic. . . . The Gospel is still the most winsome message in the world.

"We never take up a collection. The one object is to reach men, and from the beginning we have had crowds of them. The work thus far has resulted in many transformations of character. Some of those who have been greatly helped have expressed their purpose to unite with churches at once. We believe that we are carrying out Christ's idea in going to the people and not waiting for them to come to us."

All this interested Borden deeply, and further acquaintance with the work only increased his sense of its value, so that when he was asked in the fall of 1910 to become one of the directors of the National Bible Institute, it was a call he could not refuse. The position was no sinecure. It involved frequent journeys to New York to attend the Board Meetings, and the problems of the work called for much thought and prayer. A large part of his vacation in the summer of 1911 was spent in the heat and hurry of New York, taking a full share in meetings and other activities. Of this Mr. Shelton writes:

I find in my diary under date of May 8, 1911, the following sentences: "Mr. William W. Borden came up from Princeton to-day to co-operate for a few weeks in the work of the National Bible Institute. A noble, generous, Christlike young man —a rare gift of God to the work under his care!"

We placed a desk for him in my office, and he continually manifested an eager desire to enter into the work in every possible way. Responsibility for our four gospel halls was delegated to him, and he kept in close touch with the super-intendents, counselling with them in regard to all the details. He investigated men who were being considered for positions of trust. He gave much thought and prayer to drafting the "Principles and Practice" of the National Bible Institute, and prepared a document which has been of exceeding great value in its development. . . .

It is a joy to recall his first appearance at our Madison Square meeting in the open air. His address was brief, but remarkably vigorous and direct. He stood there as a witness to the saving power of Jesus Christ. As he spoke, I rejoiced that the large company of listeners had before them one of the manliest, purest and noblest of our Lord's modern witnesses. His radiant face, unaffected manner, and joyous, fervent testimony to the power of the Christian faith made the occasion memorable. . . .

As a member of the Board of Directors he was a valued counsellor. He turned the white light of Scripture on every matter that came up for consideration. His presence in any meeting was a moral and spiritual tonic.

All his work began, continued and ended in prayer. Again and again, at our office, he would suggest before taking up the consideration of any important matter that we should unite in waiting upon God. Prayer was to him the first means to be used in accomplishing any object. And how simple, direct, unselfish and childlike his prayers were! He prayed as one confident that his heavenly Father would hear and answer.

That he was thinking deeply about the work of the National Bible Institute was evident from the fact that he had arranged, before coming to New York, for a visit that he thought would be helpful from a representative of the China Inland Mission. "Owe no man anything, but to love one another," was a scriptural injunction that was authoritative with him, and he wanted the practical methods explained by which a Mission with a thousand foreign and four thousand native workers was enabled to carry it out. With an intimate knowledge of the book-keeping of the Mission, Miss Mary Brayton, the head of its accounting department in Philadelphia, had consented to make the matter plain, and it was an interesting hour in the New York office as it was all talked over in detail.

By never making a purchase, large or small, until there was money in hand to pay for it, the visitor explained, and by carefully estimating running expenses and putting aside a daily proportion of the income, whatever it might be, to meet them, there were always funds in hand for coming charges.

> One cannot be running out every day to pay one's gas bill! But we can and do put aside a dollar and a half a day, or whatever the proportion may be, toward it. We do the same for our rent, fuel, electric light, taxes on property and all other running expenses, so that the money is there when it is needed. We paid the rent on Saturday, for example, but on Monday we begin just the same putting away for the next month or quarter. And these funds are rarely drawn upon for any other purpose. We reckon that we have spent that money already. And as to other things, we never give an order unless we have actual cash in hand to meet it. We do not draw upon probabilities.

"If the China Inland Mission can do it, never making an appeal for funds nor taking a collection," Borden exclaimed, "surely we can, by prayer and watchfulness! And I do think we ought not to buy even *a broom* until we have money in hand to pay for it."

But it was not only in these ways he sought to be of use. The work was growing fast and it was hard to keep pace with its requirements. Permanent offices were badly needed, and some places in which the students could meet for their classes. A hall also was required for the old Jerry McAuley Mission which had passed into Mr. Shelton's care.

The neighborhood in which they hoped to locate was a desperate one, almost every corner for many blocks in all directions being occupied by saloons or dance halls, with a plentiful sprinkling of moving-picture houses. Thousands of young people thronged the streets at night, and there were few places open to them in which the influences were not harmful.

The time had come for action, so Borden set to work under Mr. Shelton's direction to make the needs and opportunities known and to gather a circle of praying friends. Together they investigated every street in that section of "the tenderloin," and made a map showing exactly what there was and was not—a map which was in itself the most powerful of appeals. The circular Borden sent out, signed with his own name as chairman of the Building Committee, contained the map in full, dotted over with more than three hundred hell-traps of various sorts, and the plea for the activities of the National Bible Institute where it was so much needed "as a protest against iniquity and for the reaching of the sin-sick and for the protection of the innocent."

More important still was his work that summer in forming the "Circle of Intercession." This was his own idea, born of his conviction that prayer is fundamental and not secondary in work for God. Buildings might be put up and organization developed, but unless prayer kept pace with these activities all would be in vain. So it was for prayer Borden appealed most earnestly of all.

"Our Circle of Intercession has become most dear to us," Mrs. Shelton wrote, when these efforts had been rewarded, "for we realize that it was through Mr. Borden's consecrated energy and perseverance that it was formed two years ago. That was a wonderful summer for us—Mr. Borden gave so much time and thought in Mr. Shelton's office to the work; and for me there stands out vividly the morning when he most feelingly expressed his sympathy because of a dreaded ordeal before me. Every contact with him revealed the depths of a wonderful Christian character."

Back for his last year at Princeton, Borden was harder at work than ever, preparing a course of lectures he was to deliver to the students of the National Bible Institute. The Epistle to the Galatians was his subject, and the long list of books he consulted shows how thorough was his preparation. Luther's commentary he enjoyed especially, but it was only one of several. How he could possibly make time in the midst of his third year in Seminary to complete and deliver these seven lectures is a mystery. Week by week his class in the Marble Collegiate Church numbered from sixty to a hundred.

"His handling of this difficult Epistle showed that he had completely mastered his material," was Mr. Shelton's comment. "His outlines were clear and comprehensive, and he made the book a living message to the hearers."

Early in 1912 the National Bible Institute was passing through a time of no little trial. In spite of the Directors' efforts to keep clear of debt, a deficit of five thousand dollars had accumulated. There was much prayer about it, and an earnest desire to learn by past experience. But how was the deficit to be wiped out?

A meeting of the Board was called, for it looked as though there would have to be serious retrenchment. Borden had come up from Princeton. His financial contributions to the work were considerable, and no one was looking to him to do more. The morning had passed in earnest conference and prayer.

"I must make the 2:04 train," he said at length, "and shall have to run for it."

He was writing on a slip of paper as he spoke, and pushing it across the table to the Treasurer, Mr. Hugh Monro, he made for the door. It was a check for five thousand two hundred dollars! Without a word he had taken up the entire indebtedness. It was not only the gift, but the way in which it was done that was so like him! Nobody dreamed he was writing a check, and before they realized it he was gone.

But he gave more than money. A few weeks later he was in the throes of his final examinations at Princeton. The mountains were calling him. After a heavy winter's work he was eager for a few weeks in Switzerland among the glaciers he loved. His passage was taken and everything was ready when it came to his knowledge that Mr. Shelton was on the verge of a breakdown. Calling at his office Borden found that the doctor had ordered him to take complete rest and change. The need for it was urgent, but there seemed no one to take his place.

"Looks as though I might have to change my plans a bit, and help," was the entry in Borden's journal for that day.

Quietly then his passage was given up and the trip postponed. He was sufficiently familiar with the National Bible Institute to step in effectively, and before long was fully in charge. This meant that he was responsible not only for the office work. There were the daily open-air meetings, the oversight of the students in their classes and practical training, the charge of four Rescue Missions and of the monthly magazine, as well as the financial care of all this work.

It was a serious undertaking, the more so as Borden had decided before entering upon it that he must not be his own Providence in the matter of supplies. Mr. Shelton was not himself in a position to finance the work, and when sufficient means were not forthcoming he and his helpers had no resource but prayer. To strengthen them in their attitude of looking to the Lord in faith had long been Borden's desire. He believed that the promises of God were absolutely true and dependable. Here then was an opportunity for proving the reality of his own faith as well as strengthening that of his fellow workers. He would continue to give just as he had been giving, but would not permit himself to escape difficulties by the easy method of drawing upon his own banking account. And this led to a remarkable experience, as Mrs. Shelton writes:

There followed a time of severe testing along financial lines for the young substitute. Days passed without a dollar coming in—and mission superintendents and others needing their salaries! Some time before, Mr. Borden had faced the question of making up known deficiencies in the various Christian enterprises in which he was interested, and as his gifts were always thoughtfully and prayerfully given he had decided against it. Yet here was a temptation! How much easier to put his hand in his pocket and make up this lack than to spend hours in prayer alone and with friends, awaiting God's gracious answer. But the answers came—and with them such a sense of the reality and nearness of the living God as days and hours of ease could never have afforded.

It was the hottest summer that had been known in New York for many years, and the Bordens had just moved from Princeton to a house on Fifty-fifth Street for the time being. It was convenient to be nearer the office, but the heat of the city was overpowering. In spite of this, Mrs. Borden went with her son to some of the noonday meetings and put off her sailing for Europe until he could come. But that was weeks ahead and meanwhile the pressure of the work was heavy.

"Gee," William exclaimed in the office one day, "if I had known what I was coming up against, I doubt whether I would have made this suggestion!"

Yet in addition to all his other occupations he was caring for an invalid uncle that summer. He made time to go frequently to Long Beach, where his relatives were staying, to be a cheer to his aunt and to wheel the patient up and down the boardwalk in a chair, returning to the city by an early train in the morning.

"The Price of Power" was the title of an article he was writing at Long Beach one Sunday for the paper of which Mr. Shelton was editor. It was the outgrowth of a thought that had long been in his mind. A saying quoted by Mr. Moody had deeply impressed him: "The world has yet to see what God can do with a fully consecrated man." To be such a man was his highest ambition, and he was learning how real and practical is the price that has to be paid. He was learning that it comes into everything, and that it may be expressed in the one inclusive word, obedience. Obedience toward God had come to be the keynote of his life—instant, glad obedience. To him, the Word of God was final.

"On the other hand—" some of us are tempted to say.

To him there was no "other hand."

If he saw that in anything his life did not square with the Word of God, that ended it. The secret of power, he had learned, was that secret open to all—"the Holy Spirit whom God hath given *to them that obey him*" (Acts 5:32). He was speaking from experience when he wrote:

> There must be a definite determination to do God's will— a will to obey. Christ laid down the conditions of discipleship as denying self and following Him, and that is just what is required here. Each one must examine his life and put away all sin, not holding on to anything which the Spirit tells him he should let go.
>
> One of the hardest things anyone can have to do is to confess he has wronged another. But we read, "If thou bring thy gift to the altar, and there rememberest that thy brother hath aught against thee, leave there thy gift before the altar, and go thy way; first be reconciled to thy brother, and then come and offer thy gift."[1] We touch upon this matter of confession to others because it has played such a prominent part in spiritual awakenings, and because of the conviction that lack of such confession is the cause of much powerlessness in Christian service.
>
> Questions of life-work also need to be met squarely and the enquiry honestly made: "Lord, what wilt Thou have me to do?" The answer may not come at once, but there should be a willingness and determination to do His will, whatever service it may involve, at home or abroad. These are but suggestions to indicate what is involved in absolute consecration

[1] Matthew 5:23, 24.

to Christ, which is so necessary to real obedience. Do you lack power? Ask yourself, Have I ever fully surrendered? Have I definitely consecrated myself, put myself at God's disposal, to use as He deems best?

It must be admitted, however, that there are those who at some time of vision or conflict have won a victory and taken this great step, and yet have not subsequently had real power in their lives. What is the reason? Cases differ, but may we not say that it was probably through failure to make this principle of complete obedience permanent in their lives? Christ's rule for discipleship as given in Matthew 16:24 has been referred to above. Do you know how it reads in Luke, and what the additional feature is which has there been preserved for us? It is just one word: "If any man would come after me, let him deny himself and take up his cross *daily* and follow me." Daily—that is the thing to note. It is not enough to take up the cross once and then lay it down when the burden grows wearisome.

The need for daily application of this principle appears in two ways: first, old questions which have been faced and downed as we thought, will come up again; and secondly, there will arise new problems which were not covered by the original act of consecration. Many who have faced the question of life-work, and decided for the foreign field, illustrate this. It was at tremendous cost they made the decision, and possibly there was the thought that afterwards all would be plain sailing. But no: the same old problems had to be fought out, and there were new ones too to face. The principle of Christ's supremacy could not be lost sight of for a moment. Satan, when defeated, left Christ but for a little season. How much less, when he has been ousted from our lives at some conference or on some mountain-top, will he despair of finding a foothold when we are on the plane of everyday living again. Obedience, which is the price of power, must not only be absolute but daily. Are we paying this part of the price?

It may be there are others who have consecrated themselves to Christ and do seek to make this a daily attitude of life, and yet fail to receive real power. Where this is the case, may it not be due to imperfect application of the principle of obedience? It is comparatively easy to isolate the great issues, the big problems, and to deal with them by the grace of God. But there are many so-called "little things" which are apt to be overlooked. These grieve and quench the Spirit in no less real a way than the others.[2] They are difficult to deal with, and many Christians do not seem to recognize what they are at all —though ignorance does not save us from the consequences in this any more than in other spheres. We must study the Word of God, daily see ourselves in that glass, asking God to search us and know our hearts, try us and know our thoughts, and see if there be any wicked way in us.

Mr. Speer in his *Principles of Jesus* has indicated four great guiding principles that our Lord laid down—namely, purity, honesty, unselfishness and love. These are simple and plain enough; yet how many of us are checking up our every thought and word and deed by these? How many of us are asking in everything, "Is this pleasing to Him?" Our personal habits, our amusements, all our intercourse with others, business or social, should be considered in this light. We must seek not merely to avoid quenching the Spirit; we must be careful lest we grieve Him.

Obedience, absolute and unqualified, which is made a daily principle of living, carried even into little things, this is the price of power.

Of course there must not be a selfish motive, and we must not fail to ask in definite believing prayer for the Holy Spirit. But if the conditions are met, God will make good His promise, "Ye shall receive power." How the power will manifest itself in our lives need not concern us here. The saying still holds good—"The world has yet to see what God can do with a fully consecrated man." Only as filled with His Spirit can we hope to win men from darkness to light and to faith in

---

[2] "Self-pleasing in little things brings darkness. The lightest cloud before the sun will prevent it from focussing its rays to a burning point through the convex glass. Spiritually, the result is the same even with small, thin, scarcely visible acts of self-will."—ALEXANDER MACLAREN, D.D.

Christ. Shall we not each one resolve, from henceforth, to obey Him absolutely in all things, small and great?

Reality was what gave his words their power. Before Mr. Shelton's return to the office Borden was tested, himself, in the matter of putting duty before pleasure. A great occasion was on hand, the first reunion of his class at Yale, and he managed to get away for the weekend. But the triennial banquet, the climax of the proceedings, did not come until Monday, and there was a Board meeting of the National Bible Institute that day that he felt he should attend. Great was the consternatiton of his classmates when it appeared that he was leaving before the banquet. Many old friends were there, among them his roommate, Mac Vilas.

"Indeed you won't go to New York," they exclaimed with insistence. "We won't let you go!"

"But we might as well have talked to the Rock of Gibraltar," Vilas said.

Borden managed to return the following day, and that he entered fully into the spirit of the occasion may be seen from the note in his journal: "Attended to a few things at the office and left for New Haven, getting there just in time for the picture and the parade to the field for the game, which Yale won from Harvard, 9-6. Our class wore farmers' costumes. It was a great jollification!"

The summer had taken more out of the young substitute than he realized, but even on the voyage to Europe for a much-curtailed holiday he was working at an important task. The Moody Bible Institute of Chicago, of which he was a Director, thought it timely to prepare a statement setting forth the doctrinal standards of the institution. Borden was on the committee appointed for that purpose. His application papers to the China Inland Mission had already called for such a statement, and he had with him the Doctrinal Basis of the National Bible Institute, covering the same ground, which had been largely his work. This he enclosed with his letter to Chicago, concerning which Dr. Gray wrote to Mrs. Borden: "The letter is much valued by me, and I trust that when the biographer has finished with it, it may be returned to my hands."

Kronprinz Wilhelm,
July 21, 1912

Dear Dr. Gray—In accordance with your wishes I am taking this opportunity to draw up my suggestions for the proposed doctrinal basis of the Moody Institute.

First, the purpose:

As I understand it, the need is for a statement embodying what we feel is essential to sound doctrine in the teaching and work of the Institute. This statement should be an aid to the trustees, not only as a standard for checking up the teaching staff, but also to guide them in the selection of new trustees at any time—written assent to the doctrinal basis being required of all present and future members of the Board of Trustees as well as the teaching staff, and also a pledge to give notice of any future change of opinion, and willingness to resign if requested to do so.

Second:

What is the essential to sound doctrine? I feel that the inspiration and authority of Scripture; God: His being and attributes; Christ: His person (Deity) and work (atonement); the Holy Spirit: His person and work; man's sinful state and need of regeneration; the way of salvation from the guilt of sin (justification by faith alone) and from the power of sin (sanctification); the return of Christ and future rewards and punishments are the essentials.

Third:

The order and phrasing of the statement. I would say at once that I do not feel that it will be possible to employ Scripture language only, both from the nature and extent of the ground to be covered and the exigencies of the present day with its requirement of great exactness. We should, however, seek to be as brief as may be consistent with clearness. Coming then to the actual phrasing, I would suggest the following:

DOCTRINAL BASIS

OF

THE MOODY BIBLE INSTITUTE

We believe in the inspiration, integrity, and authority of the Bible. By this is meant a miraculous guiding work of the Holy Spirit in their original writing, extending to all parts of the Scriptures equally, applying even to the choice of words. Moreover, it is our conviction that God has exercised such singular care and providence through the ages in preserving the written word, that the Scriptures as we now have them are in every essential particular as originally given, so that the result is the very word of God, the only infallible rule of faith and practice, containing all things necessary to salvation and sound doctrine.

We believe that there is one living and true God, a spirit infinite, eternal and incomparable, etc. (see Westminister Shorter Catechism). And we believe that in unity of this Godhead there are three persons, the Father, the Son and the Holy Spirit (see Episcopalian Prayer Book).

We believe in the deity of our Lord Jesus Christ and in His death on the cross as a true substitute, and that His death was a sufficient expiation for the guilt of all men.

We believe in the Holy Spirit as a Divine person, distinct from the Father and the Son, who convicts the world of sin, regenerates and dwells in the true believer, quickening and empowering him in all his life and service.

We believe that all men are by nature sinful and unable to save themselves, and that "except a man be born again, he cannot see the kingdom of God."

We believe that men are justified by faith (in Jesus Christ) alone and are accounted righteous before God only for the merit of our Lord and Saviour Jesus Christ.

We believe that sanctification is a work of God's free grace whereby, being renewed in the whole man, we are enabled more and more to die unto sin and to live unto righteousness.

We believe in the second coming of our Lord, as a personal, visible and glorious advent on this earth.

We believe in the everlasting conscious blessedness of the saved and in the everlasting conscious punishment of the lost.

As a conclusion I would suggest an adaptation of the paragraph in the Moody Church statement to the effect that while specifying these doctrines, we by no means undervalue or set aside any Scriptures of the Old or New Testaments.

Of course I do not pretend that this is final, but it embodies my thoughts for the present. I hope you can read it all. Kindly keep the enclosed typewritten statement with this letter (of which I have no copy by the way) as I would like to refer to the two together in Chicago when we meet next fall, D.V.—Sincerely yours,

WILLIAM W. BORDEN

"So often nowadays we are told that it does not matter what men think, it only matters what they do," wrote a friend of Borden's from Bryn Mawr College. "It is a striking contrast to turn back to the Gospels and find the Lord Himself reversing this emphasis. His great question was, 'What think ye of Christ?' 'Who do men say that I am?'

"This Bill realized fully. He knew that it mattered supremely what he thought. He was a great help to me always in the Christian life, and I wish that more might know of his devotion to Christ. I wish that people who say it doesn't matter what you believe could only see how much it mattered to him, and the results those very beliefs produced in his life."

CHAPTER 13

MISSIONARY OUTLOOK

1912. AGE 24

The Master said, "Come, follow"—
  That was all.
Earth's joys grew dim,
  My soul went after Him;
I rose and followed—
  That was all.
Will you not follow if you hear His call?

— Selected

COMMENCEMENT EXERCISES were especially memorable the year that Borden graduated from Princeton, as they coincided with the Centennial celebrations of the Seminary. From all over the world came congratulatory messages, for Princeton —the oldest seminary of the Presbyterian Church in America— had graduated almost six thousand students, over four hundred of whom had gone abroad as missionaries. Many distinguished visitors were there for the occasion and the Borden home was full of guests.

"President Patton was at his best," William wrote, "and preached a tremendous sermon on 'The faith once for all delivered to the saints.' "

Dr. Speer's missionary address was equally inspiring. After recalling the devoted lives of Princeton graduates in many a field, he continued:

We owe it to the fathers who went before us to stand

afraid at no opportunity and flinch at no call. They taught us the glory of unswerving fidelity. The men who have gone out from these halls have always known the duty of staying by duty until the sun went down. They were taught that God is patient and that His servants need not be anxious or afraid.

The world situation which confronts us in these days he spoke of as God's gift to us, and not God's gift only, but God's test of our worthiness to be the heirs and executors of such a past.

The Seminary has always sought to breed in her sons a dauntless and unfearing supernaturalism. The missionary enterprise is too vast for a mere human will to sustain. Its difficulties, its necessities, its problems, its ideals call for God. Its sufficiency is in Him alone. Here, men learn that God was in the beginning and that God stands back of the end. With God and for God such men have dared all things, and have not fainted nor grown weary.

In the midst of the celebrations came the granting of diplomas to the graduating students. In his Line-A-Day journal, Borden noted:

> May 6, 1912
>
> Got our diplomas in Alexandria Hall. The academic procession was quite brilliant. Four fine addresses in the afternoon. Speer's was best, on Princeton in the Mission Field.

And the following day:

> Had our final prayer-meeting of the Benham Club.

Little more than six months remained for Borden of life in his own land, but how full they were of far-reaching activities! "He fulfilled a great time in a short time," as was said of Keith Falconer. He was running a race, and his eye was on the goal.

The very day that he had taken this last examination at Princeton, for example, found him in New York with Dr. John R. Mott, deep in plans for the work he was to take up in the fall in connection with the Student Volunteer Movement. A three months' schedule had been made out for visits to many colleges. He was to speak especially on the need of the Moslem world, before sailing himself for Egypt on his way to China. It was felt that a few months at Cairo, in the language school, would be of advantage, not only for the study of Arabic and the Koran but of Mohammedanism generally, before attempting to meet it in its strongholds in Western China.

Released from his responsibilities in Mr. Shelton's office, Borden had spent a few weeks in Switzerland, climbing the Jungfrau and the Wetterhorn, and had returned to New York refreshed for his work in the colleges. Then came his ordination, which took place in the Moody Church, Chicago, as its elders recorded:

> He was one of our boys. This was the church of his childhood. . . . Here he returned for ordination after completing his Seminary course, and as we examined him in view of that step his testimony rang true as steel to every cardinal doctrine of Holy Writ.
>
> On September 9, 1912, we set him apart to the ministry of our Lord and Saviour Jesus Christ in a foreign land, little thinking that his ministry was to be to our Lord himself in the better land.

The service was simple but impressive, marked by contrasts that gave the daily papers a good deal to say at the time. That a man of his age and prospects should turn away from all the world could offer and devote himself to a life of loneliness and hardship in a remote province in China, "the darkest and meanest section of the Orient," as one paper seriously said, became a nine days' wonder. But another Chicago daily gave an account of the proceedings that must have arrested attention, printing in full on its front page the hymn that seemed to sum up all there was to be said:

> When I survey the wondrous cross
>   On which the Prince of Glory died,
> My richest gain I count but loss
>   And pour contempt on all my pride.
>
> . . . . .
>
> Were the whole realm of nature mine.
>   That were an offering far too small;
> Love so amazing, so divine,
>   Demands my life, my soul, my all.

Borden did not see the papers. That side of the matter was painful to him. In a circular letter to twelve Princeton class-mates who kept up a correspondence, he mentioned the fact of his ordination, adding:

> I am sorry there was such unnecessary publicity, and hope you fellows will discount what was said very liberally.

The real impressiveness of the service lay in the love and sym-pathy of the great assembly for one who had grown up among them, whose consecration to Christ they knew full well; in the sermon by Dr. James Gray, Dean of the Bible Institute, and the charge given by Dr. John Timothy Stone, Pastor of the Fourth Presbyterian Church, and in the prayers with which Borden was committed to the Lord, on the spot from which Moody had so often preached, as the ministers and elders gathered round him:

> We set him apart for the work to which he was called. The hands of the lowly were laid upon his head. The Holy Spirit filled him. The grace of the Omnipotent was in his life.

That grace was very real in his mother's experience as well, in the hour which was to her the climax of her sacrifice. From his childhood she had consecrated him to the Lord, and his call to missionary work had come as an answer to her many prayers. Yet, since his father's death, she had learned to lean upon him in everything, and the very thought of separation seemed at times unbearable. Firm as a rock, there had been no wavering in his purpose. He knew as well as she did that her deepest desire was one with his own. They stood together, and his strength had helped her no less than his tenderness. But the separation had hitherto been prospective. Now it was coming near. His ordination meant, as Mrs. Borden realized, that they were committed to the sacrifice that seemed as if it must cost her very life.

And then—there is no explaining it apart from the presence of the Lord Himself—as in that hour she held back nothing, a wonderful peace filled her heart. Physical weakness, even, was replaced by strength, so that she was able to meet all the demands of the dreaded situation when it came, with gladness. For there is a fellowship with Christ which infinitely compensates any cost at which it is won.

To a friend who expressed surprise, about this time, that he was "throwing himself away as a missionary," Borden replied: "*You* have not seen heathenism."

He had; and the constraining love of Christ made him, as one of his Princeton classmates put it, "a missionary, first, last and all the time."

"No one would have known from Borden's life and talk that he was a millionaire," wrote another, "but no one could have helped knowing that he was a Christian and alive for missions."

Yet, to him, souls were just as precious in America as across the ocean, and his responsibility as great for all whom he could reach. His friend, Mr. Hugh Monro, Treasurer of the National Bible Institute, said in this connection:

> Not a few of us, under the influence of evangelistic services, or some other spiritual tonic, are filled with zeal for the salvation of others. At certain seasons, when we have given ourselves specially to prayer, perhaps, and the study of God's

Word, we are awakened to a new concern about the spiritual welfare of those around us. But there was nothing spasmodic about Borden's zeal. He had that unique thing, an abiding passion for the souls of men. It was his constant thought; it seemed never absent from his mind.

Most of us look for occasions which may afford a suitable opportunity for soul-winning, and excuse our lack of devotion and diligence because we feel that such an opportunity is not present. We continually hesitate to broach the subject of another's salvation, lest the occasion should not be favourable. Yet Borden found such opportunities continually.

Visiting with his mother, for example, in the home of some relatives, he became concerned about the butler, who was giving way to drink. At dinner one evening, when not sober, he let some ice cream slip off a plate, almost ruining a Worth gown. Learning that he had been dismissed, Mrs. Borden mentioned the matter to William. It was not their responsibility, maybe, but the following Sunday his mother's maid, walking in the direction of the butler's house, heard quick steps behind her and found William at her side.

"Melanie," he said, "I am going to enquire for ——. Couldn't we have prayer together that God will speak to him today?"

"So we stopped right there on the street," his old friend recalled. "Then Mr. William went on to the house, and the butler truly turned to the Lord that day. Only a fortnight later, he took pneumonia and died."

Did Borden regret the effort he had made to see him?

It was not easy in his busy life to make time for correspondence, but did he regret the letters he wrote, at some sacrifice, to a poor fellow in jail to whom, apparently, he was a stranger?

"I think of you a great deal," came the answer from a Connecticut prison, "and I am more than thankful for what you have done for me. I have had a hard time getting back to faith, but with your help and the help of God I can call myself a Christian again. . . . I have received a letter from my wife saying that you have sent her a copy of St. John's Gospel. She is very thankful to you for it; also for what you have done for me. You cannot imagine how much the brute I feel when I think of having done what I have—leaving my wife and baby, to be locked up in a felon's cell. . . . I hope with the help of God that henceforth I will be a better man."

The real test for fitness for missionary work abroad is not so much a high educational standard as the faith and love, the prayer and devotedness, that win men at home.

Borden's message in the colleges was of the sort to appeal to a strong type of personality. Fuller knowledge had but deepened his conviction that the two hundred millions of the Moslem world offered by far the hardest as well as the most neglected field for missionary enterprise. The very difficulties attracted him.

Kansu, for example—that lonely, far-off province in Northwest China, with its three million Moslems among a hardy population of Mongols, Tibetans and Chinese—was the sphere in which he hoped to labor. Peking was much more central, strategic, some would have said. There were not a few mosques in the capital, and a post as organizing secretary for work among Mohammedans throughout China could easily have been arranged. But Borden was looking for a harder billet. Just because Kansu was isolated, thrust out between Mongolia and Tibet, because the missionaries were few and the work difficult, because the people he longed to reach were there in multitudes, and no one was set apart for work among them, Kansu was the place of his choice.

Ho-chow was there with its bigoted, proud race of Moslems, Arabs by descent. There, too, were the Tung-hsiang, remnants of the old Hun tribes in the mountains, long since converted to Islam at the point of the sword. And there were the Salas from distant Samarkand, with their Turkish speech and faces, Moslem exiles who had tramped across Central Asia, hundreds of years ago, to find a home beside the Yellow River. And these virile, dominating sons of Islam were mingled in the western part of the province with Tibetans from the border marches and Mongols from north of the Great Wall. More than this, the Great Road running through the province—itself a thousand miles from east to west—led on across the Gobi Desert to the Moslem heart of Central Asia, linking up city after city in which no missionary had ever labored, and giving access to the mingled peoples of that vast region, one of the most neglected, from the missionary point of view, in the world. That waiting heart of Asia, how it appealed to him, just because so few were willing to lay down their lives that these, too, might have the message of redeeming love!

A handful of brave men and women were there, representing the two missions working in the province, and forty days' journey westward, two lonely pioneers, almost as far from the nearest missionaries on the other side.[1] More than sixty cities in Kansu itself without a witness for Christ; four-fifths of its population still unreached; three million Moslems for whom no one could be spared, because the inadequate staff was absorbed in work among the Chinese; no doctor, no hospital in the entire province, and those vast lands beyond with millions more for whom there were so few to care—that was the sphere that attracted Borden. And that is the sphere that with but little change as regards its Mohammedan population is waiting still.

With a background of such thoughts and purposes, Borden brought to his work in the colleges a reality that could not but be felt. The joy and inspiration of a great task possessed him, and he could not speak of missionary work, even in its hardest phases, as sacrifice. To him it was privilege of the highest order,

[1] The China Inland Mission and the Christian and Missionary Alliance were the only missions working in Kansu at that time. The solitary outpost in Central Asia is the city of Ti-hwa-fu, in which Mr. George Hunter and Mr. P. C. Mather of the China Inland Mission are still holding the fort alone. Pray for them and for the people to whom their lives are given.

the privilege that comes not to angels but to men, and to us
once only, now, in this fleeting life.

Two books were his traveling companions at this time, and
give some idea as to his talks in the colleges—one, the mission-
study book for the year, Dr. Zwemer's *Unoccupied Mission
Fields of Africa and Asia,* full of facts that were the strongest
arguments, and the other a little paper-covered volume so worn
and marked as to tell its own story. Many a journey it had
taken with him, and its truths were being wrought into his
deepest life. The little book cannot be purchased but it can be
obtained as a gift from the author, and in that way is in keeping
with its theme, "The Threefold Secret of the Spirit." Divided
into three parts, it deals first with the secret of the incoming of
the Holy Spirit; then with the secret of His fullness; and lastly
with the secret of His constant manifestation in our lives.[2]
Borden's copy is marked in the way he had with all his best-
loved books, one sentence standing out as meaning much to him:

*The supreme human condition of the fulness of the Spirit is
a life wholly surrendered to God to do His will.*

"To do His will": nothing greater or more glorious could be
desired, and Borden knew of nothing that brought deeper satis-
faction. Life was not, to him, a question of being or having this
or that; it was simply a question of the will of God—knowing
it, doing it, loving it. And such a life, he knew, was possible
even in college, through the indwelling of the Holy Spirit. So
his message was one of gladness and power.

Beginning at Schenectady, New York, in September, he
managed to visit no fewer than thirty colleges and seminaries
before sailing for Egypt in December. One to three days in a
place gave opportunity for interviews as well as meetings, and
his time was so filled that it was with difficulty he got away on
his twenty-fifth birthday to spend the evening with his mother.

---

[2] A copy of *The Threefold Secret of the Spirit,* by James H. McConkey, will
be sent free, post paid, to anyone who will write to the publishers for it. Address: Pittsburgh Bible and Tract House, 422 Bessemer Bldg., Pittsburgh, Pa.

In many an interview Mr. Robert Wilder's question came to his mind, and with the background of his experience at sea he would ask:

"Are you steering or drifting?"

The question served to open up the subject of a student's choices in life. The danger of drifting was manifest. If a man said he was steering, it was easy to go on:

"What is your goal, and Who is with you on board?"

To cut out indecision was what Borden urged. In a Greek Testament given to a friend he had written: "If any man wills to do his will, he shall know . . ." (John 7:17).

"It was a favorite passage of his," wrote the classmate, "and one upon which his own Christian activities were built up. Like his Master, he realized that it was nearly always a question of whether a man wanted to or not. Bill always referred the matter back to the will. In talking over a Bible group which was failing, the leader having grown lax, I remember Bill's saying that it might have been the best group in our class if the leader had been willing to pay the price."

The uttermost for the utmost was the price as he saw it—the uttermost of surrender on our part for the utmost of what God will do in and through us. It was a high ideal. Often Borden would meet one to whom it seemed too high with another question:

"Are you willing to be made willing?"

"I remember that to some of us this directness of appeal seemed at times to lack sympathy with the other person's point of view," continued his friend. "But it was the sort of thing to draw out the best that was in a man, and gather to itself those who were willing."

One thing evident to all was that the speaker himself was paying the price and finding it a wonderful exchange. And this gave force to the missionary side of his message, which consisted chiefly in a clear presentation of facts. For Borden felt with Dr. Zwemer that we do not need to plead the cause of missions. The case is there. All we ask is a verdict.

"If ten men are carrying a log," he said, at Andover, "nine of them on the little end and one at the heavy end, and you want to help, which end will you lift on?"[3]

Difficulties he spoke of as a challenge to faith and consecration, and while not minimizing them, especially in presenting the situation in Moslem lands, he laid but the more emphasis on our Lord's own words: "The things that are impossible with men are possible with God."

Of his own spirit in this work and the impression he made on students and others, something may be gathered from the following letters. Mrs. Henry W. Frost wrote of his visit to Philadelphia:

> While in and near the city we had asked him to stay with us. One morning I met him in the hall, just starting for one of the theological schools. He stopped hesitatingly, and then said:
>
> "Mrs. Frost, would you have a little prayer with me before I go? I don't think they want me very much, as my invitation comes from quite a small group of students."
>
> We had prayer together, and I said, "Will you be back to luncheon, William?"
>
> "Oh, I don't know," was his reply: and then laughingly, "They may not want me any longer!"
>
> As a matter of fact he stayed all day and had a very interesting time.

An intimate friend heard him when he addressed the German department of the Rochester Theological Seminary.

> After the address, he said that if there were any questions they cared to ask, though he would not promise to answer

---

[3] In proportion to the population, there were five hundred times as many ministers of the Gospel in the United States as there were ordained missionaries in China.

them all, he would be glad to try. Many questions followed —wise and otherwise—and I marvelled at his unfailing patience and complete lack of pride or self-consciousness, though he, the teacher, was probably the youngest of them all. During the months since I had seen him, a wonderful grace and sweetness had come into his life, but there was not one whit less of strength or humour.

And a Yale classmate, who attempted to draw him out on the subject of marriage, wrote from New Brunswick:

At the end of November, when Bill was here to give a talk in the Seminary, he came to my room and lay down on the couch, having caught a feverish cold. We talked over many matters. In a joking way I asked him when he was going to marry. He replied seriously that he thought it was cruel for a man who was going into one of the most difficult of missionary fields to ask any girl to go with him, because the woman always fared the worst, often succumbing when the man survived; that he had no intention of marrying—it would be wrong to the girl and would hinder his highest efficiency in the field he had in view. Bill's thorough-going decision on this question, which is so hard for many to settle, is another indication of his complete surrender of himself to the great work to which he was called.

Borden strongly approved the rule of the China Inland Mission with regard to outgoing missionaries, whether men or women, that they should remain unmarried for the first two years in China, so as to give undivided attention to the study of the language and have the best opportunity of becoming acclimatized and getting into touch with the people. It hardly needed the experience of the Mission to prove that this was wise and helpful. To him it seemed common sense, and an obvious application of the Master's words: "Seek ye first the kingdom of God. . . ."

His own problem extended, however, far beyond the two years. What about the period, long or short, when he would be practically homeless and exposed to no little hardship and danger? In one of his much-read books he had marked the lines from Meyer's *St. Paul:*

> Yes, without cheer of sister or of daughter,
> Yes, without stay of father or of son,
> Lone on the land and homeless on the water
> Pass I in patience till the work be done.

After his last meeting in December, concluding his three months' work in the colleges, he was dining with Dr. and Mrs. Angell in Rochester, and the latter wrote of being "deeply impressed with the fire and ardor of his faith."

> As he sat at table with us, talking of all he hoped to do for and in China, his face became glorified, his eyes shone with a light which only divine things can awaken. At the same time there was a poise, a dignity and balance which showed that his was not the mind of a fanatic. He was one who had counted the cost but never flinched for a moment.

"Those were fruitful months," wrote Mr. Fennell P. Turner, General Secretary of the Student Volunteer Movement. "William was used to lead students in many colleges and universities to give their lives to foreign missionary service. The last letter I received from him enclosed the 'declaration card' of a Student Volunteer who had signed it after his visit, and sent it on to him in Cairo. In years to come there will be missionaries in many fields who owe their decision, under God, to William's unselfish service during his last months in this country."

One cannot wonder that the leaders of the Volunteer Movement desired the continuance of such a strong effective work. But Borden had last arrangements to make before leaving for Egypt and felt that his departure should not be delayed. It was like him not to put off going until after Christmas even. His work in the colleges did not end until the tenth of December, and it would have seemed natural to take the Christmas vacation at home and set out early in the new year. But the S.S.

Mauretania was sailing on the seventeenth and was due to reach Port Said on New Year's Day. It meant only one week for packing and final preparations, but two or three weeks longer at the other end. Time was to Borden one of his most important stewardships. His mother did not hold him back, so it was a foregone conclusion. To him could never be imputed "the ungirt loin and the untrimmed lamp."

One last touch there had been with Yale classmates, of which his friend Campbell wrote:

> On November twenty-eight, Bill was usher at my sister's wedding to Louis G. Audette. Other Yale fellows were there. We had a jolly time and Bill was in for all the fun. The wedding was an evening affair, after which Bill packed off to the city to be with his mother, as the days before he sailed were getting few.

He had kept up his visits to the Yale Hope Mission through all his other engagements and had provided, financially, for its being carried on under the care of Mr. Don O. Shelton of the National Bible Institute. Even in December he managed to run down again to New Haven, giving a Sunday evening to the dear old work. His love for it was just the same as when he had gone into it with all the hopes and fears of a beginner, six years previously. Bernhardt had been called to a larger sphere,[4] but his place was ably filled by Mr. and Mrs. William Ellis, the later saved, himself, from the depths of sin and misery. "Bill Ellis" and "Bill Borden" were a great combination when they could be together in the meetings.

"What has impressed you most since you came to America?" Dr. Henry W. Frost asked a much-traveled visitor.

Without hesitation came the reply: "The sight of that young millionaire kneeling with his arm around a 'bum' in the Yale Hope Mission."

The last Sunday of all William spent quietly with his mother.

[4] Prison Reform work in Atlanta, Georgia.

They went to church together in the morning, little thinking it was for the last time, and on the following day he took part in the meeting held regularly in their home for prayer for the Moslem world. Several friends came to dinner that evening, including Dr. and Mrs. Frost and Mr. Shelton. William was leaving the next day, and by common consent the five or six men with whom he had been most closely associated in work for God foregathered in his room for a last hour of prayer and fellowship. It was Mr. Shelton who wrote:

> We prayed that our beloved friend might be kept in safety throughout his long journey, and guided and upheld in all his ways. And then he prayed for us, and for the work we represented. He was so strong and vigorous in body and mind that night that we anticipated for him long and useful service. And in less than four months . . .

But happily they did not know it then.

In the quiet of her room that night, weary and worn and sad, Mrs. Borden fell asleep, asking herself again and again, "Is it, after all, worth while?" In the morning as she awoke to consciousness, the still small voice was speaking in her heart, answering the question with these words: "*God* so loved the world that he gave his only begotten Son . . ."

"It was strength for the day," she said, "and for all the days to come."

From childhood, William's constant prayer with his mother had been that the will of God might be done in his life, and as they parted on the *Mauretania* it was still the same. Did it come back to him afterwards, as it did to her, that their last petition together was that he might be taken to China and made a blessing among its Moslem millions—but only, "if it be Thy will"?

To the companion of his first long journey, Mr. Walter Erdman, Borden wrote after leaving:

> It is not easy. There are many temptations and adversaries. Pray for me that I may have strength.

Among the Christmas letters opened in England was a faded sheet bearing a Christmas carol, with the refrain:

> Glory in the highest and goodwill to men.
> Peace on earth, peace on earth.

Beneath the verses and on the back of the page Mrs. Borden had written:

Darling, a blessed Christmas to you! This is one of our old song-sheets used at "89," years and years ago, when we were all together. Never did I realize so clearly the missionary meaning of Luke 2:10[5] as I did yesterday morning while sitting by your side in church.

Just one word more: I will never cease to be grateful for the rich blesing you have been to me, Dear, a comfort and a strength all your years to your devoted mother. What a rich New Year is unfolding before you! It was so beautiful having you with us in our little prayer-circle—just one more of the loving touches God has put to these last days.

[5] "Good tidings of great joy which shall be *to all people*."

CHAPTER 14

STEWARDSHIP

1912. AGE 24

Who is there to-night who can always see the shadow of the Cross falling upon his banking account? Who is there who has the mark of the nails and the print of his spear in the plans and life, his love and devotion and daily program of intercession? Who is there who has heard the word of Jesus and is quietly, obediently, every day, as He has told you and me, taking up his cross to follow Him?

REV. SAMUEL M. ZWEMER, D.D.

TWO REMARKABLE WILLS were probated within a few days of each other in the spring that followed Borden's sailing for Egypt, one his own, made in the fall of 1912, and the other that of J. Pierpont Morgan, who died possessed of almost a hundred million dollars. Though a devout believer, who prefaced his will with the statement, "I commit my soul into the hands of my Saviour, in full confidence that having redeemed it and washed it in His most precious blood, He will present it faultless before the throne of my Heavenly Father," Mr. Morgan at the age of seventy-five left little more than half as much to the work of God as William Borden left at twenty-five.

Mrs. Borden and her sister, going over William's check books recently, found that during the three years at Princeton Seminary he had given away about seventy thousand dollars to Christian work, as far as the stubs in hand show. This was a surprise to them, as he never referred to his giving.

Perhaps nothing is more distinctive than the way in which people do kindnesses, especially in the matter of financial help. Easy as it may seem, it is one of the most difficult things to give helpfully. Borden's way was characteristic.

"Few Christians of ample means," said Mr. Hugh Monro, "succeed in realizing such a degree of detachment from their possessions as to remove all sense of restraint in their dealings with their fellows of every station. Borden had learned the art of administering wealth on a large and generous scale, without a trace of self-consciousness and with complete self-effacement."

And his friend Campbell recalled:

Bill always followed the injunction, "Let not thy left hand know what thy right hand doeth." He insisted that not even his initials should appear when a list of benefactions was published. It almost seemed to irritate him if he was found out. His best friends never knew even a small percentage of the gifts he was making. Many surprising incidents would come to light if all who had been helped by him could be induced to tell their stories. Bill's cheque-books show how little he spent for himself and how much he was doing for others.

Standing in the doorway of their Princeton home, Borden's love of cars was awakened one day as a fine automobile flashed by.

"Gee!" he exclaimed, "wouldn't I like a car like that!"

"Why do you not get one, William?" asked a friend who was with him.

"I cannot afford it," was the unexpected reply.

His money was not his own, and there were always ways in which it was needed for the Master. A Princeton classmate wrote:

I have been told that he felt one of his temptations was to own a car. He never purchased one, because he thought that for him it would be an unjustifiable luxury. I remember one Saturday afternoon in New York going with him to the automobile show in a hall at Madison Square Garden. He knew all the various makes, and pointed out to me the advantages of the different cars. But we left the hall to take dinner at the Y.M.C.A. and spend the evening down at the Katherine Slip and Doyer Street Missions. And he had filled his pockets and mine with copies of St. John's Gospel to use in personal work.[1]

And Mrs. Borden said:

I think William's real reason for the stand he took about a car was that he deprecated the luxury seen in the lives of so many Christians. He did not feel justified in using his money, which he held distinctly as a stewardship, for any such purpose. All the time we were in Princeton I think he was longing to get away into simpler living.

The impression that his giving made upon his own home church is interesting. Sometimes even generous gifts produce a strained relationship in church life, but there is nothing of that sort in the picture his Chicago friends put before us:

Though separated from us a good deal during the last ten years, Borden never lost his heart-interest in the work of the Lord in this place. His frequent letters and visits and his constant gifts bore witness to that. . . .

He inaugurated and supported in this church the largest Daily Vacation Bible School in Chicago, which brought more street children into our Sunday School and services than any other movement we are undertaking.

He was the largest giver to our Fresh Air Work, to our Sunday School and to the general expenses of the church during the last years of his life, and he left to this church one hundred thousand dollars, realizing the wonderful opportunity it has as a down-town church to "preach the gospel to every creature" within the reach of its influence, in this teeming city of thirty different nationalities . . . [1955: more than forty].

[1] Rev. L. C. M. Smythe of Charleston, S.C., now a missionary in Japan.

He believed that this church could do a great foreign missionary work here at home . . . but he did not stop at that. During his lifetime he made use of his money in a world-wide ministry, yet so quietly that his left hand knew not what his right hand did. After his departure, however, his statesmanlike grasp of the problem of the evangelization of the world in this generation became apparent, for he bequeathed practically the whole of his inheritance, about one million dollars, in four nearly equal parts, all for the purpose of preaching Christ—one-fourth to be used in Chicago, another quarter in other parts of the home-land, the third portion in China, and the remainder in other foreign countries. . . .

This was Borden: quiet but powerful; saying little but doing much; rich but self-denying; humble in spirit but imperial in purpose; a general in organization, but always willing to be a private in service. He declined our urgent invitation to preach in the Moody Church, on the ground that he was not capable, but he was not ashamed to tell of his faith in Jesus on the street corner. His heart went out to the uncared-for, Christless millions of Kansu, but he did not overlook the worthy widow, orphan and cripple in the back streets of Chicago, as some of us well knew. He was intent upon seeking to win for Christ and His service the young men of our colleges and universities, and to this end the last months of his life in America were given, but that did not prevent his thinking of, praying for and giving to the care of little children and the aged.

His provision for the China Inland Mission manifested the same breadth of mind and tenderness of spirit.

"I do not like to speak of his money," Dr. Henry W. Frost said in this connection. "We seldom thought of it while he was with us. But I refer to his bequest to the mission that I may mention his desire with regard to a portion of it. He asked that a hundred thousand dollars might be invested in order that the interest upon it should be used for aged and infirm missionaries. A young man of twenty-four thinking of and providing for old and infirm missionaries! Could anything be more far-reaching in thought and sympathy?"

When the provisions of the will were made public, the Rev. E. Y. Woolley, acting pastor of the Moody Church, wrote to Mrs. Borden:

"What a remarkable document it is! The *Chicago Tribune* has the best report of it, which no doubt you have seen. Its testimony to Jesus Christ as Lord and Saviour will do untold good. And what noble bequests! The whole world will be touched for Christ by your son's life and act. . . .

"Mr. Borden's magnificent gift to the work of the Lord in and through the Moody Church has inspired our people to do and dare greater things for His glory. One very poor and very sick old lady, who has been praying and giving for a new church for several years, was just transported with praise to God when she heard of this."

The Rev. Charles R. Erdman, D.D., of Princeton Seminary, in his published sketch of Borden's life, *An Ideal Missionary Volunteer,* made the following statement with regard to his will:

It is an extraordinary document, not only in view of the actual bequests which it provides, but also because of the spirit it manifests of loyalty to Christ and devotion to the work of world evangelization. It is in itself a missionary appeal. Its largest provision is for the China Inland Mission, in connection with which the donor had expected to serve and on whose Council he held a place. For the work of this mission he bequeathed the sum of $250,000; and with unique sympathy and thoughtfulness for one so young, this was added: "I suggest that $100,000 of this amount be invested, and the income thereof be used for the support and maintenance of missionaries and other workers connected with said Mission who through age or infirmity have become incapacitated for active service in the mission field or at home, and who are in need of and deserving of aid."

The sum of $100,000 was left to the National Bible Institute of New York; and like amounts to the Moody Bible Institute of Chicago, and to the Chicago Avenue Church; $50,000 each was given to Princeton Theological Seminary, to the Board of Foreign Missions of the Presbyterian Church, U.S.A., to the Board of Foreign Missions of the Presbyterian Church, U.S. (South), to the Board of Foreign Missions of the United Presbyterian Church, and to the Chicago Hebrew Mission; and $25,000 each to the Nile Mission Press, to the American Bible Society, to the Chicago Tract Society, and to the Africa Inland Mission. Of the remaining estate the China Inland Mission and the three Presbyterian Boards were made the residuary legatees. . . .

Another provision suggests that William Borden had a definite and adequate *missionary message*. Nothing troubled him more than to see men of culture, ability and devotion planning to undertake missionary work while they were evidently ignorant of the great essential truths of the gospel. He therefore requested that his money should be used in the support of only such men as held absolutely to the deity of Christ and His vicarious atoning death for sinners. "It is further my desire," so runs the will, "that the said bequests hereinbefore made be used and disposed of in accordance with the following recommendations by me, to wit: That each of said bequests be used for and in connection with missionaries and teachers who are sound in the faith, believing in such fundamentals as the doctrine of the divine inspiration and authority of the Scriptures, the doctrine of the Trinity, including the deity of Jesus Christ, and in the doctrine of the atonement through the substitutionary death of our Lord Jesus Christ."

So statesmanlike a leader as Dr. John R. Mott was profoundly impressed with the quality of this young man's living and giving, as may be seen from the following letter to his mother:

My association with William has given me a keen appreciation of the value of the service which he accomplished for Christ and His kingdom by his life, by his witness, by his gifts, and by his activities. It has been on my mind for some time to write you to express my personal conviction as to the marked contribution which he made to his generation within the sphere of his influence. He exerted a great influence in the direction of the conservation and expansion of the spiritual life of our colleges. This he did through his constant and helpful work in the Christian Association and Volunteer Movement during his student days, as well as in his many personal relationships.

The sincere solicitude he manifested that the central points of our Christian faith might be preserved in purity and reality was one of the strong personal factors of which we have not had too many in resisting the movements and influences tending to disintegrate faith. The manner in which he sought to bring to bear the vital and superhuman power of Christianity upon the needs and problems of individuals and of society both during his college and seminary days was simply splendid. From the time I became acquainted with him as an undergraduate until I last saw him, his dominant ambition seemed to be the world-wide spread of the kingdom of Christ. He did as much as any young man whom I knew to help realize the watchword of the Volunteer Movement—"The Evangelization of the World in this Generation."

There is another aspect of his life and work which impressed me very deeply, and that was his attitude and practice with reference to money. I have read many comments in religious periodicals of different countries regarding the disposition which he made of his estate in his will. Without doubt he set an example to the rapidly multiplying number of wealthy young men and women; but to my mind even more instructive than his final will was his life-habit as a young man with reference to his money. This to my mind was truly remarkable. As you know, I was brought into the most intimate relations with him on this side of his life, in connection with different Christian enterprises which he so generously helped to promote.

I would like to mention a few things which characterized his giving. It manifested foresight and rare discernment. I have seldom met a person who showed such penetration of mind in estimating the worthiness of causes, in seizing opportunity at the flood and in anticipating results. His conscientiousness in the use of his money was always apparent. His chief concern seemed to be that of not making simply a good use of the money but the very best use of it. One was conscious of the fact that he regarded himself as a trustee and in no sense a proprietor.

His thoroughness in investigating objects was nothing less than remarkable. I have known a great many wise donors, but only one or two others who employed as thorough processes in seeking to estimate the worthiness of causes and the wisest ways of helping. He had evidently chosen a few clear guiding principles to help him determine his duty as he faced opportunity to relate his gifts to the plans of the Kingdom. These principles were such as led him to devote his money to promoting the most vital spiritual processes.

These traits, together with his prayerfulness in determining what to do with his money and in following his gifts, and above all his wonderful generosity, mark him out as a model to the young men of his generation to whom God may have entrusted financial power.

PART IV

AFTERWARDS

Oh, let me live as if Christ died
   But yestertide—
And I had seen and touched His pierced side:

I would rejoice as one who knows
   How soon He rose,
To tread beneath His feet our unseen foes.

And I would work as if heaven bright
   Were now in sight!
What if to-morrow bring that great delight!

—Selected

CHAPTER 15

CAIRO

1913. AGE 25

Having set my hand to the plough, my resolution was peremptorily taken, the Lord helping me, never to look back any more, and never to make a half-hearted work of it. Having chosen missionary work in India, I gave myself wholly up to it in the determination of my own mind. I united or wedded myself to it in a covenant the ties of which should be severed only by death.

REV. ALEXANDER DUFF, D.D.

CAIRO WITH ITS BRILLIANT SUNSHINE and lure of color and all its dust and heat was not new to Borden. He had visited it with the Rev. Walter Erdman eight years previously, when they had traveled up the Nile to Aswan, seven hundred miles toward the heart of the dark continent. The colossal ruins of Karnak, the rock-hewn tombs of the kings, the temples of Thebes and Philae, the statues of Memnon and other remains of the ancient world stirred them profoundly. From Aswan William had written:

Upper Egypt completely fulfils my expectations—the Nile itself, the contrast of the fresh green fields with the quivering sand beyond, the groves of date palms, villages of flat-roofed houses, camels with their dusky riders crossing the desert which stretches away as far as eye can see. It really is delightful.

Our first donkey-ride in Egypt took us through the town and out into the desert to the Bishareen encampment. These people are Soudanese, I believe, and very different from any others we have seen. They wear their hair hanging in loose gimlet-curls, about eight inches long. They are quite black and have clear-cut features, at least those we have seen have.

There really is an awful mess of Orientals here in Egypt, very difficult to sort out! There are Egyptians and Turks as white as any of us, who wear the red fez, the only way I have of knowing them to be natives. Then there are people of various shades of blackness who wear the fez also. Besides these there are innumerable Arabs, Soudanese and other races.

But now it was as a missionary, not a traveler, that Borden was in Cairo—that great city that Dr. Maltbie Babcock wrote of as "a huge melange, an ecumenical potpourri, a huddle of the ends of the earth and the first and last of civilizations."

It was not at Shepheard's Hotel, where he had stayed before, but at the Y.M.C.A. that he took up his quarters. Met at the railway station by Dr. Zwemer, he was soon introduced to the very heart of things in the missionary community. He found himself unexpectedly in touch with China as well, for a missionary from Hongkong had discovered a Chinese student in El Azhar university, of whom he spoke to Borden on the day of his arrival. The lonely student, it appeared, was from the very province in which William was hoping to labor (Kansu), and was so cut off from his own country that he did not even know of the fall of the Manchu dynasty or the establishment of the new republic. Borden was eager to meet him, and almost the first entry in his journal was:

January 7, 1913

Went to El Azhar with Mr. Gairdner. Met the only Chinese student there—the first Chinese Moslem I have ever seen, so far as I know.

What a world of interest that El Azhar proved to be, with its white-turbaned students, nine or ten thousand of them, from many lands, including Russia, Persia, North and Central Africa, Abyssinia, India, Arabia, and a couple of hundred professors (Sheikhs) every one of whom had spent at least twelve years studying in the university itself! Old as it was, dating from the tenth century, and entrenched in Moslem bigotry and pride, it was not unaffected by the Christian influences at work around it. Only a few months before Borden's coming an article had appeared in a religious paper in which one of its professors had written:

> Do not say that it is impossible to convert an Azhar Sheikh and bring him to Christ, for with God all things are possible. Was I not a fanatical sheikh in El Azhar, and was I not by God's grace converted? To-day I pray that my fellow-sheikhs may be won even as I was.

Numbers of students were attending the Monday evening meetings for Moslems that winter, at which Michael Mansour was speaking in great power. "Mighty in the Scriptures and in the Koran as well," he was attracting great crowds. A foreign missionary was always in the chair, to keep order, and Borden was soon in his element distributing Arabic Scriptures and tracts.

From the Y.M.C.A. headquarters it was no great distance to the American Mission where Dr. Zwemer lived, and where these Monday evening meetings were held, or to the compound of the Church Missionary Society at which a good deal of Borden's time was spent. For it was there that the students of the new Study Center took their courses in Arabic with the Rev. W. H. T. Gairdner, and in Islam and practical work with other missionaries. Eight or ten were taking the complete course and were attending Dr. Zwemer's lectures at the Y.M.C.A. and in the theological seminary. It was a keen, live circle, and one to which Borden was soon contributing a good deal. Mr. Gairdner found him "brim full of energy and hope, bringing a new element into our midst." And Dr. Zwemer wrote:

> I never saw a man come to Egypt with eyes more open to see the kingdom of God. Other men come to see the dead Pharaohs,

to study history or join the great company of tourists all over the land, never once lifting their eyes to see the fields "white unto harvest." Borden had not been in Cairo two weeks before he organized the students of the theological seminary to attempt a house-to-house canvass with Christian literature for *the whole city* with its eight hundred thousand people.

Here was a man with the frame of an athlete, the mind of a scholar, the grasp of a theologian as regards God's truth, and the heart of a little child, full of faith and love; a man who was so tender in the relations of home-life that our children used to nestle upon his knee as if they had known him for years— and he a comparative stranger. . . .

Knowing that he had to learn Chinese, he came to Cairo to perfect himself in Arabic. Some people shrink from the foreign field, questioning, "Could I learn the language?" Here was a man who deliberately set before himself the task of learning not one but two of the most difficult languages in the world, before entering upon his life-work of declaring the unsearchable riches of Christ to Chinese Mohammedans. . . .

At Yale, at Princeton, in Cairo we see him digging deep, thinking deep and studying hard. . . . He did not import doubts to the Orient, he imported his great convictions of the eternal truth of God. . . . When he lived in Cairo he was a friend to the Coptic Christians and the Armenian Christians. He was a brother to the American missionaries and to the British missionaries. He attended the Scotch church and the American church, and at the last all sorts and conditions of Christians met together to do him honour.

Borden's Cairo letters are interesting in the light of these recollections, brief though they had to be on account of his studies. His eagerness to acquire Arabic may be judged from the fact that two weeks after his arrival in Cairo he was making arrangements to board in a Syrian family, so that he might hear it spoken as much as possible. The plan about which he wrote to his mother did not materialize until a month later.

Saturday we had a very interesting session at the Study Centre, and in the afternoon I went out with Mr. Gairdner to visit old Cairo and the C.M.S. hospital. As this is well on the outskirts of the city we got a good ride on our wheels. Later we called on a Syrian family in which Mr. Gairdner thought I might be received as a paying guest. They had a surprisingly nice place, and as it was an unexpected visit the cleanliness and order could not have been put on for our benefit. They insisted upon giving us refreshments, which consisted of some kind of liquid in little liqueur glasses, quite harmless, followed by a teaspoonful of grated cocoanut put into our mouths by our hostess!

Sunday, I started my first work for Moslems by distributing *khutbas,* little sermons in Koranic style gotten out by the Nile Press. It required some courage to take the first plunge, with my two words of the spoken language, "Do you read Arabic?" and begin offering these booklets on the streets. But I soon found that it went very well, and I have given out about fifty already. Only one or two have declined to take them.

Monday night I went to my first service in Arabic. It was at the American Mission headquarters and most interesting. A few weeks ago, it seems, a rumour got abroad that Mudbuli, a Moslem saint, had come out of his tomb and had taken refuge in the Greek church near by—a pretty good exchange, considering the dilapidated state of the tomb. Of course, the more educated scoffed at the idea, but multitudes believed it, with the result that there was quite a riot at the time. Soon after, in a newly published Moslem book attacking Christianity, the author said that the resurrection of Christ was just like this Mudbuli affair, the story of a lot of silly women. He called attention to this as a great joke! But there is a Moslem convert here, Michael Mansour, a former El Azhar student, who went to the place where the book was printed and got out five hundred circulars saying he would answer the above statement, debating it with anyone who would come. This was the gathering Dr. Zwemer and I attended. He was half expecting a riot, as the place was packed with Moslems. The meeting opened and closed with prayer, however, and Mansour spoke for nearly an hour, holding their attention so that there was no disturbance and only one or two went out. It was a great triumph, and though I could only understand an occasional word, I was very glad to be there.

This afternoon I had a fine time, going off into the native bazaar with Dr. Zwemer to a book shop. It was near the Azhar, and we had a fine chance to get rid of all the *khutbas* we had, to students and others, and one of them bought a Gospel. Among the books we purchased were some Korans, and when these were put in the bottom of the carriage there were strong objections immediately and they had to be put up on the seat beside the driver. The outing was great fun, for we not only did this work but had a great time together. This book-shop man, by the way, is an enquirer who has been already a couple of times to see Dr. Zwemer. Things are on the jump here, especially when you are with Dr. Zwemer.

He had not time to write about the fascination of the street-life in Cairo, with all its movement and color. "Old Cairo is a bazaar," as Dr. Babcock put it, "its narrow lanes over-hung with cornice that almost touch; with awnings of rugs, balconies, grated windows through which secluded eyes peep; booths, like mere vestibules, with no windows or doors, their owners sitting, Turk-fashion, smoking, haggling, finally demanding your 'last price,' and following you often far along the way; with camels, donkeys, dogs, water-sellers with their clanging brass cups, vendors of everything with cries to match, whips cracking like torpedoes; with Nubians, Abyssinians, Greeks, Copts, Arabs, veiled women in black silk balloons and high-heeled slippers, fellahin women with no veils but with tattooed skin and with babies on their backs, rug men and scarab-sellers, jewellers and brass-workers dragging you into their dens, beggars, cripples, children crying 'Baksheesh.' Oh, the streets of Cairo! The Mouski Bazaar no one who has seen can ever forget."

Every phase of missionary work in this cosmopolitan city interested Borden, and his sympathy and eagerness to learn were winning many friends. He was finding ways, too, in which he could wisely give financial help. At the Y.M.C.A. he was in touch with young men of various nationalities, whom he joined in sports as well as meetings. "He was a splendid young man, so healthy, mentally, morally and spiritually," wrote a Syrian friend with whom he was reading French. And the Christian Endeavor Meeting was long remembered at which he spoke on the topic, "Be a Christian: Why not?"

He laid himself out to encourage the Egyptian Student Movement. It was a gift of his that made possible the obtaining of much better quarters, including a room set apart for Bible study. Here the students of different institutions could meet in groups, one school having one night, and another school another.

"It is for this Bible room that they are asking for a picture of Mr. Borden," one of their missionary friends wrote a little later. "They say that he was such a help to them, and his blessing is still with them in their work."

He was making time also for what in earlier days he used to call his "long-distance work"—letters to people with whom he had spiritual contacts. To a Mr. H., for example, he wrote in March:

I can sympathize with you in the matter of controlling your thoughts, for that is a thing we all have to fight for. You are right in saying we may commit great sins in our minds, though we do not do so outwardly. This is the view of sin which Christ gives us in the Sermon on the Mount, Matthew 5 and 6. However, I believe that in this as in all other things we can gain the victory by faith, through His aid, who was "tempted in all points like as we are, yet without sin." . . .

The principle on which we want to work is to crowd out the bad with the good. If we merely seek to put away evil without replacing it with active good, we may find that worse things come in. I have been helped by the suggestion that when we are tempted to harbour evil thoughts we should at once think of Christ, or repeat some verse of Scripture—in this way spoiling the picture, so to speak, by letting in a flood of light. Our object must be to bring "every thought into subjection to the obedience of Christ." 2 Cor. 10.5.

Chief among his interests at this time was the distribution of the booklets in Koranic style to which allusion has been made already. The idea had come to Borden early in his stay in Cairo. Writing about it to friends in New York, Dr. Zwemer said:

"How glad I am to hear of your good prayer meetings at the home of Mrs. Borden. Her son is a benediction to the work here, not only at the Y.M.C.A. but in both the missions. He is a spiritual power and up-to-date in his methods. At his suggestion we are starting the distribution of *khutbas* all over Cairo, the students of the theological seminary working with us."

It was a movement with prayer power behind it, and before long it was taken up by others in the missionary community, so that within six months of its beginning Mr. A. T. Upson, superintendent of the Nile Mission Press could say:

"There never has been a time in the history of mission-work at this center when there were so many inquirers."

For the tract distribution led to many talks and much personal work. And who shall say how much further the results were carried, remembering that Cairo is the intellectual center of the Mohammedan world?

All unconscious of the forces his earnest purpose would set in motion, Borden was giving every hour he could spare to his own share in this work. The *khutbas* were brief pointed discourses, written by Mr. Upson and a converted El Azhar man, beginning with some passage from the Koran and leading up to clear teaching from the Bible. Borden appreciated their value. His idea was that there should be a shop-to-shop and, if possible, house-to-house distribution of these tracts. In his direct way he went to the Seminary students and put it before them.

"I will pay for the *khutbas,* if you fellows will help me carry them."

And help they did right heartily, seeking to reach out with the gospel all through that great city of Cairo. To his mother Borden wrote:

February 5, 1913

Yesterday, we had a report of our *khutba* distribution and found that all had gone off without excitement, save in the case of Dr. Zwemer and the students who had accompanied him to a fanatical part of the city. With them, too, all went well for a time, till they met an old man who wanted to know by whom the tracts had been written, and who got quite excited when he learned that it was a former El Azhar student who had become a Christian. Dr. Zwemer, seeing that there was going to be trouble, tried to get the students away and to disperse the crowd by going into a shop. But the crowd waited outside, and there was no way of escape. Finally, the old man continuing his attack, they were all marched off to the police station.

The officer looked at the *khutbas* and listened to the charge. "Why," he said, "this is nothing but Christianity! You can read about this any day." And he let them go.

The result was that the wind was quite taken out of the old man's sails, and they were able to distribute a lot of *khutbas* right in the police headquarters, which would have been inaccessible to them otherwise. They invited the people to come to the Monday night meeting for Moslems, and the man who made the trouble was there all right last Monday night. Sorry I missed the excitement! But I have another section of the city which is less liable to afford interest of this kind.

February 12, 1913

Dr. Zwemer has just started a new thing—putting Christian notices into the daily papers, inviting inquiry by letter or in person. He has already received several answers.

My Arabic is going rather slowly just at present. I seem to have struck a snag. It certainly is difficult! However, I hope to overcome by the help of God and with due perseverence. . . . Dr. Zwemer preached a fine sermon at the American Mission, Sunday night. Afterwards we met an American girl, a graduate of Holyoke, whom we had both known in Student Volunteer days. She had just arrived with a party. It was nice to see someone like that.

February 17, 1913

I have bought a "tarboush," as they call the red fez here, to wear when we go to investigate Islam in some form or other, that I may not be so liable to be the one investigated. It is really remarkable how effective such a slight change proves as a disguise. A great many of the natives wear European dress, you see, save for just this hat. So when we put it on they do not know whether we are "Christians" or not, and can be quite sure that we are not tourists. All of which is valuable.

I bought mine as we were going to a *zikr* the other night with Mr. Swan of the Egypt General Mission, but it rained so that we called it off. . . . I have not yet explained what a *zikr* is: briefly, a repetition of the Moslem creed by Dervishes, until they are exhausted. To-morrow is the Prophet's birthday, so we expect to see plenty of them, as they go on all night.

We are still distributing *khutbas,* and it is going all right. Dr. Zwemer seems to think that as they are read more and more by Moslems all over the city there may be some kind of an outburst that would hinder our distributing them freely. We shall soon have the Sermon on the Mount, however, ready for distribution in the same form, and that no one can take exception to.

March 1, 1913

Thursday night we had an interesting trip with Mr. Swan into the back streets of Cairo. The *zikr* we were going to see had been changed, we found, to another night, but just before reaching the place we came into a cemetery and heard the chanting of another *zikr* coming from a little old house off to one side. The star-lit night, the graves and their surroundings, all made a wonderful setting for the weird intonation we could hear so distinctly, even at a distance.

Mr. Swan talked with the men at the place we went to, telling them of Him who is *the* Way. The same Arabic word is used in the Bible for "way" as these Dervishes apply to themselves, in the sense of sect or order. It was really quite remarkable how they listened and seemed to take it all in. At one place, while I was waiting for the others, I was asked by a woman to read an Arabic letter for her. I was wearing the fez, of course. And later in the evening when we met a drunken Moslem who was rather talkative, he addressed me as "Mahmoud Effendi"—Mahmoud being a Moslem name!

Not only the Egyptian women took him for a native. An American gentleman and his family who visited Cairo about this time had a similar experience. They put up at Shepheard's, and in the evening went out to see if they could find any preaching going on.

"Only a few steps from the hotel," wrote Mr. J. S. Kimber, "we found one of the mission halls. Near the door we saw a man who, though he was wearing a fez, we thought might understand English. While I was asking him one or two questions, my eldest son came up and said:

"'I think I must have met you at Princeton. Are you not Mr. Borden?'

"To my surprise the stranger said he was. He then gave us all the information we needed, and volunteered to guide us amid the tremendous scenes of the celebration of Mahomet's birthday.

"Sometime later, we had been to hear Dr. Zwemer preach and had returned to the hotel, when I saw our friend in the lobby talking with a lady from the States, a young graduate from Mount Holyoke. I asked my son whether it would not be worth while for him to wait until the conversation was finished, and then to invite Mr. Borden to take a late dinner with us. After remonstrating a little about not being suitably dressed, or something of that sort, he consented. The dinner was pretty well under way when he joined us at table. He took his seat smilingly, and at once bowed his head in a reverent and silent 'blessing.' It was a beautiful sight, and one, as we remarked, not often seen at Shepheard's."

By this time Borden was living in the family to whom he had paid a surprise visit with Mr. Gairdner. He had moved from the Y.M.C.A. to this Syrian home in the Shubra quarter, glad to be entirely among Arabic-speaking people. Of the kindness of the Hassoons and the comfort of his surroundings he wrote to his mother:

March 1, 1913

While we do use a good deal of English, I hear Arabic spoken all around me, and am given lessons by various members of the family, at meals and any other time I wish. The flat is on the third floor of a house near the station, right by the tracks, but I do not mind that. I have a room facing north looking over other, lower houses, so that I get quite a view. My room is rather small for what I have in it, but as I have the use of the dining-room and library as well, for study and writing, it does not much matter.

The family consist of Mr. and Mrs. Hassoon, his sister, who goes by the name of Sitt (Miss) Paulina, and a niece, Sitt Negla. They are all very nice and most solicitous in trying to stuff me at every meal, claiming that I do not like the food unless I eat a great deal! It is really very good, and if I do not eat more it is simply because I have had enough. I have forgotten to mention the two little kiddies, Hilda and Vera. Vera, the younger, has great big brown eyes, and is really very cute. . . .

You ask if I am getting proper food, and I can honestly say that I am. Some of the dishes are strange, and one or two not much to my liking, but in the main they are excellent. Some things which at home are luxuries are in common use here, artichokes for instance, which we often have, cooked in the most delicious manner. Then we have a good deal of rice, which you know I like.

It was a time of a good deal of excitement in the city, on account of the Prophet's birthday and subsequent festivities. The Dervish dances were in full swing, attracting great crowds day and night. For Cairo, as Borden was learning, is a center of the secret organization known as the Dervishes, with its thirty-two great mystic orders, "the very warp and woof of the Mohammedan religion." While giving most of his time to the language, which he wrote was "no afternoon-tea party," Borden was making a study of this strange development in the life of the people round him. The day he moved to the Hassoons he had "put in some hard licks at Arabic," as he wrote in his journal, had called on Mr. J. Pierpont Morgan at Shepheard's Hotel with Dr. Zwemer, and was writing to his mother at night describing some of their experiences.

February 20, 1913

I mentioned in a recent letter that we were going to see some *zikrs* at the celebration of the Prophet's birthday. This we did on Monday night, and it certainly was interesting, though I fear I shall not be able to describe it at all adequately. A large piece of level ground had been taken and tents erected in a great square, an entrance being left at one side. Each of the tents was assigned to a Dervish order, or some department of the Government. The tents themselves were very attractive, made of Oriental tapestries in rich red hues, and lighted with glass chandeliers, each of which had a dozen or more big candles. The effect was very brilliant. The floor in the centre of each tent was occupied by the Dervishes, who stood or sat in a circle, or if there were many of them in two long rows facing one another.

They all repeat more or less the same things—the name of Allah, the Moslem Creed, the opening sura of the Koran, or the ninety-nine beautiful names of God—but the accompanying motions differ. Some sit and move their heads, first to one side, then to the other and down on the chest, swaying their bodies at the same time, back and forth. Others stand, bending from the waist in rhythmic motions. This was what the Merganiyeh Order were doing as they repeated:

"La illaha il Allah,
Muhammed rasûl Allah."

At first they would bend slowly, then gradually increase the pace till they were all going full speed, the leader keeping time by clapping his hands or coming in with a solo refrain in the marvellous way of intoning these fellows have. One could not watch them without feeling the grip of the thing, although knowing it was nothing but a deliberate attempt to induce a state of ecstasy or auto-hypnosis. The Government has put a stop to many of the worst excesses, so that now these big functions are comparatively tame, and they seldom go to the former extremes.

One man Mr. Swan pointed out to us is known as "the Protestant Dervish." He preached repentance from sin, very much like a Protestant minister, though, of course, without any mention of Christ as the atonement and the One who delivers from the power of sin. He had quite an audience, which he managed much as an evangelist would at home—getting responses from them and letting them ask questions, first of all telling them good stories to get them in a favourable humour. Dr. Zwemer calls him "The Billy Sunday of Islam"!

The next night, Tuesday, was the climax of the celebrations. . . . The Dervishes all paraded through the city, chanting and dancing, each Order making a company with its Sheikh riding on horseback. I followed them a long way, and saw them as they came into the grounds at Abbasiyeh. It was really very picturesque. . . . In the evening there was an immense crowd, chiefly to see the fireworks—"an invention of the evil one" that Mohammed certainly never supposed would come to be connected with his birthday. The crowds hurrying through the streets, the brilliant lights and all the excitement, reminded me very much of the festival of Juggernaut in Madras.

It was not only as a student, however, but as a missionary that Borden went "zikr-hunting" as he called it. His companion was often a young German missionary named Straub, who was with him at the Study Center. The following letter has an interest all its own, describing as it does the last night of Borden's active service.

"His zeal made me ashamed of myself," wrote Mr. Straub. "He always had his pockets full of *khutbas,* and lost no opportunity of distributing them. . . . He was greatly interested in getting acquainted with the national life and the doings of the Dervishes. For this purpose we went to Mohammedan festivals where *zikrs* were taking place, each wearing a red fez so as not to attract attention.

"The last time we went together was on Thursday in Passion Week (March 20). It was the anniversary of the saint Abul Ela in Bulak. . . . What crowds of people were there to be seen—people of all classes and ages, men and women, people who were well and people who were sick! As these occasions partake of the character of national holidays, all sorts of amusements were going on. The illumination was truly fairy-like.

"As our chief interest was in the various *zikrs,* we were drawn to one tent from which the sound of chanting reached us—'Allah, Allah!' For a long time we stood, side by side, watching the strange motions of the men who were swinging forward and backward in strict rhythm, shouting their 'Allah, Allah.' The tempo of these motions grew quicker and quicker; 'Allah, Allah' sounded hoarser and hoarser, until finally nothing but heavy breathing could be heard. Several of the Dervishes fell unconscious to the ground. We noticed one man close beside us wrought up to the highest pitch, and saw foam gushing from his mouth. We, too, felt the excitement, and were full of pity for these poor, deluded people, whose way of worship was so unworthy. . . . About midnight we started, arm in arm, for home, and had scarcely seated ourselves in the trolley when Mr. Borden took his remaining *khutbas* and handed them to those nearest to him."

His earnestness of spirit had been not a little deepened by a startling occurrence of which he wrote to his friend, Dr. Inglis Frost, in March:

> An event here in Cairo has saddened us all and made me realize afresh the heroism of the doctor in his every-day work. I refer to the sudden death of Dr. M. Pain of the Church Missionary Society, a man beloved by hundreds and filled with the Spirit of Christ. I only met him twice, soon after my arrival, and the next thing I knew he was dead.
>
> I wish I could give you the full medical particulars, as you would be interested. As far as I could ascertain he was attending a patient suffering from spinal meningitis. The patient coughed in his face, and infection followed apparently. This took place on a Sunday, and the following Wednesday, about 5 A.M., he passed to the home above.
>
> His funeral, attended as it was by a great crowd of natives and Europeans, was a most eloquent testimony to his loving faithfulness in serving his Master.

As they were leaving the cemetery Borden said to a companion: "Now we must work all the harder, for the time is short."

This made him the more appreciate his opportunities for learning the spoken language and coming into touch with the life of the people in the home of his Syrian friends. From a letter written by Mr. Gamil B. Hassoon, we may almost see him with their eyes:

> It is beyond power to describe his great zeal and diligence in studying the difficult Arabic language. But though he was so absorbed, so fond, so overwhelmed with his studies, he did not make Arabic his only aim. He looked to what was higher and nobler, and appointed a large portion of his time for reading the sacred Scriptures. His Bibles, and he had many of them, were all visited by his eyes. Many were the remarks on their margins

made in his hand-writing, and the texts underlined, which showed that he had chosen them and probably put them into memory. His reading the Scriptures was not in the order of a daily duty. He read them because he loved them.

His life and deeds agreed to what he read. He loved everybody; and as a rule when you find one who loves like that you may be sure of his love to God. . . . In a conversation I had with him I found that he loved the Y.M.C.A. with a wonderful love and when our talk turned on the Arabic branch, his love to this seemed not less than to the other. I knew from him that he wanted to strengthen the Arabic branch by all the power he could, financially, morally and mentally, so that it might attain a level with the greatest European associations, and surpass them if possible. Many times he expressed to me his pleasure in the progress this branch had taken in the short time since it was organized, despite all obstacles.

His love to Orient and Orientals was a profound, true love. He was very pleased with many of our noble habits which he had not experienced before. He was very kindly sociable in our society, and in a few days, not exceeding the number of the fingers of one hand, he became one of us—Orientalist, with the full meaning of the word. He loved to communicate and mix up himself with us and we with him, preferring to change his long-accustomed habits and acquire our ways, so that he might prepare himself with what would agree with the taste of Orientals among whom he hoped to live. . . . The kindness and sociability God endowed him with were very great.

He denied himself, and had a special motto written on a paper in his pocket: "My Lord, enable me to conquer my will and overcome my desires." And he had another motto: *"Not my will but Thine* be done." . . .

What impressed me most was his strong faith. He did not think that there was anything impossible to do in the service of the Lord. In the books he and I read, we found that it is nearly impossible to enter into Tibet or Afghanistan, to bring the gospel to the Mohammedans there. But that fact was not to shake his faith. And he went further, believing that it is most possible that the gospel shall in a few years be preached in Mecca, the centre of Islam itself. He loved to be where the fight is hottest. . . . The unoccupied fields of the Moslem world were his target, and all the time he was preparing himself for the evangelization of such fields. . . .

He was very fond of Mohammedans. Once he came home with a very pleased face.

"What is it makes you look so happy?" I asked.

He had met, he said, two Azhar Sheikhs, and stopped them by the way. They spoke to him in Arabic, something he could not understand. But he did all he could, and led them a long distance to Dr. Zwemer's house. Showing them the house, he said, *"Koll yom gomaa"* (every Friday). And he spent with them fifteen minutes by the roadside, using the few Arabic words he knew.

I asked him to repeat the Arabic he used, and we had great fun of it! But it was good enough to make those men understand that he wanted to gain them for Christ, and they parted with peace. To my full belief they went to Dr. Zwemer's on Friday. . . .

William had a winning look and an attractive spirit. He was meek and kind. My love to him is very great, and I remember every movement of his. . . . Although he was a rich man he denied himself the privileges of rich people, and lived as simply as any missionary could live. He was following the footsteps of Jesus.

Once a friend said to me; "Your guest is a millionaire."

"I do not know anything about his dollars," I replied.

When I came in I told Mr. Borden what I heard, but he did not confirm it.

"People often mistake us," he said, "for the rich Condensed Milk firm that bears the name of Borden."

This put me into an opinion that he was not so rich, and I kept on treating him as a brother, not as to please a millionaire. I am sure he liked it that way. He was perfectly at home with that poor family of mine, and we lived together with great peace and love.

CHAPTER 16

THE FINISHED COURSE

APRIL 1913. AGE 25

Greater love hath no man than this. . . . —JOHN 15:13

D R. ZWEMER had left for Jedda when a telephone call came from the Hassoon Family on Good Friday, the twenty-first of March. It was to say that their guest was far from well. Mrs. Zwemer went over at once to the house by the railroad station, and found that Borden had seen the doctor already, who had told him to stay in bed. There was headache and some fever, but nothing serious apparently. He had been out a good deal in connection with his canvass of the city and with the *zikrs* that were going on, and might have contracted influenza, which was prevalent at the time.

Next morning the message was that he was better, so that it was a surprise to hear in the afternoon that he had been taken to the hospital. It was probably heat stroke, the doctors said, but no one could see the patient.

Easter Sunday came with all its gladness, but a shadow lay on the little missionary community, for Borden's place was empty. The hospital was five miles away, but after the morning service one of his friends went out to obtain fuller information.

"He was told," wrote Mrs. Zwemer, scarcely believing it possible, "that Mr. Borden had *cerebral meningitis*—which stunned us all. I chased the doctor from place to place, and saw him personally that evening, but he would not give any hope, only that Mr. Borden was no worse, and that serum had been injected into the spinal cord."

So the blow fell, and that bright strong young life was suddenly challenged by suffering, if not death itself. Over the succeeding days a veil of mystery is hung—at least for those who were watching, near and far, with stricken hearts. As day by day the cables carried messages of alternate hope and fear, life seemed to stand still for many, and a great volume of prayer went up to God without ceasing.

One tragic element in the situation was that the relatives in America were unable to communicate with Mrs. Borden. She had already left with her younger daughter to join William in the Lebanon Mountains for the summer, sailing for Alexandria direct. They were not due in Gibraltar till the first of April, and efforts to reach them by wireless proved unsuccessful. Happily the older sister, who had just returned from India with her family, was still in London. Upon hearing of the illness she set out for Cairo at once, but it was the second of April before she could arrive.

Meanwhile Mr. Gairdner was visiting the patient daily, and Mr. Giffen of the American Mission obtained permission to see him once and again. The risk of infection was very serious, but Mrs. Zwemer could not keep away. Repeatedly she visited and prayed with him, bearing also all the burden of communication by letter and cable with those at home.

It was there in America that consternation and sorrow found their fullest expression. Miss Whiting, Mrs. Borden's sister, set aside everything to be in the Borden home in New York, answering letters and cables and keeping in touch with the large circle of enquiring friends. To her sister she wrote:

> I telephoned Mr. Frost and he came up of his own accord and remained until the following day at noon. He was most kind and could do a good deal of enquiring, writing notes, etc., while I had to be out. Mr. Delavan Pierson suggested a circle of

prayer in which he and his wife would join; so Mr. Frost arranged this with Mr. Don O. Shelton.

Mr. Shelton telephoned me that hardly anything else had been thought of for the day—all the workers of the Institute met with him in the morning, and the Board of Directors in the afternoon, and that prayer would be continued strong and steady until William's recovery was assured.

Laura telegraphed Mrs. H. who went at once to Dr. A. B. Simpson, and there also daily prayer is offered. You, of course, are as earnestly thought of as William. . . . I telephoned the Erdmans and telegraphed to many others, trying not to leave out any one you would wish to have reached. Mr. Frost wrote to Mr. Crowell . . . who would be the one to speak to William's friends at the Moody Church. . . . Charlie Campbell spent all one afternoon here. In many ways he made William seem so near!

And then, a little later:

It has been a blessing and even a joy to be here, where I could come in touch with your friends and William's, and to hear them speak the words of love and admiration and sorrow. Even the men are not ashamed to be found in tears. No one, *no* one can understand. They and we can only *know*. Dr. W. J. Erdman showed the marks of the struggle in his face and bearing as he said:

"It is the strangest, most mysterious working of the divine providence I have ever experienced. The world had such need of William!"

But in Cairo, in the shaded room at the Anglo-American hospital, who shall say that there was question or mystery? Suffering there was, intense and prolonged, for Borden was fighting the bravest fight of all his life. But he was not alone. Had not his prayer from childhood been that the will of God should be done in his life? There was no shrinking now. All those Easter days, as he lay there, he could not but think of the young doctor missionary whose sudden call had come just in the same way. Only a few weeks previously he had stood by that new-made grave. What if, for himself too, the call had come? No reserve, no retreat, no regrets had any place in Borden's consecration to God. With Adam McCall, the young leader on the Congo, falling as one of the first missionary pioneers in that great region of Central Africa, he might have said:

> Thou knowest the circumstances, Lord. Do as Thou pleasest, I have nothing to say. I am not dissatisfied that Thou are about to take me away. Why should I be? I gave myself, body, mind and spirit to Thee—consecrated my whole life and being to Thy service. And now, if it please Thee to take me instead of the work I would have done for Thee, what is that to me? Thy will be done.

Glory, not only mystery, surrounds the earthly close of such a life.

Among the friends who risked infection and were permitted to see him was his dear Syrian host, who wrote:

> As soon as I stepped into the room, he, in spite of his great suffering, gave me a wonderful smile which is printed on my memory. He then sat up in bed, but very soon had to lay himself down again. . . . I sat by his bedside for a short time and spoke to him with all the oriental and brotherly kindness I could master at that critical moment. I was greatly astonished that all his sufferings did not hinder him from showing gratitude and love. I passed my hand over his forehead and wiped away the drops of sweat that stood there, and asked God to help and cure him. He smiled again and held my hand in his and pressed it very gently but warmly, in such a manner which made me feel his love. He was not so very able to speak much, but his eyes spoke, and transmitted to my heart all that was in his heart and mind. And thus I left him for the last time.

Meanwhile Mrs. Borden and her younger daughter were nearing Cairo. Dr. Zwemer had returned from Jedda, where he had been enabled to witness for Christ within thirty miles of Mecca itself, and while in quarantine at Suez had received "the terrible tidings of Borden's illness." From the second Sunday he was with him frequently, and even then there seemed hope, at times, that the patient's splendid constitution would hold out. He recognized his elder sister who had come from London and with the nurses was doing all that love and skill could devise. He knew that his mother was expected, and asked for her in semi-consciousness, often saying: "Poor Mother! Poor Mother!" His work, too, was much upon his heart, for in delirium he talked about it constantly.

"This is the fifteenth day," Dr. Zwemer wrote early in April, "and he is slightly better tonight, although this morning the doctor had no hope. Mrs. Zwemer has done heroic work, both in visiting and in praying, as well as keeping in touch with Mrs. Borden by cable. The latter will be in Brindisi tonight and sails for Port Said tomorrow."

Three days later it was still with a glimmer of hope that he left for Port Said to meet the steamer. They had hardly cast anchor before he was on board, at five A.M., bringing what seemed good news to those who had so dreaded the arrival. In the relief of hearing that William was still living, the beauty of the spring morning and the novelty of all around them impressed itself upon the younger members of the party, one of whom wrote:[1]

> We went ashore in small boats, and everything was very interesting and strange. Our steamer was over-run with Arabs and negroes of all descriptions. The harbour sparkled with light and bright colours. The ride from the water's edge to the railway station was also fascinating, with the first high palms, the veiled women and the bright picturesque costumes of the Arabs.
>
> We left by train at 8 A.M. and had a fine run to Ismailia,

[1] A young Swiss lady, Miss Ada von Fallenberg, who had been with Mrs. Borden for some years as companion to her younger daughter.

following for many miles the banks of the Suez Canal. It was surprising to find the canal so narrow, and that yet the largest ocean-steamers can pass through. . . . Almost at once after leaving the canal, the desert began—long stretches of sand with beautiful vistas, far away, where the sand would look bright pink. Here and there would be a green patch, wherever water was to be found, while hard by the same soil was just barren wilderness. . . .

After a long time the Nile deposit began to appear—dark soil, very different from the sandy stretches, and getting more and more black as we came into the cultivated land of Goshen. There, Arab life was all around us. Already in the desert we had seen camels wandering about, either alone or with Bedouin in floating garments. Now we passed real native villages—mud huts, people sitting around, children, veiled Moslem women, men loading camels, families riding on donkeys. . . . We had morning prayers and sang hymns, that one especially with the chorus:

> "Stayed upon Jehovah, hearts are fully blest;
> Finding as He promised, perfect peace and rest."

Afterwards this meant so much to Mrs. Borden and Joyce.

At Ismailia, half-way to Cairo, a telegram was brought to us: "William not so well." Dr. Zwemer said it had been like that all the time. Having reached a certain satisfactory level, he would drop below that level every second day, improving again the next day, so that we need not be over-anxious. . . .

We went on. It was only a few stations farther that a second telegram came to Dr. Zwemer, right to the car. It was the end.

I cannot tell you about that next hour or so on the train. Dr. Zwemer was the greatest comfort—but oh, it was dreadful! It broke my heart to see Mrs. Borden and sweet little Joyce. We reached Cairo at 1 p.m. William had passed away at 9 a.m. I cannot believe it even yet. . . .

The funeral had to be the same afternoon. His death was absolutely peaceful, without any struggle; he just simply stopped breathing. Dear, dear Mrs. Borden—what a sorrow, what a loss!

When she could write, ten days later, Mrs. Borden herself told all the rest there was to tell—and it was everything:

I do not want you to think of us as overwhelmed, for we are not. God's loving care and mercy have been evident on every side; and it has been a real joy to be in the place where William, in those few short weeks, became so honoured and loved, and was so *happy!* The missionaries have all been most kind and thoughtful, and Dr. and Mrs. Zwemer wonderful in their loving sympathy and untiring efforts on our behalf. Dr. Zwemer has been son and brother in one. He loved William and could scarcely speak of him with unbroken voice. Mr. Gairdner, head of the language school where William was studying, visited him daily through all his illness, though it is considered dangerous to go near the sufferer. The nurses they tell me were devoted, and so were the Arab boy-attendants, night and day, keeping the flies away. As yet, it is all more like a dream than reality.

But I wanted to tell you just one thing that you may not hear from anyone else: and that is that, when we saw him, it seemed as though William had been transformed into the very likeness of Christ, through suffering. I should never have known him, his beard and moustache had grown and the contour of his face was changed.

We had been in doubt as to whether to go to the hospital to see him, altered as he would inevitably be; but thank God, we did—Joyce and I with Mr. Gairdner. We were told not to go near the bed, but that at a distance it would be safe. We approached a long, low building, standing right on the ground, so that it seemed as though we might be going to the tomb itself, and the question "Who will roll us away the stone?" was almost on my lips. The door was opened, and immediately we were in the presence of all that remained here of our William.

I was so shocked at the change that I turned to beg Joyce not to look or to come in, but she had already done so, and said in the gentlest voice—afterwards, I thought, like the voice of an angel:

"But Mother, did you see how he looks like all the pictures of Christ—the crucified Christ?"

I looked again, and then indeed I saw.

One hardly dared speak of it to others, fearing it would be thought irreverent or fanciful. But I did mention it to Douglas in Mr. Gairdner's hearing, who quietly said:

"Yes, and you only stood at the threshold. If you had gone nearer you would have seen the resemblance more clearly."

I said that, standing there, I could only think of the words: "His visage was more marred than any man's."

"Yes," said Mr. Gairdner, "*His* visage—more marred than any man's."

It put such a holy, wonderful touch upon it all.

"*Perfect through suffering.*" It was as though we had been permitted a glimpse into the mystery of suffering, human and Divine, and had seen that through it God had, so to speak, given the final touches to William's life.

"Christ Jesus my Lord—for whom I have suffered the loss of all things, and do count them but refuse, that I may win Christ, and be found in Him."

"And Jesus, looking upon him, loved him."

CHAPTER 17

"FOUND FAITHFUL"

His servants shall serve Him and they shall see His face . . .
—Rev. 22. 3, 4

Far away in Kashmir, a Yale man, one of Borden's friends, was anxiously awaiting tidings. The mail arrived, bringing home letters, and was leaving again in a few hours. In his loneliness, Sherwood Day, the young missionary, wrote:

I cannot realize it yet. Last week when your letter told of Bill's illness, I knew that the crisis must be over, and asked that all might be well; and it has been so, I am sure. I feel that I want to be by myself a while and think, yet this must go to-night. I cannot say all I would, but you will understand.

Somehow, as I read your letter, I have a sense of victory and power that seems to bring that "Other Room" very near. Bill seems nearer and more gloriously living than he did at Yale or Cairo. . . . I cannot put on paper what his change of field means to me. He is the first of my friends whom I really loved, to be in that Other Place, and it makes that place very real. In fact, except for the pain to Mrs. Borden and his family, I am very happy in it all—a happiness that hurts, but one that rejoices in the victory of the thing. All victory is gained through pain, but it is a pain that spells joy—one of those strange things in life.

I have absolutely no feeling of a life cut short. A life abandoned to Christ cannot be cut short. "Cut short" means not complete, interrupted, and we know that our Master does no half-way jobs. We must pray, now, that those to whom God wants this to appeal, may *listen*. I am sure we can feel that He wants to use it, and that He counts on us to help.

I am glad for Bill! In His immediate presence—no longer a clouded, imperfect experience, but a wholly satisfying one. What his life means to us all! I mean the life we knew, the one he has finished, or the part he has finished. Put that loyalty, that staunchness, the quality for which weaker men called him "narrow," over against the "modern" line of things, and how Bill's life stands out! A splendid mind, a splendid body and a great soul—all handed over to the One who does *all* things well. It will mean more and more to me, as I try to do what my Master wants of me in this country, to know that Bill has finished his job and is just Over There. It all seems so near! . . . I feel this is the greatest thing Bill ever meant to me—a sort of volunteering for another, shall we call it, "foreign field"?

Amid the flood of sorrow that flowed so deep and wide, *this* was the conviction that seemed to dominate all others.

"There could scarcely a greater loss befall us than this," wrote Dr. Robert E. Speer, in the first shock of grief. "William Borden was one among a million. There was no better among the younger men who have gone out from our colleges in the last ten years. . . . It seems impossible that all that strength and devotion can have been taken away from the work of the Church down here. Evidently there are missionary undertakings of even greater importance elsewhere."

And to Mrs. Borden:

"You do not need to be told anything of your son's noble qualities of character, his simply rock-like faith, his loyalty that knew no limit, his remarkable abilities and above all the unreserved devotion to his Master. It is not possible to understand the providence that has taken him, except on the supposition that God has more important missionary work to be done elsewhere than it is possible for men to do here on earth, and that He needed your son in the ministry of those who serve Him day and night, and who look upon His face as they do service."

In Cairo also this note was struck of triumphant faith. It

was so manifest in Mrs. Borden's life that the Syrian friend whose home seemed so empty could write of *her* help in *their* grief!

"I shall not forget that smiling, loving face of yours as long as I live. You were a great comfort to us, and we thank God for your coming to Cairo in the time of our trial."

From the hospital, the nurse who had been in charge wrote of "the memory of a brave man who had faced illness with fortitude and patience, and never grumbled or complained, and a brave mother who did not make other people suffer because she was heart-broken."

"The funeral was very informal," a friend who was with Mrs. Borden could write. "The Anglo-American hospital is beautifully located on the island of Gezira, in the midst of green meadows, palms and roses. From there we went to the American cemetery. How strange it was to have Arabs doing everything! A great many friends and missionaries were present, the Syrian gentleman, too, in whose family William had lived. They are lovely people, simply devoted to William. Mrs. Zwemer says that the conditions in their home were perfectly all right, and that there was no risk to health in being there. The food was good, and William was in no way tired or run-down when he contracted the disease.

"Mr. Gairdner read the service and the Scriptures. Dear old Dr. Watson prayed, and so did Dr. Giffen and Dr. Zwemer. We sang 'Face to face with Christ, my Saviour.' I shall never forget it as long as I live. We stayed to the very last. The sun was going down, and the glow in the west was wonderful. They planted flowers on the grave, and it looked very beautiful."

A missionary who was present added:

As we sang hymns during the service the Mohammedan grave-diggers, standing a little way back, looked astonished, for it was all in such sharp contrast with the hideous and meaningless wailing which takes place at a Moslem funeral. Still greater was their astonishment as they watched the little company of native Christians weeping over the grave of a foreigner —one they had learned to love as a brother. Never shall I forget the feeling that came to us with our closing hymn:

"Sing it softly through the gloom,
   While the heart for mercy craves;
Sing in triumph o'er the tomb—
   Jesus saves, Jesus saves!"

Our very souls were lifted out of their mourning into a glad and glorious triumph, and we could indeed say: "O death, where is thy sting; O grave, where is thy victory?"

Even the rude, varnished coffin could bring no pang to the mother's heart, different as it was from the casket that would have been provided at home. As she saw it lowered into the grave, containing all that was mortal of her son, a feeling not of pain at the outward lack of harmony swept over her, but a wonderful joy and comfort in the thought of that entire life spent for Christ, scarcely a moment of it wasted.

The surroundings were very different in Princeton when the Memorial Service was held that gathered professors, students and friends in one common grief, but the note of victory was the same. Miss Whiting wrote:

Some day you will read the true and appreciative words spoken at Princeton on Friday, but I wish you could have been there to feel the spirit of love and reverence. Dr. Charles Erdman said it was the most wonderful testimony and tribute he had ever listened to. . . .

The day was ideal—Princeton in its first spring beauty; the hour, five o'clock, was perfect. Dr. Patton himself conducted the service in a way so dignified, reverent and affectionate that nothing more seemed needed. The chapel was nearly filled with students who had known William, and the service throughout was simple, strong, solemn, tender and triumphant. . . . As I listened, the whole of William's life seemed to sweep before me. There was not one word too much, nor undeserved. I marvelled that they had understood so truly and loved so deeply in the space of but three years.

Another Memorial Service in Princeton had a significance all its own. It was held in the little African Methodist Church, where Borden had taught in the Sunday School for two winters. The pastor learned in that meeting, for the first time, that Borden had been wealthy in his own right. They had loved him for himself:

"For his deep consecration and unassuming Christlike life. We never at any time asked him to contribute a single dollar. We asked him to teach, not to give."

So the colored children sorrowed for the loss of their friend.

At New Haven too, in the Yale Hope Mission, a touching service was held, the room packed with men of the very class Borden had sought to reach. One after another told of the new life that had come to them because of what he was and did, and one of the professors who had differed from him widely as to theological views, spoke of the house being filled with the fragrance of his love and service.

There and in the Moody Church in Chicago men were riveted by the story of what the grace of God had done in one they had known so well. A friend who was present wrote:

2 Chron. 16. 9 has been in my mind ever since Friday evening. God is ever intently looking for those whose hearts are right toward Him, that in and through them He may "show himself strong." And oh, the joy of his heart when He finds such a one! As William grew in knowledge of God, he lived up to that knowledge; as he learned more of God's will, he obeyed that will. He followed the Lord wholly. As with absorbing interest the great company listened to what God had wrought, one could not but feel that the fire of a holy purpose was lighted in the hearts of some of those young men and women.

In the Marble Collegiate Church, New York, crowded to

its full capacity, the number of students present and their interest were also remarkable. Mr. Charles Campbell was among the speakers and Mr. Delavan Pierson, Editor of *The Missionary Review of the World,* who was impressed with "the strong note of triumph and praise to God." Mr. Don O. Shelton presided. The words of Mr. Hugh R. Monro had special weight, as the testimony of a businessman well known in the great city:

> The thing that impressed me in my contact with William Borden was the fact that he was living the Christian life successfully. I suppose we all recognize the deep and abiding blessings of our discipleship. Some of us have a continuous consciousness of the abundant grace brought to us in Christ. Yet even in advanced Christian experience there is often an overpowering sense of insufficiency and failure, so that we are constrained to confess and bewail our weaknesses. Where there is triumph in one direction there may be failure in another. But more than any other young man I have ever known Borden seemed to have continuous victory. His life was so truly under the control of divine power that it breathed the spirit of the conqueror. It was an imperial spiritual life.
>
> To myself there comes a new sense of assurance as I think of it, because I recognize that this overcoming life was not lived in the strength of any innate ability or natural gifts. It was the grace of God in him that made his life victorious and such a benediction to those with whom he came in contact. The same resources are available to your faith and to mine, so that while his life is a rebuke to the poverty of our spiritual experience it is a summons also to a closer following of the Saviour. . . .

So it was in other Memorial Services, in Japan, Korea, India and South Africa, for the circle touched by this young life was practically world-wide. As to America, a friend could write, "All the papers in the country seem to have told about William"; and another, "I never heard, on all sides, such regret and sorrow expressed over the death of any young man. . . . Surely you must feel the volume of prayer that is rising for you from many hearts."

"How strong his influence is, even in this remote corner!" wrote a missionary in Korea. "Many of our Christians know of him and his faithful consecration to the Lord. So he continues to live here below in many souls made better by his example."

And from Cape Town came the following:

"You have no idea, Mrs. Borden, what William's life has meant to the South African students who knew him at Princeton, and what it means just now to the whole Dutch Reformed Church out here. Next Sunday the story will be told to the children practically throughout the whole Union of South Africa, in hundreds of Sunday schools."

More permanent records, also, carried the message of his life far and wide, in several languages. Two of his own addresses were put into Arabic by Dr. Zwemer's arrangement,[1] who wrote of the booklet: "It will make a fine message. I am calling it in Arabic: *Two Questions by a Young Man to Young Men.*"

A sketch intended especially for Moslem readers was prepared by Dr. St. Clair Tisdall and published in English and in Arabic. A little later it was translated into Persian and Hindustani and circulated by the thousand, then into Dutch and Chinese. Of the latter translation made by a master of that difficult language,[2] Mr. F. H. Rhodes of the China Inland Mission said:

> As the first Chinese booklet published for free distribution among Mohammedans in China, this story of Borden's life marks a distinct advance in bringing the gospel to these neglected millions. Requests for the book have come from practically all the districts where missionaries are in contact

[1] *What It Means to Be a Christian* and *The Price of Power.*
[2] The Rev. F. W. Baller.

with Islam, and some even from Mohammedans themselves who have heard of the memorial. Thirty-five thousand copies have been put into the hands of Moslems, and as they are now being read, passed on to others and carried farther into regions where Christ is not named, we trust that the number who will hear the message will be much larger than the number published. Already the story seems to have opened the way for several missionaries to get into closer touch with the followers of Islam in their fields.

Thus in nearly every province of China proper, in Manchuria and far out on the great road across Central Asia, Borden's love to Christ was the means of making known the love of God in Christ to followers of the Prophet. It was a wonderful ministry, wider possibly than he might have accomplished in person, and its outcome who can tell?

But to come back to America. A sketch of Borden's life by Dr. Charles Erdman appeared in *The Missionary Review of the World,* and was so much valued that it had to be published separately in pamphlet form. Yet another, written from the point of view of the college student, came from the pen of Charles Campbell, with all the freshness of a classmate's understanding and appreciation.

A volume in itself might be made of the letters that flowed in—letters from leaders in the front rank of Christian activity, as well as from fellow-students and friends of his own age. From the National Parliament in Peking and the House of Commons in London, from great city churches, oriental universities and lonely mission-stations came the same testimony.

"Mr. Borden has become a national character in his life and influence," said a leading man in Chicago. "It gratified me to hear him speak as he did," wrote Dr. J. Timothy Stone, "because he is careful as to what he says, and views everything with a broad and real justice."

From the Fifth Avenue Presbyterian Church in New York, Dr. Jowett wrote:

"His life just now is standing before the American people like some perfumed flower from the garden of God."

"Apart from Christ, there is no explanation of such a life," said Professor Charles Erdman at Princeton.

"I know of no young man in this country or in England," wrote Dr. R. A. Torrey, "from whose life I expected greater things. But God has His own way of carrying out His purposes. He has some larger plan of usefulness through your son's departure than could have been realized by his remaining here."

"The loss is wholly inexplicable," came in a letter from Dr. Charles R. Watson of Egypt, "but the thing which forbids doubt or criticism is, from the human side, William's own spirit of perfect surrender. He had given himself to his Lord for life or for death, and where he trusted we cannot but share his trust."

On his return from Asia, Dr. John R. Mott said that missionaries in every part of the world bore testimony to the influence of the life of William Borden, and that at the Student Conferences that summer (1913) no appeal was being used with such power as the story of his consecration.

"Many young men live stronger, purer, more yielded lives," wrote a fellow-student, "because of the life your boy lived and because of the death he died. You cannot *hear* of them all. You will know some day. The name of Will Borden was more used than any other during the recent great Convention in Kansas City. Japanese students remarked that the investment of life as Borden invested it was the greatest of all investments. The memory of such a son must be a blessing. I am glad he lived *and lives.*"

"At Bryn Mawr," a girl friend wrote, "when Dr. W. J. Erdman preached here in May, he told of William as an example of the Spirit-filled life—and oh, Mrs. Borden, it was a marvelous witness! I know it must have struck deep into many hearts."

Dr. Henry W. Wright, of Yale University, said:

"No undergraduate since I have been connected with Yale has done so much for Christ in four short years as Bill did. I feel very lonely trying to work without his visible presence to cheer and inspire me."

Mrs. Walter Erdman wrote from Korea:

"William's life has touched many of whom you have never heard, and no one can measure its influence. As for Walter, you can hardly realize what a blow it has been to him. It is the loss of a cherished brother, rather than a friend."

And the Rev. Walter Erdman himself:

"We have been praying tonight that you may be comforted in the assurance that the love of God does *not* change, even when our understanding is baffled by His acts, and that our lives may be purified and made stronger through the inspiration of William's friendship and love and his loyalty to Christ. I learned more things from William about simplicity of faith and steadfastness of purpose than he did from me, during the year we were together while he was still a boy, and the memory of our comradeship will be dearly prized until we meet again. . . .

"I have been thinking more and more, since the news came, that the length of time God permits us to stay here is not related to a certain amount of work He wants us to do, so much as to a certain closeness of relationship to Himself He wants us to attain. Some of us who are less useful, perhaps, are allowed to live on longer that we may learn more and be perfected in understanding. And as for the mystery of the interruption of such a work as his was and promised increasingly to be, while there is no explanation now, I like to think that it is *not* interrupted, but that as he desired to serve so he will be permitted to serve, only with higher powers. I think of him as still working for Mohammedans in some relation to the proclamation of the gospel."

Mr. Fennell P. Turner of the Student Volunteer Movement wrote of the fellow-worker he had loved:

"Few men plan their preparation with such care and earnestness or carry out their plans with such faithfulness. What great things we expected of him, and how he is missed! But we have this assurance: the life so truly given to God was His life and the work William was preparing to do was His work. On *His* heart rests a far greater burden for the Moslems of China than we can possibly feel. He will not permit His work to suffer or be hindered because His servant was not allowed to enter upon it as he had planned."

And a class-mate who had preceded Borden to China wrote from Nanking:

"Somehow, already, I seem able to look down the years a bit and see, not one, but *many* giving their all to the Master to take up the work for Mohammedans here in China which William had planned to do. Just as Keith Falconer and Horace Pitkin did more even in death than in life, may we not believe that God will, out of seeming loss, get great glory to Himself and call many to fill the breach? William was taken while doing with great joy and enthusiasm the work to which God had called him. When my call comes, I pray that I may be found doing my Lord's work with like faithfulness and devotion."

Finally our thoughts are carried back to Cairo, for the words of Dr. Zwemer linger longest, spoken in the place and among the friends Borden had last loved. There in the American Mission were gathered, representatives of all forms of Christian service through the city, and with them men wearing the fez and the white turban of the Azhar student. Few leaders had influenced Borden more than Dr. Zwemer, and none could have had truer insight as he spoke at that Memorial Service from the words: "I have fought a good fight, I have finished my course, I have kept the faith."[3]

[3] II Timothy 4:7, 8.

One of the great characteristics of this life we mourn and in which we rejoice is that our friend and brother was a soldier, every inch—a soldier of Jesus Christ. Those who knew him best knew that he was fighting, and now he "has fought."

He won that greatest victory of all, the victory over himself. Charles Kingsley, who knew that life was not a bed of ease or a garden of roses, wrote:

"The very air teems thick with leaguèd fiends;
Each word we speak has infinite effects;
Each soul we pass must go to heaven or hell. . . .
Be earnest, earnest, earnest—*mad* an thou wilt:
Do what thou doest as if the stake were heaven
And this thy last deed ere the judgment day."

And Borden was earnest. No one could say of him that he trifled with the thing men are trifling with all around, the great talent of life.

He won the victory over his environment. By some the victory has to be won over poverty; by others over heredity, or over shame and temptation; but Borden won the victory over an environment of wealth. He felt that life consisted not in "the abundance of things a man possesseth," but in the abundance of things which possess the man.

He won the victory in great measure over sin and temptation. There is not a young man living in America today who has not to fight a deadly battle for character. Borden fought and won—for two reasons: he always carried his sword and looked up for strength. He was a man of the Bible, as his Greek Testament and the Bibles he used for study and devotion show, and he was a man of prayer. . . . Even in the smallest details of life he looked up for wisdom and strength.

Another great thing that comes into a man's life is "urgency." At college as well as here in Cairo, Borden felt the call of urgency, and to him this was linked with thoughts of the Moslem world. I found underlined in his Testament: "I must work the works of him that sent me while it is day."

The real secret of this full-orbed life was that, like St. Paul, Borden could say, "I have kept the faith." How many men in these days—men at the beginning of their ministry, or in pulpits, or at the end of their service—have to cry, "God knows, I have lost the faith." Borden held to the Bible. He believed it from cover to cover. His faith had been tested, for he had met destructive criticism in his college course. He had a grasp of the oracles of God, and to us it was a great joy to see that *belief in the Book* had made him a missionary.

He gripped the essentials; he had no shibboleth; his was no narrow creed. This gathering is indicative of his wide fellowship. His Egyptian brethren could never have told to which regiment he belonged in the army of God. He was too big a man to wear the distinctive colours of any regiment. He kept the faith—but he did not keep the faith to himself. Ask the man who met him.

"Henceforth there is laid up for me a crown of righteousness." He now wears the crown of life and glory. "O God, to us may grace be given to follow in his train!"

Only today I was reading in *Pilgrim's Progress* of the death of Valiant for Truth:

" 'My sword I give to him that shall succeed me in my pilgrimage, and my courage and strength to him that can get it. My marks and scars I carry with me, to be a witness for me that I have fought His battles who will now be my rewarder.' . . . So he passed over, and all the trumpets sounded for him on the other side."

CHAPTER 18

THE UNFINISHED TASK
1926

What though he standeth at no earthly altar,
Yet in white raiment on the golden floor,
Where love is perfect and no footsteps falter,
He serveth as a priest for evermore.

—Selected

IN FARAWAY KANSU some new influence is telling. Since Borden passed to the place of higher powers a great change has come over the province to which his life was given, so that far from being what it was, one of the most barren fields in China, it is becoming fruitful. Wonderful things are happening there, right in the midst of that great Mohammedan population, that put to shame our small expectations and little faith.

But the position is critical. That part of China is becoming one of the most charged with high explosive powers in the world. Bolshevism has to be reckoned with there now, as well as Mohammedanism and the most bigoted forms of idolatrous worship. The doors are open still for the most widespread proclamation of the Gospel, and hungry hearts are welcoming the Bread of Life. Men, women—yes, and many children—are coming to the Saviour who never had a chance to hear of Him before. But who can tell how long the doors may remain open?

God needs lives that count, up there in these days—the

world needs them, China needs them, Mongolia needs them, Tibet needs them unspeakably, the Moslems of Central Asia need them, waiting in agelong darkness.

> From many a mosque there comes the call to prayer;
>   I hear no voice that calls on Christ for light—
> But still I wait
>   For the messenger of Christ who cometh late.

Remote as it is, that province is on the firing line today. It is strategic in the most vital sense. Russia knows this, and is tightening her grasp upon the great highway that runs through Kansu into China. China knows this, and is making her railway and motor road as rapidly as possible, to connect Peking with this imperiled line of communication between her populous provinces and vast outlying dependencies. Islam knows this, and is appropriating every place of power, firmly intrenched already in that western corner of the republic. There is no time to be lost. Already the tension is great, and the few missionaries who are toiling amid wonderful opportunities write of an outlook that could hardly be more serious. Bolshevism is coming in like a flood. Look at that long frontier line of Russia right up against China, north and west, for thousands of miles, and consider what the pressure must be where the one road runs through that is most practicable. This must be the route of the coming railway. Already General Feng's officers are there putting through the line. Their Christian influence is telling. It was a cheer to see two of them come in to the most remote of all the little Christian churches out on the great road, to join reverently in the Communion Service not long ago.

The last station in the province at which there are foreign missionaries (men) is away back at Liang-chow, more than two weeks' journey from the outpost missionary women have reached at Su-chow, the Western Gate of China. The next station beyond, in the heart of Central Asia, is forty days' journey farther west, and there are no witnesses for Christ (missionaries) between, or northward in Mongolia or southward in Tibet for hundreds and hundreds of miles. The population is not great:—no, but it numbers millions. The field is hard in every possible way:—yes, it needs lives that count, "steadfast through union with the Anointed One".[1]

Think of the band of preachers sent out by that last little church to be founded in the far northwest, a church only six years old, but which is evangelizing the whole region with its own unpaid, voluntary workers, men and women. Think of the need of prayer—for them, for their leader, the young Chinese doctor who was used to bring the Light, for the missionaries who are helping them, three ladies all alone. Think of the longing of the heart of Christ over that waiting world of Central Asia in all its darkness, sin and need, and over the Moslems of Kansu itself, three millions, for whom one young missionary has recently been set apart.

Think of him and his wife and little children (boys of three and five years old) in the first Christian home in the crowded Moslem suburb of Ho-chow, the Mecca of China. And round that little new light-center is a population of hundreds of thousands of Moslems, possibly a million, within easy reach. Are not lives that count needed there? Will you by constant, earnest prayer help to make and keep those young missionaries spiritually, mentally, physically efficient? For there are prayers that count as well as lives that count. Will you pray such prayers?

Borden's life counted because it was rooted in Christ, fed daily upon His Word, was subject to His Spirit, breathed the atmosphere of prayer, was poured out for others.

Each of us can put a fullness of meaning all our own into his simple act of faith (p. 116):

[1] II Cor. 1:21; Rotherham's version.

Lord Jesus, I take hands off as far as my life is concerned. I put Thee on the throne in my heart. Change, cleanse, use me as Thou shalt choose. I take the full power of Thy Holy Spirit. I thank Thee.

We too, "may never know a tithe of the result until morning."